NEUROLINGUISTICS
HISTORICAL AND THEORETICAL PERSPECTIVES

APPLIED PSYCHOLINGUISTICS
AND COMMUNICATION DISORDERS

THE ACOUSTICS OF CRIME
The New Science of Forensic Phonetics
Harry Hollien

APHASIA AND BRAIN ORGANIZATION
Ivar Reinvang

APPLIED PSYCHOLINGUISTICS AND MENTAL HEALTH
Edited by R. W. Rieber

COMMUNICATION DISORDERS
Edited by R. W. Rieber

NEUROLINGUISTICS
Historical and Theoretical Perspectives
Charles P. Bouton

PSYCHOLOGY OF LANGUAGE AND THOUGHT
Essays on the Theory and History of Psycholinguistics
Edited by R. W. Rieber

A Continuation Order Plan is available for this series. A continuation order will bring delivery of each new volume immediately upon publication. Volumes are billed only upon actual shipment. For further information please contact the publisher.

NEUROLINGUISTICS

HISTORICAL AND THEORETICAL PERSPECTIVES

Charles P. Bouton
Simon Fraser University
Vancouver, British Columbia, Canada

Translated by

Terence MacNamee

PLENUM PRESS • NEW YORK AND LONDON

Library of Congress Cataloging-in-Publication Data

Bouton, Charles P.
     [Neurolinguistique. English]
     Neurolinguistics : historical and theoretical perspectives /
Charles P. Bouton ; translated by Terence MacNamee.
          p.   cm. -- (Applied psycholinguistics and communication
     disorders)
     Translation of: Neurolinguistique.
     Includes bibliographical references and index.
     ISBN 0-306-43691-4
     1. Neurolinguistics. 2. Neurolinguistics--History.   I. Title.
II. Series.
QP399.B6813   1990
153.6--dc20   90-7853
                                                            CIP

ISBN 0-306-43691-4

© 1991 Plenum Press, New York
A Division of Plenum Publishing Corporation
233 Spring Street, New York, N.Y. 10013

Printed in the United States of America

PREFACE

A discussion of the relationship between the human body and language seems to be the inevitable result of any reflexion by man on his particular condition. This has held true since the earliest records in written tradition.

It may be an excessively ambitious undertaking to try to catalogue the themes in that reflexion and reconstruct its successive stages within the confines of a book of fairly modest proportions such as this one; but the challenge has been stimulating enough to call for a response.

The long research work that preceded the writing of this book and the large collection of source material accumulated over a period of several years at least afford the writer the satisfaction of appreciating more than anyone else the care for accuracy and completeness that went into the gradual reduction of this text to manageable proportions.

Moreover, it is hoped to make available to all those interested at a later date the rich and rare corpus of documents that forms the basis of this book, in an anthology of selected readings. It was originally intended to publish these documents in a companion volume to this book.

The method followed here in chronicling facts and interpreting them and the ideas they have given rise to perhaps owes more to that of archaeology than history or linguistics. Attention is paid to the links discernible between particular concepts and the ideology predominant at the time they were developed. On the other hand, care was exercised to avoid a "finalistic" view in which one considers past contributions as a series of achievements and discoveries dominated by a logic of progress and leading necessarily to the present. If the book occasionally favours such an interpretation, it is where rhetoric has won out over strict objectivity.

Some recent work, closely related in subject-matter to this book, points to the growing interest in this area of scholarly endeavour. The present publication owes much to Simon Fraser University, its tactical support and the research assistants who have worked with the author, among them Terence MacNamee, who has written an excellent dissertation on the history of disordered language from the 16th to the 19th centuries, and who has prepared the English version of this book. The book owes much, in a special way, to Eliane Bouton, her advice and her patient rereading of a complex text that without her would not have reached fruition.

CHARLES P. BOUTON
VANCOUVER, BRITISH COLUMBIA, CANADA

CONTENTS

I
THE PREHISTORY OF NEUROLINGUISTICS

1. EARLY BEGINNINGS

THE BIRTH OF WRITTEN TRADITION

> The practice of medicine is divided among them [the Egyptians], so that each physician is a healer of one disease and no more. All the country is full of physicians, some of the eye, some of the teeth, some of what pertains to the belly, and some of the hidden diseases.
> Herodotus, II, 84

In the Eastern Mediterranean, where the history of Western thought begins with the first accounts committed to writing, there are two cultures that show evidence of having engaged in systematic study of the human body, based on a tradition of practical experience.

Between the parallel valleys of the Tigris and the Euphrates, from the fourth millennium onwards, developed the civilization of Sumer, which was passed on to the Babylonians and in turn to the Assyrians. The code engraved on the stele of Hammurabi[1] (about 1750 B.C.) states the physician's responsibility to his patient, and his fee. The tablets remaining from the rich library of Assurbanipal at Nineveh tell us that the blood was regarded as the vehicle of vital functions and the liver as the essential organ from which these functions derived.

On the banks of the Nile, in the Egypt of the Pharaohs (Third Dynasty - about 2700 B.C.), a system of knowledge grew up about the human body and disease which has come down to us through the so-called papyrus of Imhotep,[2] a copy of a lost original which dates from around 1700 B.C. This papyrus contains the oldest description of what in modern terms would be called traumatic aphasia:

> He who has a wound on the temple perforating the temporal bone, while losing blood from both nostrils, suffers from a stiffness of the neck and cannot speak. This condition cannot be treated.

Other cases are mentioned, accompanied by similar statements. Out of 48 cases described in the text, 27 involve traumas of the head and 6 involve injuries to the spine. Each case is presented in the same format: title, clinical examination, diagnosis and treatment.

Another papyrus provides additional information on the medical thought of ancient Egypt. It is known as the Ebers[3] papyrus and was written at one of the shrines of Imhotep. In it we find statements such as the following:

> There are vessels (nerves) which go out from the heart to all the
> limbs... The heart is the centre of all the vessels in the whole body.

Souques [374a], noting that the hieroglyph translated by Ebers as "vessels" is translated as "nerves" by Stern, comments:

> In my opinion this can be readily understood. The fact that they used
> only one word probably means that they did not distinguish between
> nerves and vessels. ([374a], p. 126)

Such problems of lexical interpretation are common, not only with Egyptian hieroglyphs but with Greek and Latin texts - or quite simply with anything prior to the 17th century.

There can be no doubt that, long before the dawn of Greek philosophy, the Egyptians possessed detailed medical knowledge, though it was couched in terms of their philosophy and religion which is still largely a mystery to us. It would appear that breathing was regarded as the vehicle of all vital functions and that the concept of pneuma provided the focus of their system of neurophysiology, the circulation of the blood thus being considered less important than breathing. It is difficult, however, to recast into modern terms a set of concepts that belong to a world-view vastly different from our own and about which, for the most part, we are reduced to mere conjectures.

NEW BEGINNINGS IN GREECE

> Anaximenes of Miletus, the son of Eurasystratus, regarded air as the
> principle of everything: everything comes from it, and everything returns
> to it. Just as our soul, which is of air, sustains us, so also breath or air
> surrounds the whole world; breath and air are used synonymously.
> Aetius I, 3, 4 (Dox. 278) [2]

Like Imhotep, Asclepius[4] was deified in recognition of his achievements; but unlike the legendary Egyptian healer, he left no written record of the kind of knowledge he bequeathed to posterity. It was outside the shrines of Asclepius, in fact - among lay philosophers and physicians - that the first ideas of Greek medicine developed. Though specific texts are lacking, we find allusions to this long-lost body of knowledge in Greek literature. Homer tells us of the generally-held view that the brain is contained in the skull and the spinal cord in the vertebrae. On the other hand, the word "nerve" in Homeric usage is applied without distinction to all fibrous tissues; and the function of the brain remains unclear, the seat of sensation being mostly identified with the liver, the diaphragm, and especially the heart.

Observations like these tell us that a system of knowledge about the human body had already come into being. The thinkers who preserved and contributed to it are in many cases known to us by name: Thales of Miletus, Heraclitus of Ephesus, Anaximenes of Miletus, Diogenes of Apollonia, Empedocles, Democritus, Alcmeon and numerous others on down to Hippocrates.

There were some detailed investigations, but at least until Hippocrates the Greek mind constantly went beyond such investigations in leaping to universal, cosmic interpretations. These philosophers, whom Aristotle calls "physiologists" or "physicists", opened a way of thought different from that of theologians. Conceptions of man and the world were freed from the mystery of the gods to become an object of reasoning.

Retracing the discontinuous path of this tradition of philosophising about man and the world that was constantly being taken up anew and reinterpreted in different ways, we can attempt to discern the stages through which it developed.

Sensation was apparently the only nervous system function that attracted the interest of these early Greek thinkers, who regarded it as the source of intelligence. They assumed the existence of channels linking the peripheral sense organs to a sensorium located by some in the heart and by others in the brain. In fact, the mechanism of sensation gave rise to less controversy than its location. The functioning of the mechanism can be summarized as follows: atoms (a highly abstract concept, but a widely used one) emanating from objects which give them their shape, arrive at the peripheral sense organs where an impression is registered. These atomic corpuscles are carried by the "channels" already mentioned to the sensorium, where sensation results from the collision of homeomorphic[5] atoms.

Alcmeon[6] was probably one of the first to carry of dissection and vivisection of animals, and thus to base his theoretical claims on direct observation. He may also have been the first to attempt to demonstrate that the brain is the seat of the sensorium. In fact, he went so far as to posit a link between the eye and the brain which he termed poros or channel.[7] Generalising this claim, he laid down the relations between the sense organs and the brain, where he proceeded to place the seat of sensation. The concept of a channel and the representation that derives from it - a flux of atoms (Anaximenes' air or *pneuma*) moving through a hollow pipe - would influence all later conceptions of nervous system physiology.

From Theophrastus[8] we know that Alcmeon, unlike Heraclitus, Parmenides and Empedocles, made a distinction between sensation and thought, basing his opinion on the observation that man's intelligence is more powerful and more encompassing than the animals', and that whereas all animals feel, only man thinks. With this bold theory, he was opening up new possibilities.

4   CHAPTER 1

A UNIFYING VISION OF MAN AND THE WORLD

> Socrates:
> Is it the blood, or air, or fire by which we think? Or is it none of
> these, and does the brain furnish the sensations of hearing and sight
> and smell, and do memory and opinion arise from these, and does
> knowledge come from memory and opinion in a state of rest?
> Plato ([318a] I, p. 331f.)

The reasoning which Plato ascribes to his teacher Socrates in the above quotation is a precise summing-up of the Greek intellectual journey down to his time. It was Empedocles who believed that blood was the basis of mind; Diogenes of Apolloni (among others) said it was air; Heraclitus, fire; and it was Alcmeon who attributed the thought function to the brain - an attribution that would be hotly disputed for the next two thousand years. Indeed, the whole debate prior to Socrates turns on a theory of sensation based on a broader theory of knowledge and the world.

But once sensation was taken to be the source of knowledge, the question arose as to how and why the process worked. Hence the series of speculative constructs recited by Socrates. These philosophical theories, with their numerous variations and restatements, projected the illusion of appearances onto an imaginary inner space; but like the procession of shadows on the wall of Plato's famous cave, they only hinted at the reality beyond.

The atomic theory provided Democritus[9] with the conceptual basis of his representation of the world, which he saw as an open system, and its relationship with man, a closed system. In this way he attempted to account for the mechanism of sensation, and the more deeply hidden mechanism of knowledge. Atomic theory rests on two principles or postulates, the atom and the void. The human body is an aggregate of constituent atoms with empty spaces between them.

Democritus, using a term already coined by Alcmeon, though giving it a rather different meaning, called these empty spaces "pores" (poroi). Within this interstitial or interatomic network, vital and psychic atoms disseminated in the atmosphere are in constant circulation. Democritus imagined a World-Soul, a fiery element, Parmenides' "Being",[10] distributed in an infinite number of atoms, each of which embodies the One on an infinitesimal scale. This is what he referred to as the Divine. The soul of each individual corresponds to this World-Soul. The essence of Soul, which is made of the most mobile substance - smooth, round, subtle atoms - is its quickening and moving force. Thought itself is movement. The action of breathing draws fresh igneous and psychic matter into the body to replace lost atoms. The soul is the essential part of the body, if only because it is itself the most perfect kind of body. Sensation, reduced to the changes which external impressions make in us, is contact, so the senses are all just variations on the basic sense of touch.

The broad outline of this theory recurs in all of the Presocratics, with variations in motif added by each thinker. The concept of effluvium is often used to account for the relationship between matter and sensation. These effluvia, which somehow retain the form of the objects from which they emanate, are transmitted by the peripheral sense organs to the sensorium, where like matches up with like. On this last point, though, opinions differed. Heraclitus[11] and Anaxagoras[12] preferred to assume a sorting of contraries rather than likes, since only the contrary knows its opposite. As Anaxagoras explains, an object applied to the body surface is felt to be hot only if its temperature exceeds that of the outer skin.

The model propounded by Democritus seems to have had the most long-lasting influence. In one way, however, his theory was less advanced than Alcmeon's. While not lumping thought and sensation together like Parmenides, Heraclitus and Empedocles, he failed to distinguish them as clearly as Alcmeon. For Democritus, sensation and thought were purely mechanical events with a common origin - collision of atoms. He identified the heart as the organ of anger and the liver as the organ of desire; we are thus far from the organic unity of mental life envisaged by Alcmeon. Importantly, however, Democritus pointed out the subjective nature of knowing. Colour, he explains, does not exist per se; it comes from parts in motion; the same with taste. Sweet and bitter, hot and cold exist in men's opinion. For Democritus, nothing exists in reality but atoms and the void.

Empedocles of Agrigentum,[13] Anaxagoras of Clazomenae and Diogenes of Apollonia[14] each proposed a theory of sensation. Empedocles in his theory gave pride of place to the peripheral sense organs. Smell and taste result from the action of odorous and gustatory particles on the nostrils and the mouth. Hearing takes place in the auditory passage when particles of air set in motion by sound penetrate the membrane of the ear. Though all organs, the brain included, have a part in intelligence, according to Empedocles, the heart is its principal seat.

Anaxagoras assumed a formal distinction between mind and matter. Matter and νοῦς are the twin causes of the universe. Matter is inert, and it is made up of an infinite number of identical elements whose varied combinations form all the objects in the world. He called these elements "germs" or seeds"; they are also called *homeomereis* ("things like each other, or the whole"). Human bodily organs are made up of such identical particles. As for νοῦς (mind, soul, intelligence), it is an all-pervading fluid substance that regulates all things, from the rotation of the heavenly bodies to sensation, motion and intelligence in living beings. Thought has its seat in the brain, according to Anaxagoras, but he does not seem to have localised it exclusively there any more than Democritus had.

According to Diogenes, who followed the views of Anaximenes of Miletus, air, which is in eternal motion, constitutes the prime matter of everything. It brings forth earth and fire, the heavenly bodies and the human body, the movement of the planets as well as intelligence. Though brain be the center of sensation, it is not the cerebral substance itself that feels, but the intercerebral air.

One of the more helpful commentators on early Greek neurological thought, Souques points out with some irony modern man's mystification in the face of these "obscure aphorisms" of the Presocratics, which he dismisses perhaps too quickly as flights of imagination.

> These old thinkers elaborated obscure philosophical myths about the origins of the world, its beings and the things in the universe.
> ([374a], p. 13)

Though to modern ways of thinking these theories seem strange, we should not be put off just by the language they use. To be sure, Democritus' atom is not the same as the atom of modern science, but it is its remote ancestor. For these early thinkers, sensation was carried by the primary elements of the universe as they believed they had identified them by the sole power of reflection. And perhaps the theories of knowledge developed by the early Greeks are not so far from our own after all. Democritus' dictum "to think is to feel", echoed by Aristotle in somewhat different terms, would later be taken up by Locke and Condillac. A modern restatement would be that thinking obeys the laws of association of sensation, but we really do not know what such a claim amounts to in terms of the inner workings of the nervous system. Souques' conclusion regarding modern views is perhaps worth quoting:

> Basically [they] know no more than the Ancients did about what goes on in the depths of the sensory nerves, brain cells and motor nerves when sensation, knowledge and voluntary motion take place. They hide their ignorance behind such terms as 'waves', 'nervous influx' and 'transformation of energy', as the Ancients hid theirs with talk of colliding atoms and the action of like on like. ([374a], p. 21)

NOTES

1   The 2.25 m high stele of Hammurabi was discovered at Susa in 1901-1902, and is now in the Louvre Museum.

2   This papyrus was found as Luxor in 1862 by Edwin Smith. It was translated into English in 1930 by James H. Breasted, who states that the document was found to contain both the original text, dating from 3000-2500 B.C., and 69 commentaries or glosses added several centuries later. There are four medical papyri existent: the Edwin Smith, the British Museum's, the Berlin Museum's, and Ebers'.

3   Georg Ebers, German Egyptologist (1837-1898). The papyrus which bears his name dates from the 16th century B.C. The writer's name was Neb-Sext, and it was written at one of the shrines of Imhotep. For the history of the various Egyptian medical texts, see Lefèbvre [228].

4   Or Aesculapius; legend makes him a kind of Thessaly, both warrior and healer.

5   I.e. having the same geometric shape. Man is a microcosm containing all the elements of the Macrocosm on a reduced scale. Modern concepts of "tropism" and "biochemical affinities" basically amount to the same thing, though these terms borrowed from the exact sciences naturally confer an added aura of scientific validity.

6   Alcmeon, 500 B.C. See Freeman [136], Guthrie [169], Kayserling [205] and Schumacher [363].

7   Souques ([374a], p. 14) suggests that Alcmeon may have seen the narrow divide that separates the pial sheath from the dural in the optic nerve.

8   Theophrastus (369-288 B.C.), Peripatetic philosopher.

9   Democritus of Abdera (460?-370? B.C.).

10 Parmenides of Elea (6th cent. B.C.).

11 Heraclitus of Ephesus (born early 5th cent. B.C.).

12 Anaxagoras of Clazomenae (5th cent. B.C.).

13 Empedocles of Agrigentum (484-424?B.C.).

14 Diogenes of Apollonia was a contemporary of Anaxagoras and knew his system.

2. Observation and Theory: Reciprocal Influences

The Data of Perception

Socrates:
Now, do you think one can acquire any appreciable knowledge of the nature of the soul without knowing the nature of the whole man?

Phaedrus:
If Hippocrates the Asclepiad is to be trusted, one cannot know the nature the body, either, except in that way.

Socrates:
He is right, my friend; however, we ought not to be content with the authority of Hippocrates, but to see also if our reason agrees with him on examination.
Plato ([318]. p. 549)

That a physician named Hippocrates[1] made a decisive contribution to medical science is hardly open to dispute, though it is now difficult to determine exactly what that contribution was. The textual evidence leads us to think in terms of a Hippocratic School, which handed down a set of writings known as the Hippocratic corpus.

Even with this considerable body of material, it is not easy to make a coherent picture of the knowledge possessed by physicians of the Hippocratic School, for several reasons. First, the documentation is fragmentary, and probably crucially incomplete.[2] Secondly, the medical knowledge contained in the corpus is couched in a vocabulary inscrutable even to specialists; similarities with modern medical terms can be both deceptive and misleading.[3] Again, Hippocratic medicine is based on a system of concepts and beliefs that remains obscure to historians of the period.

Since dissection of human remains was forbidden, it must be borne in mind that Hippocratic anatomy is derived from dissection of animals. Furthermore, working from lifeless specimens makes it difficult to distinguish anatomy and physiology, and in point of fact this distinction was practically non-existent for a very long period.

Vagueness of observation encouraged vagueness of terminology. The word "nerve" is used by the Hippocratic writers with a meaning just as vague as in the Homeric texts. The term "pores" (poroi) made nerves into hollow vessels enabling the passage of pneuma. Arteries were believed to be vessels containing air, and veins to be vessels containing blood. There was clearly debate as to where these vessels originate: some authors say the

9

brain, some say the liver, and others the heart, depending on their overall conception of animal or human physiology.

Failure to understand the nerves made sensory and motor physiology incomprehensible; but the Hippocratic writers did note that injuries to one side of the head cause disturbances on the opposite side of the body, and that paralysis occurs on the side opposite that of a cerebral lesion. Aretaeus[4] would later attempt to provide an anatomical explanation of this physiological phenomenon.

The nervous physiology of the Hippocratics was limited to the study of brain functions, which is to their credit. Hippocrates and his followers proclaimed the brain as the seat of sensation, including our feelings and our awareness of them. By virtue of the brain, says Hippocrates, man thinks, understands and distinguishes ugly from beautiful, evil from good. It is the brain that makes us mad or delirious, that inspires us with terror or fear, and which, by day or by night, brings us sleeplessness or anxiety.[5]

The Hippocratics regarded the brain as a gland, to which air (according to the author of the *Sacred Disease*)[6] imparts intelligence, while the author of the *Breaths*[7] considers that nothing contributes to intelligence more than the blood. As a result, only the supposedly empty spaces of the cerebral ventricles seem to have received the attention of these writers. This is hardly surprising. All theories of knowledge in this early period tended to focus on the exchanges between the human body and its environment, based on the imaginary idea that air is the agent of these exchanges. The hollow ventricular spaces irresistibly suggested themselves as the site where the exchange process occurred.

The Hippocratic tradition continued for a further century without notable progress. It was not until the reign of Ptolemy I at Alexandria that knowledge of the human body achieved a breakthrough within the space of a single generation, though that breakthrough was to have no sequel. It was the result of two favorable circumstances: the protection of an enlightened monarch who authorised the dissection of human remains, and the presence in Alexandria of two particularly brilliant anatomists, Herophilus[8] and Erasistratus.[9]

Herophilus saw no distinction between nerves, tendons and ligaments. He claimed the existence of hollow cavities in the optic nerves, necessary for the passage of *pneuma*. Rufus of Ephesus[10] would later make the same claim. Herophilus' skill as an anatomist, and his sagacity as an observer, led him to the discovery of the peripheral nerves and the establishment both of their cerebrospinal origin and their twin sensory and motor function. Herophilus went further than simple observation of the brain, which he regarded as the most noble part of the human body; he made sections precise enough to reveal the existence of ventricular cavities in cerebrum and cerebellum.

It was here that Aristotle had suspected the force governing animal and mental life resided a false perception that would long weigh on the anatomy of the human brain. Continuing in that direction, Herophilus made a careful study of what would later become the *rete mirabile*, the network forming the divisions of the carotid and vertebral arteries in the pia mater. In the modern toponymy of the sinuses of the dura mater, the term *torcular Herophili* still recalls the accuracy of the Alexandrian anatomist's observations.

Erasistratus corroborated and extended Herophilus' observations on the peripheral nerves. He revealed his own genius as an observer by noting the importance of the cerebral convolutions and the role of the cerebellum. Whereas for a long time after him the arrangement of the cerebral convolutions would be dismissed as insignificant by other observers, Erasistratus claimed a relationship between the development of intelligence and the complexity of the convolutions. According to Erasistratus, intellectual development in a cross-species perspective corresponds with increasing gyral complexity or "richness", as he termed it. He also found that cerebellar organisation is more complex in fast-running animals. In a remarkable anticipation, he assigned basic functions involving motor activity and equilibrium to the cerebellum. It was not until the 19th century, with the experiments of Flourens and Bouillaud,[11] that Erasistratus' flash of intuition would be verified.

Unfortunately, the golden age of Alexandrian medicine did not last beyond the generation of Herophilus and Erasistratus.

Dissection was again banned by law, and, until Galen,[12] research stagnated. Speculative thinking, for a time held in check by empirical inquiry, would now continue to govern man's self-perception, and more often than not lead him astray.

SPECULATIVE VIEWS

This word logos, men never understand it, neither before hearing it nor afterward. Although all things happen in accordance with this word, they seem to have no experience of words and facts as I expound them, distinguishing and expressing the nature of each thing. But other men do not know what they do in a waking state, as they forget what they do during sleep.
Heraclitus [180]

We have already gained some appreciation of the power of *logos* over human perceptions. As a factor conditioning medical perceptions it predates the Alexandrian school, and it will continue to crop up in various historical contexts.

More than a century before Herophilus and Erasistratus, Plato[13] and Aristotle[14] had made their weighty contributions to the debate.

Plato, in the *Timaeus*, presented a bold cosmological epic. "The god" allowed his own children to fashion the race of man, and they fashioned him in the likeness of the divine cosmos. Thus the head is round, in imitation of the heavenly sphere of the universe. It is the seat of the most noble part of a threefold mortal soul having its other two parts in the thorax, the area of the heart and lungs - this is the so-called "irascible" soul - and in the abdomen, the area of the liver and spleen - the "appetitive" or "imaginative" soul. This diffuse triple soul seems to be closely associated in Plato's thinking with the spinal marrow,

> for it was in this, [he tells us,] that the bonds of life by which the soul
> is bound to the body were fastened, and implanted the roots of the
> mortal kind.[15]
> ([318], VII, p. 191)

We have here a text rich in speculative imagination where mythic elements common to various ancient cosmologies of East and West are reflected; it would surely be a mistake, however, to see in it a human anatomy or physiology in the making. It might perhaps be more realistically regarded as an attempt at a general psychology - later to be invented (or reinvented) by Sigmund Freud.

Aristotle's approach is at first sight more rigorously empirical, but the appearance is deceptive. Man's brain, Aristotle declares, is in the front of the head whereas the back part of it is empty. The brain has no blood, for it contains no vein. That is why, he says, it is cold to the touch. The spinal cord differs in nature from the brain, since it is warm. The heart is the seat of the *sensorium commune;*[16] it is thus the organ of sense. Aristotle says that two senses are found to have their root in the heart, taste and touch; so it is to be expected that the other senses have the same root. The translation has it that Aristotle did a lot of dissecting.[17] He probably did dissect - but only animals. One might wonder what animals he dissected so as to arrive at such confident conclusions as this one: "The correct view [is] that the seat and source of sensation is the region of the heart" ([11a], p. 175); or when he declares that the function of the brain is to modify the heat of the body, and that "inspection shows that the brain has no continuity with the sensory parts" (p. 149), which is why cold-blooded animals have no brain. It is a matter for conjecture here as to whether Aristotle was arguing on the basis of his experiments or a misreading of the Hippocratic texts.

Aristotle's gift for speculative systematization at times serves him better than his skill as a scientific observer. Take for example his attempt to explain visual sensation, in which he seeks to reconcile the views of Empedocles and Democritus. Does vision come from the eye itself, or do we see by virtue of the motions of objects? Aristotle declares that vision crucially presupposes motion caused by vibration of the air placed between eye and illuminated object. The same holds true for smell and hearing. Sensation is thus the sole source of knowledge, and Aristotle is not far from guessing its functional mechanism. On the other hand, he distinguishes sensation and knowledge, the body and the "thinking soul".

The thinking soul, in order to discharge its function, requires images, since these play a fundamental part in all intellectual activity, even the most abstract. The question is to discover the nature of these images, which are not to be identified with immediate sensation but are rather the record of sensation. "In vision, air modifies the pupil, and the pupil something else; it is the same with hearing; but the final term is one."[11e] This "final term" is the sensorium, where the movement taking place "impresses a sort of shape like the one impressed on wax with a seal-ring". [11e]

In such contexts of discovery, everyday experience provides analytical thought with the metaphors it needs; man finds his nature mirrored in the tools he himself has created.

Some of the most conscientious anatomical observers in the history of the field have been unable to resist the attractions of neat systematization which, precisely because of its neatness, seems to possess explanatory power. This seems to have been the process at work in the formation of Erasistratus' theory of *pneuma*. According to Erasistratus, the enormous volume of air we breathe constantly is intended to fill the arteries, which are dedicated for air (in contrast with the veins, which are for containing blood; for it is not possible that Nature could have created two different kinds of vessel for the same function). Drawn into the trachea by respiratory action, air fills the lungs, and, by means of the pulmonary vessels, proceeds into the left ventricle of the heart, where it is transformed into *vital pneuma*. At each contraction of the heart the pneuma is expelled into the aorta and its branches, which transmit it to all regions, and there it is fed by the blood; heat, energy and bodily life result. However, one part of this pneuma rises to the encephalon, first crossing the *rete mirabile*,[18] then entering the cerebral ventricles, where it is transformed into *psychic pneuma*. It is in the cerebral ventricles - particularly the fourth - that the soul is situated. Here the psychic pneuma encounters the effluvia and vibrations of external objects, and that sensation and knowledge occur. From the brain it proceeds down into the motor nerves, which, like the veins and arteries, must be hollow in order to convey the commands of will to the muscles.

To sum up, animal life is a property of vital pneuma, while mental life is the result of psychic pneuma. This theory of pneuma or 'spirits' would

hold, with little modification, down to the time of Harvey, accepted by
physicians and philosophers.
(Souques [374a], p. 130)

We shall find that the clinical area is the most tellingly illustrative of the
interplay of observation and theoretical expectations in the history of brain
anatomy and physiology.

OBSERVATION AND THEORY IN THE CLINICAL CONTEXT

> For us, the human body defines, by natural right, the space of origin
> and distribution of disease: a space whose lines, volumes, surfaces and
> routes are laid down, in accordance with a now familiar geometry, by the
> anatomical atlas. But this order of the solid, visible body is only one way
> - in all likelihood neither the first, nor the most fundamental - in which
> one spatialises disease.
> Foucault ([132a], p. 3)

Pathological data are observable. They are seen and described. But they
call for an explanation. They are then interpreted and related to other such
data in systems where theoretical interests have full play.

Detailed clinical observation is frequent in the Hippocratic corpus. Take
for example the case of language loss in a pregnant woman, discussed in
the Epidemics.[19] She was affected by fever, and suffering back pains. On the
third day, the pain focussed in the area of the neck and head. Language
loss occurred concurrently with convulsions and paralysis of the left arm.
On the fourth day, speech returned. The correlation between right-sided
paralysis and language loss is not remarked on,[20] and the nature of the
language loss remains unclear. Hippocrates uses the terms *aphonos* and
aphonia, but philologists are unsure of the exact meaning to be given to
these particular words - "loss of voice" or "loss of speech".

Mention of voice loss also occurs in other Hippocratic texts. Under the
name hysteria or "uterine suffocation", the author of the treatise *On Diseases of Women* describes a condition in which voice loss is the major symptom.
His explanation of this phenomenon is that the womb has moved to the
liver. The notion of the uterus migrating throughout the entire female body
becomes the last resort for the explanation of women's ailments in this
treatise. The same notion recurs in Galen.

Epilepsy occupies a key position in the Hippocratic writings between
the magical and the scientific conceptions of disease, since it presents both
physical and psychological symptoms. These symptoms are described by the

authors in considerable detail. The brain is recognised as the focus of the disturbance - a highly significant observation in itself. As regards etiology, the role of heredity is clearly identified, but further study of the root causes of the disease brings us onto the cosmic stage, where Elemental Powers have dark and complex effects on man, these being the sources of all pathology. Sometimes the cause of disease is the winter, or the seasons generally, sometimes winds and bad weather, or the subtle influences of the heavenly bodies. In the treatise on *Airs, Waters and Places*, Hippocrates stresses the importance of a knowledge of meteorology and astronomy for any would-be contributor to medical science.

One of the first explicit ideas about language impairment in the tradition came from the draconian practice of cutting out the tongues of certain types of criminals. This gave rise to the idea that all language disorders had their origin in constitutional anomalies of the tongue. Hippocratic pharmacy provides a number of prescriptions designed to correct excessive moistness of the tongue. Aristotle corroborates this particular viewpoint.

Erasistratus, for his part, also resorted to imaginative speculation in his interpretation of the causes of disease. Paralysis was explained as the result of the penetration of the nerve-channels by humours which obstructed the passage of pneuma - or in other words the transmission of motor commands.

For Asclepiades of Bithynia,[21] founder of the "Methodist" school of physicians,[22] all disease was due to the contraction or dilation of interatomic channels. Athenaeus,[23] founder of the "Pneumatist" school,[24] one of whose members was Rufus,[25] the author of a careful description of the brain, and Aretaeus[26] were of the opinion of the Stoics that Nature was made up of two principles: matter and pneuma. Pneuma is the vital force, the World-Soul of which each individual soul is an emanation. It dispenses health or disease. Deficiencies of pneuma are the source of all pathological states. Its accumulation in the bodily organs causes epilepsy. If it is trapped in the womb, hysteric attacks are the result.

Even Galen,[27] who single-handedly promoted medicine to the status of an "art", if not quite a science, was not immune to the spell cast by speculative thinking over the slow, plodding work of clinical examination. Dreams played an important part in his life. He took up the study of medicine as a result of a dream of his father; and one night when he was in pain with a liver ailment, Asclepius appeared to him in a dream and told him to have a vessel between the thumb and forefinger of the right hand opened. On waking, he did this and was cured. Later he performed the same operation with similar success, he tells us. Towards the end of his life he wrote an essay on *The Diagnosis of Illness by Means of Dreams*.

NOTES

1   Hippocrates, born c. 460 B.C.
2   The Hippocratic Corpus: see [240] and [374a], p. 35.
3   In the preface to his monumental edition and French translation of
    Hippocrates [240], the great lexicographer and medical scholar Littré
    declared that: "the collection of Hippocratic books is an incoherent
    muddle where it is difficult to find one's way at first".
4   Aretaeus of Cappadocia, 81-138? or 131-200?
5   This is a summary of a passage (text established by Littré, vol. VI)
    from the *Sacred Disease*, probably written by a pupil of Hippocrates.
6   See note 5. "For these reasons I consider the brain to be the most
    powerful organ of man's body, for when it is healthy it is our inter-
    preter of the impressions produced by the air; now, the air gives it
    intelligence." ([76], translated from Littré's version).
7   "Blood in man contributes the greater part of intelligence; some
    even say that it contributes all of it."
8   Herophilus, c. 300 B.C.
9   Erasistratus, c. 260 B.C., born at Julis on Chios. Pliny claims that he
    was the grandson of Aristotle.
10 Rufus of Ephesus, end of 1st century. See [352]
11 See notes 11 & 12, p.7
12 See p. 27.
13 Plato: 428-348 B.C.
14 Aristotle: 384-322 B.C.
15 Later in the same text (p. 191 of the Loeb edition), Plato refers to
    "the marrow...a universal seed-stuff for every mortal kind".
16 Aristotle seems to use this term with a more precise new meaning, one
    which it would henceforth retain: the seat of the internal senses, where
    information coming from the five senses is received and images are
    formed.
17 According to an ancient tradition revived by Cuvier in the 19th cen-
    tury, Alexander the Great gave his old teacher a menagerie which he
    stocked with exotic animals, as well as a botanical garden.
18 Herophilus was the first to examine this imaginary locus of human physi-
    ology.
19 In the *Epidemics*.
20 However, in his description of traumatic meningitis, and in the treatise
    On the Wounds of the Head, Hippocrates notes that "if the wound is on
    the left side of the head, the convulsions will appear on the right side
    of the body, and conversely."

21 Asclepiades of Bithynia, in Rome c. 120 B.C.

22 This school claimed to have the best method for learning and practicing medicine. The doctrine was based on atomic theory, by which it sought to explain sensation, thought, movement, and the pathogenesis of any disease.

23 Athenaeus was a physician in Cilicia and a contemporary of Pliny.

24 Athenaeus taught that the true elements are not earth, water, air and fire, but hot, cold, moist and dry, and added a fifth, spirit (pneuma), whence the school's name. This doctrine is closely connected with Stoicism, but its remote ancestor is Anaxagoras of Clazomenae (see p. 13, n. 12).

25 See n. 10 above.

26 See n. 4 above.

27 Galen: 127-199 A.D.

3. EMERGENCE OF MAJOR THEMES

GALEN'S NEW SYNTHESIS

> Moreover, if anyone thinks that nothing is known, he does not even
> know whether that can be known, since he declares that he knows noth-
> ing. I will therefore spare to plead cause against a man who has put his
> head where his feet ought to be.
> Lucretius ([245], p. 313)

A superficial reading of Galen might lead one to believe that the most
illustrious physician of the Hellenistic period, the confidant of Marcus
Aurelius, was only the faithful follower of his teachers. For Galen, the nerves
are hollow tubes, as they were for Alcmaeon. For Galen, as for Herophilus,
these nerves bring the muscles energy which they draw from the brain like
water from a well. In spite of Erasistratus' efforts, Galen had no interest in
the solid parts of the brain; in accordance with prevailing tradition, what
interested him was the ventricular cavities where the mysterious pneuma
was thought to reside.

Galen correctly believed that anatomy and physiology are the foundation of medicine. Respectful of taboo, however, he dissected only animals,
making the hazardous assumption that human anatomy is no different from
animal anatomy. This approach led him into numerous errors. He assigned
the *rete mirabile* the impossible function of producing *pneuma*. In fact, the
development of the *rete* in man does not have anything like the importance
it has in such mammals as the ungulates.[1]

His overall conception of the nervous system rested on an equally false
idea: difference in the consistency of its various parts. According to this
criterion, the cerebrum and the sensory nerves are soft - for what is soft
feels and receives impressions - while the cerebellum, the spinal cord and
the motor nerves are hard - for what is hard moves and is strong. At the
junction of the brain and spinal cord there are nerves that are not part of
this classification and belong to both categories at once.[2]

The brain, says Galen (in a remote allusion to Plato's *Timaeus*),[3] is formed
out of the purest part of the human seed. It is the greatest of the viscera.
Here again, ideological interests diverted scientific perception into false consciousness. As Daremberg [92b] comments, Galen:

> hastens to open up the brain and penetrate its cavities, to discover
> communication channels, to find out how they correspond to the main
> functions they have to carry out... He starts in the place where the spirit

19

arrives, the anterior ventricles, which receive it by way of the olfactory
meatus; then he examines the middle ventricle, the passageway for
pneuma, which from there travels to the fourth ventricle through a tube,
whence it issues forth into the nerves, giving them life and power.

But for Galen, as Souques [374a] points out, all the brain's pneuma does
not come from the olfactory meatus. The main part of it is formed by the
rete. This conclusion means that, in Galen's view, the pneuma has to travel
a complex route, reaching the rete via the carotids after coming from the
left side of the heart which receives it from the lungs. Galen also believed
that this pneuma is abundant in the cerebellum, which must be basis of all
the body's nerves.

In the midst of all these erroneous deductions, Galen showed himself to
be an anatomist of genius in his description of the system of nerves originating from the spinal cord. The cord, he tells us, arises from the brain
"like a trunk rising up into a great tree". From this trunk, extending down
the spine, he sees various nervous offshoots, "which, like boughs and branches,
divide and subdivide into thousands of smaller ones". Because of these, he
says, the whole body is involved in movement and sensation. He marvels at
this ingenious arrangement. If the cord did not exist, either all the parts of
the animal below the head would be completely devoid of movement, or
else nerves would have to descend from the brain to each of them separate-
ly. To stretch a fragile nerve from the brain to each of the parts would be
the act of a Creator little concerned with the safety of his creatures.

> Therefore, [he concludes,] it was preferable that the cord, arising from
> the brain like a river flowing from its source, should send a nerve to
> each of the parts as a channel of sensation and voluntary motion.[4]

Leaving aside Galen's teleological reasoning, it must be said that his
presentation of the spinal nerve system is surprisingly accurate. He was the
first to draw attention to the arrangement of nerves in symmetrical pairs.
He correctly described seven pairs of cranial nerves. Oddly enough, he did
not include the olfactory nerve, which he regarded as a stretched-out extension of the brain.

The function of the recurrent nerves of the voice especially interested
Galen. He was able to show that section of the laryngeal muscles, which
contract and tense during voice production, results in loss of voice. He
noted that section of the recurrents produces the same effect by paralysing
these muscles, and that section of the pneumogastrics also rapidly brings
on complete loss of voice. Since recurrents and pneumogastrics come from
the brain, he concluded that it is there that the true seat of the vocal faculty resides.

Against the authority of Aristotle, who had favoured a cardiocentric theory of sensation and thinking, Galen took the side of Hippocrates and Plato, ascribing the supreme role to the brain on the basis of empirical evidence. Among his numerous remarks on the subject, Galen writes that,

> we should agree with Plato and Hippocrates, as against Aristotle and Chrysippus,[5] that the brain is the source of voluntary movement, while the heart is the source of involuntary movement.[6]

By way of generalization, Galen arrived at the view that the nerves transmit energies from the brain into the parts and relay messages from the parts up to the brain.

Hippocrates may have guessed at the reality of chiasmus, as may Aretaeus, but it was Galen who first actually saw it. He was able to give an accurate description of the phenomenon, but he could not see the reason for it. His demon would later explain it to him as he slept - thus giving rise to a theory of vision that would last into the Middle Ages.[7]

Galen tended to offer teleological interpretations for everything he studied.

> The reason why Nature has not made the phrenics come from the brain, [he declared,] is because the nerves of the cervical cord are stronger, harder, and more suited to active movement.[8]

Such reasoning is no longer a part of science, but if we leave this aside Galen's knowledge is often surprising in its depth and accuracy. One case history will serve to illustrate these qualities. Pausanias the sophist was suffering from loss of sensation in the last two fingers of the right hand. Questioning him, Galen discovered that he had fallen from his chariot and that his upper back had hit the ground. By applying the medication which had previously been put on the patient's fingers on his upper back instead, Galen was able to cure him completely. Galen recounts that following this cure a fierce debate arose between himself and the physicians as to where a paralysis of sensation alone could originate.

> I wanted to embarrass them, [Galen goes on,] and I asked them how they could explain the loss of movement alone. Seeing that they could offer no reply, I explained to them that there are nerves that are connected to the muscles and others that are connected to the skin. When the first kind are affected, movement alone is lost; when the second kind are, it is sensation that is interrupted.[9]

As soon as Galen had been told the details of Pausanias' mishap, he had realized that the nerve at the seventh cervical vertebra (which was the place of the injury) had been affected. Thus he had achieved a sufficiently accurate representation of the nervous system to be able to obtain effective medical results, using the power of deductive reasoning coupled with anatomical knowledge more detailed than that of his contemporaries.

While other medical figures fell into oblivion despite the reputation they enjoyed in their lifetime, Galen's name would forever after be linked with the idea of a classic phase of ancient medicine. Centuries would go by without eroding the monolithic authority of Galen's medical writings. Every new discovery would have to be fitted into the Galenic framework, and any questioning of the framework itself would be regarded as bordering on sacrilege.

THE INNATENESS HYPOTHESIS

> Now careful consideration will show that the mechanism of speech displays a skill on Nature's part that surpasses belief. In the first place, there is artery passing from the lungs to the back of the mouth, which is the channel by which the voice, originating from the mind, is caught and uttered. Next, the tongue is placed in the mouth and confined by the teeth; it modulates and defines the inarticulate flow of the voice and renders its sounds distinct and clear by striking the teeth and other parts of the mouth. Accordingly, my school is fond of comparing the tongue to the quill of a lyre, the teeth to the strings, and the nostrils to the horns which echo the notes of the strings when the instrument is played.
> Cicero, *De Natura Deorum* II, 148 ([73], p. 267)

In Biblical tradition, speech is given to man by a God who defines Himself as the Word. Genesis tells us that God first created plants and animals, then man; but that man was entrusted with the task of naming the living things of Creation over which he was to reign in the Garden of Eden. There is accordingly a fundamental ambiguity in Judaic thought about the relationship between man and language: language is God's gift, but man is left free to use it as he wills in naming the things of his world.

Herodotus'[10] oft-quoted story of the Pharaoh Psammeticus has two points. The first is the belief in an original language, the oldest human language. This idea is found developed later in Plato's *Cratylus*,[11] with the interpretation that we have already noted regarding the relationship between word and object, and it would haunt philosophies of language till the 18th century.[12] The second point of the story is implicit acceptance of the innateness of man's language ability. For the narrator of the story, and also presumably for its originators, there was no doubt that speech so closely conforms to human nature that it appears spontaneously at the appropriate moment, without any necessity of stimulus from the social environment.[13]

But these two points further suggest that individual development is

understood as a repetition albeit an abbreviated one of the development of
the species, since the first word pronounced by the children in the story is
regarded as belonging to the most ancient language of mankind. Modern
genetics has the logical concept that ontogeny repeats phylogeny.

Herodotus' Egyptian tale is of prime importance, for it reveals a conceptual system about language that has been expanded on down through the
ages. That conceptual system is contradicted by another system that represents language as a social fact, the fruit of human ingenuity.

According to Pindar,[14] man's faculties are the gift of the gods. In modern
terms, this means that they are innate, that they cannot be acquired but
only developed. For Pindar as for Heraclitus,[15] the order of things in human societies belongs to the sphere of *nomos*, the will and decree of the
gods. But for Heraclitus, again, fate is *logos*, the maker of all existences.
Everything happens in accordance with fate, which is identified with necessity. The entire substance of the universe is shot through with logos. Fate,
with logos its essence, is the ethereal body, the life-giving germ of all things
and the measure of their allotted span.[16]

It is against this archaic backdrop that the understanding of man's relation to language and the relation of language to the world gradually un-
folds through the long debate between "physeists", for whom words have
meaning by nature, and "theseists", for whom word meaning is a matter of
convention without there being any logical relationship between word and
object. In the Middle Ages, "Realists" became the party of physis, and
"Nominalists" the party of thesis.[17]

Whenever Western thought has leaned towards the theseist position, this
has led to an emphasis on the social learning aspect of language, and has at
the same time raised a fundamental question: if language is conventional,
how did it originate?

Since, in early Antiquity at least, language was accepted as a "given", we
can readily understand that philosophical discussion was largely concerned
not with the origin of language that was divine but with the relationship
between language and world, between word and object. For Parmenides,
Anaxagoras and Empedocles, names were to be regarded as synonyms for
concepts; but these same philosophers also believed that defining names
were frequently assigned to objects as a result of an initial erroneous judgement of their nature. Thus the order of *nomos* became the order of uncertainty, error and approximation, in contrast with the true order of nature,
physis.

In the *Cratylus*, *Parmenides* and *The Sophist*, Plato attempts to resolve
these opposing viewpoints by the use of dialectic. To summarize his argument, if the name of a thing is determined by the thing's nature, then language belongs to the world of *physis*, and we may conclude that it reflects

the true nature of the thing; but if names belong to the world of *nomos*, they cannot lead us to true knowledge. Plato tries to show that, although the name does not truly represent the thing, it is to be regarded as the equivalent of the idea we have of the thing itself. This is perhaps not altogether convincing as a solution of the *nomos-physis* problem. Building on this line of argument, however, Plato takes the position that the name is only a phonic symbol that does not in itself reveal the truth of the idea it represents. This way of looking at the problem has had a decisive influence on subsequent philosophizing. It placed the sign system of language in a semiotic perspective and thus opened up a path to be followed by many thinkers on language, from Augustine to Saussure.

In the period dominated by Plato, a new representation of the world of language-signs developed. Nomos became a social inheritance that almost seemed to overshadow the physis bestowed by the gods. In the *Cratylus*, Plato has Socrates say that speaking of a divine origin of naming is merely a way to evade objective examination of its origin and development. Eighteenth-century readers in particular would take this lesson to heart.[18]

Aristotle's position on the subject of language is a rather complex one. For him, the language faculty belongs to the order of *physis*, that is, to the very laws governing human nature. But the actualizations of this single faculty in the various languages of mankind belong to the order of *nomos* (a term which, by the way, Aristotle avoids, preferring *thesis* instead). The language faculty is man's distinguishing characteristic: Aristotle defines man not as a rational animal (this is an incorrect tradition) but as a speaking animal. The undeniable fact that there are different human languages belongs to the sphere of the social, the conventional, manners. Aristotle develops his views of logos most fully in the *Rhetoric*. In that treatise language is presented as a tool of thought which can be mastered through training. One can learn to speak "dialectically" to others as subjects who can respond to what has been said, or one can speak "rhetorically" to the whole man, capable of judgement but also of emotions which the speaker must know how to arouse or appease. This would appear to be how Aristotle arrived at his distinction between what is innate and what is learned in human language. The faculty is innate, whereas the variety of language, and the uses to which language can be put, are facts belonging to the social world.

The Stoics attempted to reassign language to man alone. Epicurus[19] was the first to put forward the idea that man owes the faculty of speech neither to the gods nor even to his own reason, but merely to a biological function similar to the functions of sight and hearing. Zeno[20] later proposed a more balanced view in which language emerges from reason while reason itself develops out of the complexity of social relations.

Much of our information on the thinking of the Stoics comes from the late Greek writer Diogenes Laertius.[21] He tells us that Chrysippus[22] had bypassed the problem of the word-object relation and chosen to start with the much more complex phenomenon of meaning that arises from the combination of words in sentences. For Chrysippus, context effectively did away with naming ambiguity. He had also put forward the rather significant idea that language does not follow logic, an anticipation of modern views. Diogenes Laertius expounds the various opinions of the Stoic philosophers in a chapter entitled Language Theory.

> In the opinion of most, [he says,] dialectic speculation begins with the question of the voice. Voice is air receiving a shock which is perceived by the hearing, as is said by Diogenes of Babylonia.[23]

We note the desire to remain within the confines of that definition at the physical and physiological level. After mentioning the voice of animals, Diogenes Laertius gives this definition of human voice: "the voice of man is articulate and is brought forth by thought". Further on he states: "Voice is a body, in the Stoic view" this is what Chrysippus in particular says in the second book of the Physics,

> for every active agent is a body; now voice acts by travelling from the speaker to the hearer.

Then these definitions follow:

> The word is a voice made of letters, like 'day'. Language is a meaningful voice brought forth by thought, like 'It is day'. Dialect refers to words bearing the mark of a people, such as Greek, or a particular region's dialect words.[24]

In these extracts, as in the Cicero quotation that heads this chapter, we find the same desire to place language in an objective light, and to situate it within the realm of natural phenomena. This is what Lucretius, too, was saying in his *De Rerum Natura*:

> But the various sounds of the tongue nature drove them to utter, and convenience moulded the names for things...
> (V, 1028-1029)

Several factors contributed to this evolution of thinking on language. The discovery of changes in languages over time, and the work of philologists on old texts, tended to weaken the position of those who regarded words as expressing of a profound congruence with objects, and who saw language itself as divine gift. These same factors buttressed the arguments of those who regarded language and all its manifestations as purely human phenomena, social phenomena, and thus as closely tied to a given environment, a culture, or a historical period.

In the Ancient period we thus find a full circle being reached that would be reached again several times over, in a kind of intellectual recursivity, down to our own time. To this extent our investigation deals not with evolution of ideas but with repetition and constant reworking of the same themes, and constant restating of them in accordance with the habits of thought and the metalanguage of the day.

THE HEART VERSUS THE BRAIN

> Tell me, where is fancy bred? Or in the heart, or in the head?
> Shakespeare, *Merchant of Venice* III, 64.

If speech is derived from an innate language faculty, what is the seat of that faculty? The question is part of the wider debate on the relation between mind and body which has been carried on down through the centuries, and in which Pythagoras[25] had already seemingly taken sides when he placed the rational part of the soul in the brain.

As we have seen, observers noted the correlation between wounds of the skull and disturbances of language, though at the same time the tongue was regarded as having a central role in language production.

During the entire period we have covered, linking language to the human body was not a major issue for thinkers who accepted the idea of the soul having a place in the body, and who saw in language no more than an epiphenomenon of thought whereby thought communicated itself.

The first approach to that issue would have to be an effort to clarify the meaning - in physiological terms - of the idea of a soul housed in the body space. Ancient philosophers came back to this problem again and again, but they could not resolve it decisively on the basis of their evidence. Depending on the particular time and place, opinion tended towards one or the other option - the heart or the brain. These came to be thought of as the main sites of intellect and emotion, while the soul that nourished them wandered in imaginary inner space.

We saw Hippocrates[26] awarding to the brain the distinction of being the seat of higher human faculties, thus taking the opposite side from those who ascribed the preeminent role to the heart. However, we must be careful not to read too much into his position, since it is based only on correlations such as the one he established between the brain and epilepsy.[27]

While Plato exalted the head (and therefore the brain), Aristotle regarded the brain as no more than a secondary organ where the pneuma is cooled, and thought the heart to be the seat of the *sensorium commune*.

Cardiocentrists were in fact much more numerous than cerebrocentrists. The assumption of the heart's preeminence derives ultimately from folk belief. The heart is in an obvious sense the organ of life: if the heart stops beating, it indicates death; when the heart-beat accelerates, it expresses strong human feelings and sensations. Herophilus seems to have decisively refuted the cardiac theory of sensation by showing that the heart had no sensory function, and Erasistratus agreed with him; but the remarkable progress in human anatomy and physiology we owe to the two Alexandrians unfortunately ended with them.

In the realm of folk belief, the heart has always retained pride of place in the human body. Our language today expresses this viewpoint as much as it did in the first centuries of our era. In the Gospel of Luke (who is said to have been a physician) we find this kind of statement when Mary finds her Son teaching the Doctors in the Temple: "But his mother kept all these sayings in her heart".[28]

Galen believed he had irrefutable proof that the brain was the organ of thought. In the course of a polemic against the opinion of Erasistratus that the arteries contained air or "spirits", Galen showed that while pressure applied to the heart did not deprive an animal of sensation or movement, pressure on the brain did. Therefore the largest concentrations of "spirit" were not in the heart but in the brain.[29]

In the *Use of Parts*, Galen, who returned to the attack, refuting the cardiocentric position stated by Aristotle, declares:

> The head seems to many observers to have been created for the brain, and thus to contain all the senses, like servants and retainers of the great King [i.e. the brain]. However, crabs and crustaceans have no head. The part which governs the senses and voluntary motion is situated in the thorax. Thus what in us is found in the head, or the brain, is found in the thorax in these animals. However, if it is not the brain but the heart that is the origin of these phenomena, it is with good reason that in the acephala the sense organs have been placed in the thorax; for in this way they are in direct contact with the heart situated near them, and one must then say that it is untrue that in others they are located in the brain. Those who hold this opinion must regard the head as quite superfluous, since they are unable to assign any function to the brain or to situate the sense organs in it. In fact, to imagine that the brain was created just to cool the natural heat of the heart and regulate its temperature is totally absurd. If so, instead of placing the brain so far away from the heart, Nature could have placed it as a kind of cover for the heart, as it did in the case of the lungs. At least it could have situated it

in the thorax; but it would not have situated the origins of all the senses
in the brain.

Galen waxes ironic in his attempts to demolish Aristotle's thesis and
adds:

> Do not think I am joking for an attentive examination will show you
> that a refrigerative action would be more efficient in reaching the heart
> if it came from the heels rather than from the brain.[30]

Nevertheless, the cardiocentric theory persisted long after Galen, because
of the authority of Aristotle. Avicenna[31] for one repeated Aristotle's teaching: he held that the heart is the first organ to develop in the embryo, and
that as a result it exercises an influence on the growth of all the other
organs - including the brain.

In the middle of the 16th century, Andrea Cesalpino[32] still believed that
the nerves came from the heart. In fact, the cardiac theory of mind would
have its supporters even at the beginning of the 19th century. Bichat, Pinel
and Esquirol, the great pioneers of psychopathology, still regarded the heart
as the centre of emotional life.

NOTES

1   Ungulates are "... a diverse group of placental mammals characterised
    as hoofed, herbivorous quadripeds".
    Encyclopedia Britannica (Micropedia).
2   Souques [374a] remarks: "In Galen's terminology 'encephalon' means
    the cerebrum and 'parencephalon' means the cerebellum... He puts for-
    ward the rather surprising idea that the head was made, not for the
    brain, but for the eyes, since the eyes must always occupy a salient
    position to the front of the body, the direction of movement. They
    could not be placed in the back of the head because they had to re-
    ceive a soft nerve, the optic nerve, which cannot come from the cere-
    bellum as it only produces hard nerves" (p. 192, n. 2).
3   See p. 21.
4   A summary is given here of Use of Parts XII, 11 (Daremberg 1854-
    1856, II), the text quoted by Souques (p. 196ff.)
5   Chrysippus (281-205 B.C.), Greek philosopher of the Stoic school.
6   This viewpoint is developed in [141c], pp. 278f.

7   Galen devotes a great deal of space to the function of the optic nerves. In the *Dissection of Nerves*, 2 (Khn II, 833), he states that the optic nerves are hollow: "but in these nerves alone, there is a clearly perceptible channel..." He adds: "The organ of sight contains a luminous pneuma which emanates continuously from the encephalon, and the optic nerves are hollow to receive this pneuma."

8   *Use of Parts* VII, 14-15 (Daremberg) [92b].

9   Souques ([374a], pp. 203f). Galen adds: "The physicians do not even know that there are special roots sent out to the skin of the whole upper limb, from which it receives sensation, and others which give rise to the branches that go to the muscles." Galen's basic ideas about nerve function are found in The Seat of Diseases IV (Daremberg 1854-1856, II, 58ff.)

10 Herodotus ([184], vol. I, pp. 275ff.). Psammetichus desired to learn which was the oldest nation on earth. He devised a plan whereby he took two newborn children and gave them to a shepherd to bring up among his flocks. He charged that no one should speak any word in their hearing. Two years passed, and then one day the children ran to the shepherd and said *bekos!* On hearing of this, the king summoned his wise men to tell him what language bekos belonged to. He found that it was the Phrygian word for "bread". Herodotus says: "Reasoning from this fact the Egyptians confessed that the Phrygians were older than they. This is the story which I heard from the priests of Hephaestus' temple at Memphis..."

11 Socrates: "... manifestly the gods (this is certain at least) use names correctly, that is to say, those that are correct by nature..."With a very clever use of dialectic 'Socrates', in the presence of Hermogenes and Cratylus, demolishes the basis of this position, and in its place proposes a theory of naming by imposition, along with some striking observations about the suggestive power of sounds.

12 See p. 62.

13 The German Emperor Frederick II and James IV of Scotland performed the same experiment.

14 Pindar, 518-438 B.C.

15 Heraclitus: see p. 7, n. 11.

16 I, 7, 22 (Dox. 303)

17 See Robins [345], chapters 2 and 4.

18 See p. 64.

19 Epicurus, 341-270 B.C.

20 Zeno, 335-264 B.C.

21 Diogenes Laertius, beginning of 3rd cent. Almost nothing is known of him, but his *Lives and Opinions of the Philosophers* has survived.

22 See p. 28, n. 5.
23 Diogenes of Babylonia, 240?-150? B.C. , a disciple of Chrysippus.
24 This is a summary of the account given by Diogenes.
25 Pythagoras, 6th cent. B.C.
26 See p. 9.
27 See Penfield [305c]. It is hardly admissible to interpret the thought of such a remote period in modern terms without further ado.
28 Luke 2, 51.
29 Galen, *On the Opinions of Hippocrates and Plato* II, 8 [141c], pp. 185ff.
30 Galen, *Use of Parts* VIII, 2, 3 [92b], vol. I, pp. 527-530.
31 Avicenna, 980-1037.
32 Andrea Cesalpino, 1519-1603.

II
THE MYTHOLOGY OF BODY AND MIND

1. LANGUAGE AS A DETERMINANT OF PERCEPTION

IMAGINARY ANATOMY

> Then these verbal wizards produce another argument. Man, they say, is especially gifted with understanding of the sciences so that they can help him to compensate by his wits for what Nature has denied him. But does it seem likely that Nature would be so alert and careful about things like midges and grasses and flowers, and yet be caught napping over man alone, so that he has need of the sciences which the notorious Thoth, the evil genius of the human race devised to be its greatest curse? These are quite useless as regards happiness; they are in fact an obstacle to the very thing for which they were specially invented...
>
> Erasmus, *Praise of Folly*, trans. by Betty Radice, London, The Folio Society, 1974, p. 55

Galen (Souques[1] tells us) filled the noses of several slaves with strong smelling substances. When he asked them to hold their breath, they smelt nothing. When he instructed them to breathe, they had a very penetrating sensation. For Galen, the conclusion to be drawn from this was that the brain breathes. With each breath, air enters the anterior ventricles, and leaves on the out-breath. The pituitary membrane is porous; the best proof of this is the frequent and sudden evacuation of nasal mucus. Smell is closely connected with breathing. Galen expands on this theme.[2] He expresses his admiration for:

> the Creator of living things... because he fashioned a unique instrument capable of fulfilling various functions.

He observes that:

> Nature provided a bone, the ethmoid bone, with holes like a sponge, to protect the brain [or more specifically, the anterior ventricles, during breathing] by keeping out hard bodies that might injure it, and by obstructing the flow of cold air into the ventricles.

Erasistratus' interest in developing a taxonomy of cerebral convolutions[3] raised Galen's irony:

> ...When he [Erasistratus] claims that the 'epencranis' (parencephalon) and the encephalon itself are more complex in man than in the animals, because his intelligence is greater than theirs, it seems to me that his understanding of the facts is incorrect; for even the ass, which is supposed to be a stupid animal, has a very complex encephalon, whereas

33

from this point of view it should be among the most simple. It would be
much more accurate to say that intelligence depends on the quality of
the thinking matter [i.e. the psychic pneuma that determines the quality
of the thinking].[4]

Thus it was that medical science came to attribute only minimal importance to the visible anatomy of the cortex and applied itself from now on
to developing a ventricular theory, as required by the very notion of pneuma.

At every developmental stage of thinking about the nature of things and
their order, man has projected notions derived from what he knows of the
physical world onto whatever phenomenon he is studying. Galen made use
of contemporary notions about fluid mechanics in his attempt to conceptualise the nervous system's exchanges with the rest of the body.

The brain was to be regarded as a kind of distillery which takes in the
prime matter and sense impressions from the air surrounding the body and
out of them makes pneuma, which gives rise to motion, sensation and
consciousness within the body space.

The Middle Ages came to prefer the term *animal spirits*[5] to pneuma, but
it was only a change of name. In the search for a better understanding of
how the fermentation process worked, anatomists looked to the place where
the spirits were produced and refined. This explains the importance attached
to the study of the *rete mirabile*. Cerebrocentrists and cardiocentrists took
opposing viewpoints on this line of research; some tried to eliminate the
conflict by proposing a single function for the rete. Ignorance of the real
mechanism of the circulation of the blood did not in fact allow of a clear
understanding of blood flow in the brain; only progress in the knowledge
of fluid dynamics would later make this possible.[6]

It was at brain level that the vascular network with its serried links called
the rete mirabile was supposed to develop, creating an inner sanctum where
part of the spirits was distilled and mixed with air breathed into the cerebral ventricles through the porous base of the skull.

After the *rete*, the ventricles enjoyed pride of place in the anatomical
discussions of the Middle Ages. They were quite simply the most important
structures. In the spaces they enclosed, there took place what one might
call (in excessively modern terms, perhaps) the functional differentiation of
the pneuma. After Galen it was claimed that the anterior ventricles received pneuma carrying sense data, and, together with the apparatus of the
rete, formed the *sensorium commune* or *sensus communis*, while the posterior ventricles were the location from which the motor pneuma was dif-

fused. The credibility of this anatomical model was based on the tradition of medical teaching and on the texts rather than on empirical study. Avicenna,[7] in his Canon,[8] provides only a compilation of Greek authors (Aristotle and Galen in particular) from whom he draws all his anatomical and physiological information. In deference to Aristotle's views he adopts the cardiocentric position.

Two centuries later, Mondino de Luzzi[9] began practicing anatomy. He was even the first to introduce the discipline at the University of Bologna, where he had studied and later taught. His anatomical treatise [274] remained an authoritative work until the sixteenth century.[10] However, what Mondino believed he saw mainly conformed to the teaching of the past. He recognized the ventricles, noted the existence of the *sensus communis* in the middle of the brain, and indicated the presence of the *rete mirabile* at its base.

There was no doubt in the minds of medieval anatomists that Galen had based his account of the nervous system on the dissection of human cadavers. The existence of the *rete mirabile*, the linchpin of the whole neurophysiological model represented by the pneuma theory, could not therefore be questioned. The phenomenon of life, both animal and human, could not be understood without the anatomical assumptions underlying the physiological model. Those assumptions had been made since Hippocrates, and Galen had only confirmed them and clarified their implications - seemingly by observation and experiment.

Now while the medieval anatomists (if they can be called that) were convinced that Galen had done their observing for them as far as the human body was concerned, there was to be understanding later on that this was not the case. Galen, bound by the taboos of his era, could exercise his anatomical skills only in dissecting mammals, especially ungulates in which the vascular network of the *rete* is readily observable. He never sought to hide the fact.

Jacopo Berengario da Carpi[11] and Andreas Vesalius[12] were the first to deny categorically that the *rete* existed in man. Vesalius realized the source of the error: it was that Galen had never dissected a human cadaver. "He described", said Vesalius, "the brain of an ox, not that of a man"[13].

Vesalius, his contemporaries and his seventeenth-century successors did not, however, abandon the theory of *animal spirits*; they had no other model available. Imaginary anatomy led to imaginary localisations, while language continued to condition scientific perception.

IMAGINARY LOCALIZATIONS

> But, in order to understand in greater detail how the mind, located in
> the brain, can thus receive impressions of external objects through the
> mediation of the nerves, it is necessary to distinguish three things in
> these nerves: these are, first, the membranes which enclose them... ;
> second, their interior substance... ; and finally the animal spirits, which
> are like a very subtle wind or air which, coming from the chambers or
> concavities in the brain, flows away by these same tubes throughout the
> muscles.
>
> Descartes ([99b], p. 87f.)

Galen had been able to distinguish sensory and motor pathways in his
description of the central nervous system.[14] The sensory pathways, he believed, led to the anterior cerebral ventricles, and the motor pathways came
from the posterior ventricles. A functional role for the ventricles had already been proposed by Herophilus,[15] who had placed the seat of the soul
in the fourth ventricle.

During the fourth and fifth centuries, the Fathers of the Christian Church,[16]
basing themselves on the speculation of pagan Antiquity (particularly the
teaching of Aristotle), undertook an initial systematization of the localization of the internal senses and the mental faculties in the cavities of the
brain. These cavities or ventricles were held to be three in number, each
one being the seat of one or several mental functions.

In the two lateral ventricles (regarded as forming a single cavity, the
first), sensations were received from the five senses; they constituted the
sensus communis. The images produced by these sensations were formed in
the back of the first cavity, or in the second (the third cerebral ventricle, in
fact). This second cavity was also the site of reasoning, judgement and
cognitive thinking. The third cavity (fourth ventricle) was the seat of memory.

This arrangement was adopted with minor variations in all models of
the brain, both in the Christian West and Muslim East, which became quite
numerous between the eleventh and the fifteenth centuries. Conspicuous
by its absence in these representations is any indication of the division of
the hemispheres.[17]

An important aspect was added to this conception of brain localization,
however, when the focus of theory building shifted from static to dynamic
models. The shift occurred around the tenth century, and it was based on
contemporary discussions about the process of digestion. The new theoretical model suggested a series of transformations taking place between the
first ventricle (or rather, cavity), the second and the third: images created
by sensations in the first cavity (*sensus communis*) were "processed" in the
second cavity (the site of reasoning), and what was left over was registered
in the third cavity, the site of memory.

It was of course the Ancients who provided the foundation for this imaginary construct elaborated by medieval theorists, both European and Arab. However, both Aristotle himself and Avicenna, who revived Aristotle's ideas, caused the commentators no end of difficulty. Because of the vagueness of his pronouncements,[18] Aristotle often gave rise to divergent interpretations. It must be remembered that nothing in the works of Aristotle suggests that he conceived of any kind of anatomical or functional connection between the peripheral sense organs and the brain proper, whereas he placed the *sensorium commune* in the heart.[19] Avicenna[20] subscribed completely to Aristotle's opinion. However, the Galenic theory gave him pause, and he concedes that,

> many philosophers and all the physicians follow Galen, who holds that each faculty has its own 'principal member' whence the function originates.

He goes on to say:

> According to these views, the faculty of judgement resides in the brain, and its functions come from the brain.

Subsequently, though, he reiterates that,

> the vital faculty maintains the integrity of the pneuma and is the vehicle of sensation and movement... The seat of this faculty is in the heart. Of course, [he concedes again,] the physicians still support the idea that the brain is the principal focus of sense life, although the great Aristotle thinks that the heart is the source of all these functions. But, [he decides,] if the physicians thought through the whole problem again as carefully as possible, they would quickly come around to Aristotle's point of view. They would then realise that they had fastened onto appearances instead of taking the essential reality into consideration. [21]

This rather complex if not ambiguous position allows Avicenna to develop a theory in which five internal senses - sensus communis, imagination (this means "formation of images"), judgement, fantasy and memory - are localized in the three Galenic ventricles, the anterior, the middle and the posterior. The "common sense" receives the forms of objects from the five external senses, and assembles or separates these forms so as to arrive at some initial comparative information. It will, for example, generate the decision that, given two red apples, the second is sweeter than the first. Next, these forms are input to the imagination, which is regarded as a centre for accumulating and processing images without reference to time. The judgement collects "intentions", which do not belong to the domain of the senses, and transforms them into information enabling the individual to choose a response. Thus the sheep flees at the approach of the wolf, because it judges that the wolf's intention is to harm it. The fantasy combines items of information without being limited by the constraints of reality; it combines forms and intentions to create non-existent things, such as a man flying or a mountain made of gold. Memory stores the information output by the other internal senses, thus making possible temporal reference to the past and past experiences.

Over a period of about twenty years Albertus Magnus[22] vacillated between three different classifications: the threefold division of John Damascene[23] and Nemesius of Emesa[24] (imagination, cognition and memory); a fourfold classification attributed to Gregory of Nyssa,[25] which he adopts in the *Summa*[26] (imagination, fantasy, judgement and memory); and a five-fold classification in accordance with Avicenna and Algazel[27] which he uses in the *De Anima* (common sense, imagination, fantasy, judgement and memory). Steneck[28] provides some explanation of this apparent inconsistency: "common sense", depending on the model adopted, is regarded as belonging sometimes to the external senses, sometimes to the internal senses. Basically, however, the models are unconstrained in their variability for the precise reason that they are purely verbal constructs not connected with real anatomy.

When the expression "internal senses" appears in Latin it refers to a faculty of the mind assumed to receive and interpret sense data. St. Augustine used *interior sensus* and *interior vis*, and these terms were used as equivalent to Aristotle's "common sense", again implying such a faculty. The lexical variants as well as the increasing number of faculties that were identified within the common sense or alongside it show that the medievals tried to be rigorous and refine their thinking, but, again, since the models were purely verbal the only progress achieved was a refinement of terminology.

Albertus Magnus introduced a new concept into his own classification: abstraction. This was intended to harmonize the three-, four- and five-fold models. The fact that the common sense apprehends the form of an object only if the object is physically present places it along with the five external senses at the first level of abstraction. Imagination is the second level, since it can generate a representation of the form of an object even if it is not present. Fantasy and judgement make up the third level. They can even represent what is not expressed by sensible forms, and are therefore near the level of cognition. As for memory, which belongs with the faculties of apprehension grouping all the internal senses, its chief characteristic is that it functions *ad rem*, in contrast with the other internal senses which function *a re*.[29]

The thinking of the High Middle Ages imported substructures into the ventricular spaces, varying in number with the ventricle concerned. Here, too, nothing is well defined. The writings of Albertus Magnus reflect this uncertainty[30]. He claims the existence of a system of localisation unique to man which can be represented by a three- or fourfold organisation. (Avicenna's classification, on the other hand, is with reference to the brutes, which have no intellect.)

Analysis of the passage[31] seems to suggest a sixth internal sense, a "cogitative power" occupying the middle ventricle of the brain. This possibility is discussed by Averroes[32] and Thomas Aquinas[33] in particular. But according to Albertus Magnus, the cognitive ability or cogitative power is just another name that can be applied to any of the effects of the internal senses. The meaning of the expression varies depending on whether it is applied to the animal brain or man's: in the first case, it is instinct, in the second, reason. For Albert, then, there is really no internal sixth sense, despite appearances.

Taking his lead from the *De differentia animae et spiritus* of Costa Ben Luca,[34] Albert ascribed an essential role to the pneuma (or, if preferred, the "animal spirits") in the functioning of the nervous system. The pneuma first activates the territories of the first ventricle, where sensory data are received; then the common sense; then imagination, in the middle of the frontal space of the brain; and finally, fantasy and judgement, in the posterior part of the frontal space of the brain.[35] In fact, these ventricular pneuma-refinements vary in appearance: the frontal and posterior spaces are really ventricles, although the first is larger than the second; but the middle ventricle is more of a way-station providing communication between the frontal and the posterior spaces.

> Hence this ventricle is regarded as the seat of the powers of cognition and imagination which are produced in this passage by the movement of spirits. ([4d], I, 3, 1)

The middle ventricle is thus the key to the cognitive power. Albert provides a detailed description of the physiology of this middle ventricle; it turns out to be a rather picturesque representation of the functioning of all three cavities. An intricate system of valves permits the opening or closing of the orifices communicating between the ventricles so as to control or stem the flow of spirits. This is why, he adds,

> when a man wishes to recall a memory or the creations of his imagination, he shakes his head, and this movement aids in opening the passages which communicate between the cavities of the brain.[36]

Because the medieval thinker constructed speculative models without reference to real anatomy or physiology, he was driven to seize on odd facts like this and claim them as proof. Theory-building and observation, both cut off from empirical reality, could only reinforce one another.

MAGICAL SPEECH

> For all such words by which we mentally speak of objects (i.e. by which we think them) are likenesses and images of those objects for which they are words. And every likeness and image is true in proportion to the exactness with which it imitates the thing whose likeness it is.
> St. Anselm, *Monologion: Anselm of Canterbury*, Vol. I: ed. and trans. by J. Hopkins & H. Richardson: London: SCM Press: 1974: p. 45

To ascribe to man's speech the attributes of God's - such an identification becomes all the more tempting and easy when one believes that the word participates in the qualities of the thing it represents. To all intents and purposes, medieval thought was locked into this magic circle of language. Referring to the heart - brain controversy, Clarke and O'Malley ([76], p. 25) remark:

> The experimental data provided by Galen were not considered necessary by the medieval philosopher who was content to solve the problem by disputation (*disputatio*) alone. In his eyes this was a more worthy and reliable method of tackling a controversial issue.

This interpretation is corroborated in all other areas of inquiry. The two preceding sections of the present chapter afford ample illustration of it. In the medieval period, of course, the frontier had not yet been established between metaphysics, which can accommodate semantic fictions, and science, which should reject them. Neither is there any reason for such demarcation, if the relationship between word and object goes beyond convention to take on the character of logical necessity. We are perhaps too quick to classify the medievals as either Realists or Nominalists.

The medieval Realists, like the Physeists of Antiquity, are generally supposed to have been the only school to have believed that reasoning about the word was the same as reasoning about the thing it referred to. In terms of the epistemology of the Middle Ages, however, we must remember that characterisation applied almost equally to those who regarded themselves as Nominalists, the successors of the Theseists of Antiquity.

The reality of phenomena - ignored by some thinkers, and seen by others only through the prism of doctrines handed down by the Ancients - is regarded by all of them as a text whose hidden meaning can only be elucidated by the work of commentary. But when we come to consider this commentary on the relation of mind to body, we find that logical coherence is the only guarantee of truth. Every philosopher accordingly strives to improve on the scheme laid out by his predecessors; the problem is constantly being restated, but no more than that.

The draughtsman's pen is guided by the philosopher's, for empirical observation has to yield pride of place to speculative imagination.[37] Since the empirical reality remains hidden and is not in any case considered important, illustration does not claim to reproduce it. The illustrator makes visible ideas that owe nothing to the eye.

Empirical observation would not assume priority over verbal speculation until the sixteenth century, but it does appear sporadically before that time. It is not a question of "progress" or of an evolution of rationality, but rather a tendency that seems to assert itself almost instinctively from time to time - but insistently and increasingly. Thinkers began to measure the distance between the imaginary and the real, or their understanding of it. A slow change in mental attitude began to emerge: verification by observation was becoming the guarantee of correctness in the interpretation of phenomena. But what is verified? Over a fairly long period reaching from the sixteenth century to the eighteenth, science studied the human phenomenon in search of the imaginary entities that Western cultural tradition had projected onto it. Once the validity of sensory data was unconditionally accepted, the empirical element once more became integrated into scientific statement, though coherence and consistency of statement would long remain the only proof of truth. The insistent questioning - from the end of the seventeenth century on - of the value of sense evidence would only serve to put scientific inquiry back on the track of imaginary entities.[38]

Thus the heart - brain controversy would not be settled by simple empirical observation. Vesalius would need a lot of prestige to combat the illusion of the rete mirabile, and in the end he would only succeed in convincing those whose positions were already close to his own. Animal spirits would not disappear from physiology with empirical observation either. Major authors would continue to accept them as a valid explanatory principle regarding sensation and movement. Only with the discovery of electricity would they finally be relegated to mythology.

Even the development of optical instruments to amplify the power of observation would often be no more than a novel means - and a more convincing one, because of its apparent objectivity - for speculative imagination to clothe reality in its own colours.

NOTES

1   Souques [374a], p. 215f.
2   Particularly *Use of Parts*, Book VIII, i, 470, 471, 472.
3   Erasistratus: see p. 20.
4   Galen, *Use of Parts*, Book VIII, i, 488.
5   Note that this term is just the Latin equivalent of the Greek word *pneuma*.
6   "The system of brain function introduced by the Alexandrians and elaborated by Galen gave the blood and its contained spirits a vital role to play so that blood vessels and blood flow in the cranial cavity, like the ventricular system and its humors, had to be studied in as much detail as was then possible. However, those who adhered to the Aristotelian theory of cardiac dominance interpreted the cerebral vessels as merely conveyors of blood to be cooled by the otherwise functionless brain." ([76], p. 756).
7   Avicenna, 980-1037.
8   The *Canon* is a collection of writings borrowed from Greek medical tradition, anatomy and physiology. This work had a profound and lasting influence in Europe and the Eastern Mediterranean. See Gruner [166].
9   Mondino de Luzzi (Mundinus), 1270-1326. See [275].
10 We find in it notably an accurate description of the overall outward appearance of the brain. However, the author is interested mainly in the ventricles, through which the spirits pass, and in the sensus communis.
11 Berengario da Carpi, 1460-1530.
12 Vesalius, 1514-1564.
13 *De humani corporis fabrica*, 1543 [409].
14 See pp. 19-20.
15 See p. 10.
16 Nemesius (end of 3rd, beginning of 4th century): one work by him has survived, *On the nature of man*. St. Augustine, 354-430.
17 On this point see 77, especially chapter III, pp. 10-45.
18 See *De partibus animalium*, *De Anima*, and, in the *Parva Naturalia*, *De memoria et reminiscentia*.
19 For Aristotle, the visual, auditory and olfactory pathways end at the veins of the *pia mater*, and do not enter into direct contact with the brain. As for smell and hearing, the pathways for these senses, which are full of natural breath and are in contact with the outside air, end at the small veins rising from the heart in the vicinity of the brain ([374a], p. 107f.; [375b], pp. 546- 670).

20 See p. 35.
21 A paraphrase of sections 138-141 of Book I of the *Canon*; see n. 8 above.
22 Albertus Magnus, 1193-1280.
23 John Damascene, 674-749. His main work is *The Source of Knowledge*.
24 See n. 16 above.
25 St Gregory of Nyssa, 335?-395?
26 Summa I, 37, 1-i; 38, 3-i; 40, 3.
27 Algazel (Abu Hamed Muhammad Al-Ghazali), 1058-1111.
28 Steneck [383].
29 This means that memory recognises an object by matching it with a "form" recorded beforehand, while the other senses acquire knowledge of it from the outside world. *Summa* I, 42, 2 and *De Anima* III, 2, 19.
30 See [386] and [425].
31 [4a], I, 40, 3.
32 Averroes, 1126-1198. Cf. Klubertanz, *The Discursive Power*, St Louis, The Modern Schoolman, 1952, pp. 109-121 and 161-176.
33 St Thomas Aquinas, 1227-1274.
34 Costa Ben Luca (Constabulus), *De differentia animae et spiritus liber translatus a Johanne Hispalensi*, ed. C.S. Barach, *Bibliotheca Philosophorum Mediae Aetatis*, vol. VII, Innsbruck, Wagner, 1878, pp. 124f.
35 [4c], I, 2, 4 and [4d], XII, 2, 4.
36 *De Animalibus* XII, 2, 4 [4d].
37 See n. 17 above. This work [77] reproduces about 70 drawings made from the 9th century to the 15th both in the West and in the Arab world.
38 Descartes [99d] and La Mettrie [264b]. See pp. 48 and 79.

2. Paths of Seeing

From terms to objects: a shift of focus

> Then carefully revisit the books of the Greek, Arab and Latin physicians, without dismissing the Talmudists and Cabalists; and by frequent anatomies get thyself perfect knowledge of the other world which is Man. Rabelais, *Pantagruel* viii

In the year 1531, François Rabelais,[1] later to become a famous name in literature, was conferred with a bachelor's degree in medicine by the University of Montpellier, and almost immediately found himself on the teaching faculty. The basis of medical education at the time consisted of reading and commenting on the works of the Ancients and the Arabs in Latin. Practical exercises on skeletons were rare, and even rarer, dissection of cadavers - anatomy. Rabelais carried on the tradition, but he introduced an important innovation: instead of using the bad Latin translations current at the time, he decided to present Hippocrates and Galen in the original, according to Humanistic method. In Rabelais' science, philology had as great a role as observation and experiment, and the text of the Hippocratic *Aphorisms* which he subsequently published[2] shows in its accompanying notes his abilities as a classical scholar. In 1537, Rabelais was conferred with an M.D. Thanks to his reputation, he could now openly practise the direct observation method of human dissection.

Rabelais' example illustrates the new look of scientific knowledge brought about by the Renaissance. The ancient writings at that time formed a unified corpus to which all knowledge must refer, but the human body itself now became a text in which a new science was being enunciated.

Sir Francis Bacon,[3] in his *Novum Organum*, identified the true task of science as interpretation naturae: this is not exactly "interpretation of nature", but "the reading, or spelling out of (the Book of) Nature". The metaphor of the Open Book sums up the epistemology of Renaissance science; it is also used by Galileo.[4] Through texts and commentaries the Renaissance scientist, as Foucault[5] has described him, strives to work back to the *Original Text*. The human Microcosm is a text with a meaning, like the Macrocosm, the Universe. This attitude of mind is still discernible in Descartes, at the outset of the *Age of Reason*.

With Leonardo da Vinci,[6] the imperatives of observation took decisive priority over the constructions of speculative imagination - at least in one great lifetime. The artist's mastery of his art was what made his drawing true to life; now, by means of that drawing, what the eye saw could be recorded and elucidated.

Leonardo did not attain this clarity of vision right away. We have a diagram
of his, dating from 1490, of a sagittal section of the head, where he tries to
illustrate in the greatest detail Avicenna's description of the brain.[7] Between 1504 and 1507, however, Leonardo devised a technique for injecting
wax into the cerebral ventricles of cattle and sheep. This way he obtained
molds which provided the first evidence of the true shape of the spaces
revealed to the eye by dissection. Despite these technical advances, Leonardo
did not diverge from tradition when it came to interpreting what he could,
for the first time, see better than anyone else. Twenty years later, Berengario da Carpi[8] had the same attitude. Scientists' minds were hesitant in
following the path their eyes opened up for them.

Vesalius'[9] position on brain function makes him the exact type of the
thinker in a transitional period. In [409], he recalls the instruction he received in the ventricular doctrine, referring to a "philosophical pearl".[10]
His own contribution to brain anatomy may be regarded as the most significant of his time. The practice of dissection gave him a clearer idea of
the shape of the ventricles and enabled him to study what he took to be
ventricular organisation. He has no hesitation in assigning them a role in
the manufacture of animal spirits, but he also declares that in his opinion
there should be no further talk of localizing the faculties of the mind in the
ventricles. The higher mental faculties - man's crowning privilege - are denied
to the animals. Now, dissection shows that man is not distinguished from
other species by the possession of a particular ventricle. Not only is the
number of ventricles the same in man as in the animals, but the whole
organisation of the brain seems to be identical.

This standard of observational rigour led Vesalius, along with Berengario da Carpi,[11] to cast doubt on the existence of the *rete mirabile* in man
- not without a long period of soul-searching, for he must have found it
difficult to make the claim that the Ancients could have been mistaken. In
fact, Vesalius failed to convince many of his contemporaries. A century
later, Thomas Willis[12] would still find it necessary to discuss the question
of the existence of the *rete* in man, concluding that, in some views, it might
be present occasionally in subnormal human beings due to their affinity
with animals!

Using his gifts as an anatomist, Vesalius showed that the assumed ducts
of the interventricular wall of the heart did not exist. Such a finding attacked the very foundation of the whole physiological theory of the formation of spirits, which was supposed to occur when the pneuma from the
lungs was mixed with blood travelling from the right ventricle of the heart
to the left ventricle by way of these non-existent ducts.

Physicians and anatomists (the pursuits were usually combined) tended
to be more circumspect than philosophers. Caspar Bauhin,[13] following the

path opened up by Galen and now by Vesalius, had no hesitation in criticising the ventricular theory and claiming that if the animal spirits had any physiological reality, they could only be generated in the brain substance itself. Thus the focus of interest began to shift from the contents to the container that held them.

Despite the accuracy of his observations on the structure of the brain, Vesalius did not pay much attention to its surface features.[14] In his anatomical illustrations, the cortex still looks like the intestine *in situ*. What was seen at this time appeared to have no permanent configuration; the term "enteroid process" well expresses the negative reaction felt by observers. On the other hand, Vesalius noticed the *corpus callosum*: he does not actually name it, but shows it in his illustrations. He also noted the difference between the white and grey matter.

Arcangelo Piccolomini[15] was the anatomist who clearly established the distinction between *cerebrum* (the cerebral grey matter) and *medulla* (the white matter). Costanzo Varolio[16] was more explicit than Vesalius in stating that there is one single mental faculty in the brain, which functions as a whole. Varolio and Bauhin were practically contemporaries, and their approaches are quite similar. Neither of them, however, paid much attention to the cortex.

On this last point, the seventeenth century brought change. Sylvius[17] and Willis[18] both put forward the view that the cerebral cortex could have specific functions. Having rejected the rete mirabile as a manufacturing centre for vital spirit, each of these anatomists was in fact looking for another possible site for that function, as Bauhin and Varolio had been. Rediscovering Erasistratus' insight, Willis even went so far as to suggest a direct correlation between gyral complexity and intelligence.

The philosopher Gassendi[19] thought that animals must have a soul, since, like man, they possessed memory, judgement and other "psychological" attributes. Willis posited the existence of two souls in man, the corporeal and physical soul ("the soul of brutes"), common to man and the animals, and the rational soul, unique to man, to which the brute soul is subject. The higher functions of reason and sensibility depend on this immortal soul. Willis obviously wanted to preserve God's rightful place - beyond the reach of the anatomist's scalpel. The anatomist, however, retained the privilege of speculating on the localization of the brute soul. By resorting to this ingenious system, Willis cleared the ground for a re-localization of the three mental functions that had previously been consigned to the ventricles: the "common sense" in the *corpus striatum*, "imagination" in the *corpus callosum* (by which Willis actually meant the whole of the cerebral white matter between the basal ganglia and the cortex), and memory, in the cortex itself. While the brain was in charge of voluntary motor activity, Willis held, the

cerebellum regulated the vital functions. Till Haller[20] attacked his doctrine
of cerebral localizations, Willis' position retained considerable authority.

From Rabelais to Willis, empirical observation would seem to have gained
priority over respect for traditional taxonomies and the teaching of the Ancients. But even the most painstaking observer (which Willis was, as can be
seen from his anatomical diagrams)[21] is not proof against the temptations
of speculative imagination when it takes on the reassuring appearance of
rigorous, coherent statement. Descartes,[22] the man whose name would become synonymous with reason in later generations, provides ample illustration of the phenomenon in his *Treatise on Man*, published posthumously in
1662.

THE LIMITS OF REASON

> Imagination - that dominant part in man, that mistress of error and
> falsehood, all the more mischievous because she is not always so.
> Pascal, *Pensées*.

In a letter to Mersenne dated November 23, 1646, Descartes refers to a
description he had made of all the functions of the human body, some twelve
or thirteen years before. The manuscript was so full of corrections that, he
confesses, "I would have difficulty reading it myself." He recalls having later
entrusted it to "a close friend" who "made a copy of it, which has been further transcribed by two or three others, with my permission."

The close friend was probably Clersellier, who in 1664 (fourteen years
after Descartes' death) published a volume entitled *Man, by René Descartes,
with a treatise on the formation of the fetus, by the same author*. A Latin
translation, *De Homine*, had already been published in Leyden by Florens
Schuyl in 1662. Descartes' well-known reluctance to publish explains why
this text had only limited circulation in its author's lifetime.

The *Treatise on Man* overlaps partly, however, with the fifth chapter of
the *Discourse on Method*.[23] In that work, Descartes written:

> But after I had spend some years pursuing these studies in the *Book
> of the World* and trying to gain some experience, I resolved one day to
> undertake studies within myself too and to use all the powers of my
> mind in choosing the paths I should follow. ([99a], p. 116)

It is enlightening to keep this statement in mind when reading the *Treatise on Man*. The *Treatise* represents a movement away from reliance on
observational experience, and towards abstract, speculative modelling with
a view to accounting for the functioning of all the forces hidden from the
observer's eye which determine human behavior.

Treatise on Man is the sequel to another treatise: *The World*, by Monsieur Descartes *(De Mundo)*. Bridoux, in his critical introduction to the text ([99], p. 805), pointedly remarks:

> In moving on to man, Descartes does not change his topic. It is still an artificial world constructed by the philosopher in imaginary spaces, which is not the real world we live in, but as it were points towards it.

The piece-by-piece reconstruction of a hypothetical human being that Descartes lays out is intended to afford a better understanding of the original by virtue of the effort of invention required by the artificial modelling process. The human organism is regarded as a "black box", and the mechanical model is supposed to shed light on its workings.

The analogy with the mechanical world is used by Descartes right from the first page, where there is mention of clocks, artificial fountains and mills.[24] The trouble is that the entire intricate engineering of this physiological machinery is based on very questionable anatomical data - even making allowances for the state of the anatomical art at the time. For example, the digestive process is handled by a kind of filtering mechanism in which the wall of the intestine is made out to be a sieve.

When it comes to phenomena that are infinitely more difficult to account for - sensation and knowledge - Descartes finds an explanatory common denominator in the animal spirits,[25] and his conception of these is a very traditional one. The heart and the blood, along with the lungs and air, have the essential roles in the manufacture of spirits, and the nerves channelling the spirit are still hollow pipes. Descartes is closer to Aristotle than to Vesalius, and Galenic tradition seems to have made little impression on him.

The *Treatise on Man* nonetheless finds its unity, and probably its tacit justification, in the philosopher's constant effort to show that natural explanations are entirely adequate for the functioning of human neurophysiology. Descartes may have found the germ of his thought in Santro[26] (especially [356]), but the achievement of developing a complete system out of it is his alone. This system is built on the simple idea that all the activities of the organism can be reduced to movements subject to precise physical and mathematical study. Descartes is accordingly one of the founders of iatrophysics; also of iatrochemistry, by his remarks on the chemical phenomena that have their place in the organism.

False consciousness is masked by the reassuring force of words - as in this passage, where a highly dubious hypothesis is presented as truth in the most matter-of-fact way.

> Secondly, concerning the pores of the brain, they must be imagined as no different from the spaces that occur between the threads of some

tissue [for example, a woven or felted fabric]; because, in effect, the
whole brain is nothing but a tissue constituted in a particular way, as I
shall try to explain to you here. ([99d], p. 77)

Nothing mysterious here, then all that is required is a little thought and
a knowledge of physics.

The treatise *Passions in the Soul* further elucidates and complements the
Treatise on Man, though it purports to deal with the real human organism
rather than the previous mechanical model, which adds to the ambiguity.
After deciding axiomatically that, "the soul is united to all parts of the
body conjointly" (art. 30), the author dismisses the possibility of locating
its seat in the heart, and postulates that "there is a little gland in the brain
where the soul exercises its functions more particularly that in the other
parts of the body" ([99c], p. 340, art. 31). This little gland is the pineal
gland or *conarium*. According to Descartes, it is the principal seat of the
soul - and he thinks it can be proved. Art. 32 is headed: How we know that
this gland is the principal seat of the soul. Descartes' certainty is based
firstly on the position of this gland in the brain:

> ...situated in the middle of the brain's substance and suspended above
> the passage through which the spirits in the brain's anterior cavities
> communicate with those in its posterior cavities. The slightest move-
> ments on the part of this gland may alter very greatly the course of these
> spirits and conversely any change, however slight, taking place in the
> course of the spirits may do much to change the movements of the
> gland. ([99c], p. 340, art. 31)

Secondly, "all the other parts of our brain are double" (art. 32, p. 340),
whereas there is only one pineal gland:

> ...but, insofar as we have only one simple thought about a given object
> at any one time, there must necessarily be some place where the two
> images coming through the two eyes, or the two impressions coming
> from a single object through the double organs of any other sense, can
> come together in a single image or impression before reaching the soul,
> so that they do not present to it two objects instead of one. (ibid.)

It would be hard to imagine greater self-confidence in scientific argument to prove something that - after all - is not the case.[27] One might
wonder if Descartes was the first to propose this localization. Soury[28] reports that Jean Cousin[29] had discussed in his 1641 thesis whether the seat
of the soul might be in the conarium, and reached a positive conclusion;
however, Descartes' correspondence shows that he had held this opinion
several years before.

The pineal, because of its uniqueness in a system where all other organs are twofold, sums up in itself all the basic psychological functions. Its mobility is the crucial feature by which it discharges its functional role. It moves about as a result of three factors:

(1) the action of the soul;
(2) the difference in relative force between the minute parts of the spirits which raise and support the gland; and
(3) the action of objects touching the senses.

Species (which in the traditional vocabulary of metaphysics are merely the representative images of external objects) imprint the shapes of objects on the nerve endings at the periphery, and then a movement transmits them instantly to the central nerve roots. This movement enlarges or widens the orifices of the pores on the inner surface of the brain, and at the same time imprints on this inner surface a second shape identical to the first. Immediately the spirits contained in the cerebral ventricles rush to these entrance points, receive the imprint of the second shape, and then proceed to transfer it to the surface of the pineal gland.

The pineal, accordingly, is the centre of all sensory impressions coming from the external senses, as well as being the centre of natural appetites and passions. It is, in other words, the seat of the "common sense". This is why Descartes regards it as the principal seat of the soul, its action on the body being explained by a decidedly mechanistic theory. When the soul wishes something, it causes the small gland with which it is closely associated to move in the manner required so as to produce the effect corresponding to the wish.[30]

Article 44 of *Passions in the Soul* bears the title "Each volition is naturally joined to some movement of the gland, but through effort or habit we may join it to others." This heading is somewhat vague, though the body of the article is quite explicit.[31] A mechanistic explanation is proposed for the acquisition of new habits. Descartes provides the outline of what would be called in modern terms a learning theory, the somatic basis of which lies in the gland's ability to acquire new movements. Descartes gives as an example the learning of speech production automatisms:

> Again, when we speak, we think only of the meaning of what we want to say, and this makes us move our tongue and lips much more readily and effectively than if we thought of moving them in all the ways required for uttering the same words. For the habits acquired in learning to speak have made us join the action of the soul (which, by means of the gland, can move the tongue and lips) with the meaning of the words which follow upon these movements, rather than with the movements themselves. (p. 344f.)

Descartes' ingenuity in reducing all the phenomena of intellectual and emotional life to movements of the pineal gland can be understood only as the expression of a tacit ideology that aims to explain man by man alone. The automaton he proposes as a model of human functioning is supposed to represent a simplified version of the actual organism, but, as we have seen, the distinction fades in the transition from the *Treatise on Man* to *Passions in the Soul*.

What remains of this sometimes laborious intellectual construction, intended to form the basis of a purely mechanistic conception of man, is the fascinating use it makes of the achievements of contemporary physics. As with Harvey, who portrays the heart as a suction-pressure pump, Descartes' view of spirit mechanics is closely related to contemporary work on fluid statics and the then new science of hydraulics. Descartes remains first and foremost a physicist.[32]

However, the physical analogies quickly get out of hand and lead the philosopher astray. For, in the final analysis, his cerebral machinery is all wrong. Empirical observation here leads only to imaginary anatomy. It promotes an evanescent *form* - the pineal - to the status of a gland within a larger gland, the brain.[33] It locates this *form* in a mythical space, the vault of the cerebral cavity. It makes it closely dependent on a *rete* that exists only in the mind of the medical traditionalist. And finally, the very function of the *rete* in hallowed medical tradition is transferred to the pineal itself, by the sole arbitrary decision of the author.

When Descartes observed, he really only saw what he knew he should see, or what he imagined he should see. From his reading of Greco-Roman medical literature, he was a believer in the *animal spirits*, whose movement provided an explanation both of sensory pathways, which he understood to some degree, and of motor pathways, which he understood very little. It was when he forgot the lessons of tradition that Descartes' rationalizing imagination served him best. For instance, he foresaw the necessity of having a single somatic infrastructure for the moral, emotional and intellectual faculties. He unambiguously identified the brain as the seat of these functions, rejecting the claims of the heart (*Passions in the Soul*, art. 33). By virtue of the functions which he assigned to the pineal gland, Descartes further rejected the theory of the threefold soul, which had been the Platonic alternative to the notion of unity of the somatic infrastructure.

Descartes, again by the sole power of speculation, arrived at a theory of memory that felicitously anticipates the engram[34] concept. For him, the species (see p. 102) retained in the memory are "like creases left in a sheet of paper that has been folded"- in a letter to Mersenne, he speaks of "memory creases". Besides this intellectual memory, Descartes conceived of a local, muscular kind of memory, the automatism, which he found particularly evident in the acquired movements of the eye (described in the *Optics*). He further noted the interdependence of memory and the association of ideas.[35] Not too successful as an anatomist because of his careless habits of observation, Descartes, whose single-minded ambition was to reveal truth as self-evident, found truth himself, ironically enough, only by flights of imaginative speculation beyond the empirical realm.

Faced with an organic phenomenon whose complexity he could scarcely conceptualize and which was still largely inaccessible to his anatomical technology, the philosopher - like the humanist poring over his text - reinvented and fantasized it in the struggle to understand it. With reason eclipsed by imagination, scientific debate at this prescientific juncture was fated to remain a matter of philosophical concepts rather than empirical realities.

THE BEGINNINGS OF OBJECTIVITY

> When water curves a stick, my reason straightens it; reason decides, as the mistress; my eyes, aided by this intervention, never deceive me while always lying to me.
> La Fontaine, *Fables VII*, XVIII

Besides the Cartesian approach of constructing a model whose logical well-formedness was thought to underwrite its fidelity to nature, the seventeenth-century mind sometimes took another approach in which thought was adapted to the object of investigation rather than the converse. In the anatomical literature of the period, this tendency is nowhere more apparent than in the work of the Danish medical scientist Nicholas Steno.[36]

Steno was living in Paris between November 1664 and September 1665. He was then only 26 years old. He delivered his famous *Discourse* [384] on April 6, 1665 to a meeting of the learned society which met at the house of Melchisedec Thévenot,[37] a high-ranking official under Louis XIV, and which later developed into the Académie des Sciences. It brought together some of the most distinguished minds in the scientific world of the time. Anatomy was practised there, according to Thévenot's own statement. *The Treatise on Man* must have been debated by the group from the time it was published in 1664. It is not surprising that Steno, whose youthful reputation had gone before him, was welcomed into this environment open to new trends in science.

To appreciate Steno's contribution to seventeenth-century brain science at its true value, we must remember that knowledge of anatomical detail was still sketchy (as the *Treatise on Man* clearly reveals) and any attempt at dissecting the brain encountered technical and ethical problems that most considered insurmountable.[38] But anatomists less well-remembered than Steno had been contributing bit by bit to the development of a body of knowledge in brain anatomy since the beginning of the century, and Steno was to some extent the product of their teaching.[39]

In Thevenot's academy, Steno found himself drawn willy-nilly into the controversy between supporters of Descartes and supporters of Gassendi that had been revived by the publication of the *Treatise on Man*. Gassendi, a vitalist, rejected the animal-machine, the basic idea of the Cartesian system. Gassendi also emphasized the value of experiment and observation rather than deductive reasoning. Reasoning, for him, was not a method in itself. It could not occur unless based on immediate knowledge acquired from sensory data. Paradoxically, Descartes, who would later come to be regarded as the father of experimental science, was attacked in his own time for approaching problems in a way that undermined the validity of the experimental method. Gassendi appears the more modern in comparison.

Descartes' was a physiological theory based on hypothetical functions. In place of the hydraulic movement which he had decreed for the nervous system, Steno posited static but real structures. Descartes had provided a method for the mind; Steno provided one for the scalpel, as a guide to the mind.

As early as 1662, the *Treatise on Man* had been criticized by Chapelain,[40] who was not himself a medical man, however. The medical community does not seem to have taken Descartes' views all that seriously. Steno, who impressed medical colleagues with the objectivity of his approach and the precision of his technique, clearly shared their assessment.[41] For Steno, Descartes remained an amateur in anatomy; he, on the other hand, while correcting Descartes' mistakes, did not presume to set himself up as a philosopher. *The Discourse on the Anatomy of the Brain* is quite candid in this respect.

With a note of irony, Steno begins by admitting his ignorance about the structure of the brain, and declares that everyone should imitate:

> The sincerity of Silvius[42] who never talks positively concerning the brain, though he has been at more pains about it, than any man that I know. ([384], p. 1)

With the modesty of Silvius he contrasts the presumption of the philosophers:

> The number of those who think everything is easy is infinitely the greatest, and they give us the History of the Brain and Disposition of its parts with the same confidence and assurance, as if they had been present at the Formation of this surprising Machine, and had been let into all the Designs of the Great Architect. (p. 1f.)

One conclusion is immediately apparent:

> I am very much convinced that they who search for solid knowledge,
> will find nothing satisfactory in all that has been written about the Brain.
> (p. 2)

Although the brain is "the principal Organ of our Soul", the anatomist
scarcely knows what to make of it:

> On the very Surface you see varieties which deserve your admiration;
> but when you would look into its inner Substance you are utterly in the
> dark. (p.2).

Objective information boils down to very little - the existence of two
substances, grey and white, and the continuity of nerves with the white matter;
but the nature of this grey matter, and the connection of the nerves to it,
are unknown. On the other hand, much of the information current turns
out to be imaginary; for this, faulty dissection methods are at least partly
responsible.

The ventricular theory of the Ancients does not stand up to critical examination, and there is no real evidence for the localizations made,

> for there is nothing satisfactory in all that has been hitherto said in
> favour of it; and as that fine arched Cavity of the Third Ventricle where
> they placed the Throne of Judgement does not so much as exist, we may
> easily see, what Judgement is to be pronounced on the rest of this Sys-
> tem. (384) p.11

Willis' system[43] is no more reliable. He finds two kinds of striations in
the corpus striatum, one ascending, the other descending; now the separation of the grey from the white matter shows that the striations are just all
of the same kind. In view of the anatomist's error, what credence can be
given to the theorist who places the common sense in the *corpus striatum*,
imagination in the *corpus callosum* and memory in the grey matter?

Steno finds that Descartes avoided such pitfalls in his *Treatise on Man*
by describing not man but a machine that mimics him. He faults those who
take the machine for man himself. Steno points out that Silvius[44] has shown
on several occasions that Descartes' description is not in agreement with
the dissection of the bodies it refers to. He takes the pineal as an example,
and contrasts what Descartes says about it with what it is in reality, as
demonstrated by objective anatomical investigation. The inner space where
Descartes situates it and its position in this space are figments of the mind.
The third ventricular cavity appears only by virtue of an anatomical manipulation:

> By forcing in Air through the Fissure between the Tubercles of the second Pair, we raise the Fornix, and thus by breaking the Filaments which connect it to the Basis, a large cavity is formed; from whence some have imagined that when the Spirits swell the Cavities, the Fornix rises, and all sides of the Surface of the Gland are turned towards the Cavities. (p. 13f.)

Thus the imaginary physiology of the pineal goes on in an imaginary space.[45]

Anatomy indicates a reality totally incompatible with the complex mechanics of the Cartesian model. But Steno hastens to excuse Descartes, the amateur anatomist: "there is nothing more common than not to perceive the mistakes we commit in dissecting the Brain" (p. 16). In exposing the tentative quality of what was known about an object unclearly perceived and frequently distorted by the violence done to it under experiment, Steno pointed to the importance of technique and the need to improve technique with better tools. So doing, he revolutionized the whole mental attitude of his time with regard to experiment. The fact that he himself had raised the anatomist's art to a level of accuracy never reached before only lent additional weight to his analysis. It was Steno's anatomical achievement that provided him with the kind of exact knowledge he needed to expose the contradictions of the scientific systems of his age (particularly the *Treatise on Man*).

That same knowledge impelled him to criticize the traditional nomenclature of the parts of the brain. He pillories unbridled metaphor as causing errors of interpretation and encouraging fanciful speculation:[46]

> The third Ventricle is a very equivocal term. M. Silvius calls the third Ventricle a Canal found in the Substance of the Basis of the Brain, between the Infundibulum and the Passage which goes under the two posterior Pairs of the Tubercles of the Brain, towards the fourth Ventricle. Some anatomists having separated the Bodies of this second Pair of Tubercles, take the space between them, which is owing to their manner of dissection, for the third Ventricle, which is consequently sometimes the Fissure above and sometimes the Canal below... We have therefore the three third Ventricles, the second of which alone is the true one; the first and third arising entirely from the methods of preparing the parts. ([384], p. 21f.)

Steno describes a kind of Observer's Paradox in which the anatomical procedure generates the imaginary forms that the mind of the anatomist is looking for:

> Every Anatomist who dissects the Brain demonstrates from experience what he advances. This soft and pliable Substance so readily yields to every motion of his Hand, that the Parts are imperceptibly formed in the same manner as he had conceived them before dissection; while the spectator who often sees two contrary experiments made on the same Part, is either puzzled very much to know which he ought to embrace, or obliged to reject both to make himself easy. (p. 30)

Steno acutely analyses this cycle of error in which the experimenter is caught. Anatomy after Steno's *Discourse* would have to become more circumspect and more rigorous in weighing the validity of evidence. To this extent Steno may be regarded as having laid the foundations of an epistemology of dissection that would only be completed in the eighteenth and nineteenth centuries.

> There are but 2 ways of coming at the knowledge of a Machine, either to be taught the whole contrivance by the Maker, or to take it quite to pieces, and to examine each Piece by itself, and as it stands in relation to the rest. ([384], p. 23)

No better way to advance from the letter of Descartes' teaching to its spirit! Previously, Steno observes, anatomists had only observed the movements of the Machine, and on the basis of these observations alone they had built systems purported to be true representations of nature. The critique of Descartes in Steno's discussion is never direct but it is nonetheless telling. The conclusion of that discussion is expressed in a repetitive and unambiguous statement:

> As the Brain is a Machine, we must not flatter ourselves that we can discover the Contrivance of it by any other means than are made use of for knowing other Machines; and we have no way left but to take it to pieces, and to consider what every part is capable of in a separated and in a united state. (p. 24)

The *Discourse* had a wide influence, and the welcome it received shows that contemporaries immediately grasped its importance. It was not, however, the last word on the empty spaces of imaginary anatomy. The new mythology that was to develop derives directly from Descartes, but it also derives from Steno, inasmuch as, by virtue of the terminology he used, he became its accomplice. That mythology was the mechanistic conception of man and the brain, the mythology of physical language. To the extent that observation would triumph over speculation (in large measure, as we shall see, due to technological developments), Steno's teaching would be accepted by those who trusted their eyes to see.

NOTES

1   François Rabelais (1494-1553).
2   In 1532, on returning to Lyon.
3   Sir Francis Bacon (1561-1626).
4   Galileo Galilei (1564-1642).
5   [132b], p. 56.
6   Leonardo da Vinci (1452-1519).
7   This drawing is to be found in [77], p. 32, as no. 43.
8   See p. 42, n. 11.
9   See p. 42, n. 12.
10 See [336]. Fig. 117 of that work is one of the best efforts at represent-
    ing medieval notions. These are superimposed on a crude imitation of
    Greek anatomy.
11 See p. 35.
12 Thomas Willis (1621-1675): see [423a].
13 Gaspard Bauhin (1560-1623): see [22].
14 His drawings prove this. See [409].
15 Arcangelo Piccolomini (1526-1586).
16 Costanzo Varolio (1543-1575). Note that he is the originator of the
    "cortex" metaphor: he was the first to describe the outer envelope of
    the brain as a kind of protective bark (cork).
17 François de la Boé, or Sylvius (1614-1672).
18 See n. 12.
19 Gassendi (1592-1655).
20 Albrecht von Haller (1708-1777).
21 Thomas Willis: see [423b].
22 René Descartes (1596-1650).
23 "I explained all these matters in sufficient detail in the treatise I previ-
    ously intended to publish" ([99a], V, p. 139).
24 "We see clocks, artificial fountains, mills and similar machines which,
    though entirely by man, lack not the power to move in various ways"
    ([99d], p. 4).
25 Thus the spirits are used to explain the mechanism of sight: [99d], p.
    857.
26 Santrio Santro (1561-1635).
27 See [374b].
28 Soury [375c], [375a].
29 See the Bulletin de la Société Française de l'Histoire de la Médecine,
    March 1938.
30 [99c], art. 42, p. 343f.
31 Souques comments: "Thus the soul uses the gland like a helmsman his

rudder or a driver his steering-wheel, to direct the spirits towards a particular region of the ventricles" ([374b]).

32   The *Treatise on Man* becomes clearer in the light of the fact that the 17th century saw the birth of modern theories of hydraulics. Cf., in particular, p. 100: "Indeed, one may compare the nerves of the machine I am describing with the pipes in the works of these fountains..."

33   The anatomical metaphor from which the term "pineal" derives is enough to make one suspicious. It is, to say the least, a peculiar place for the soul. Galen, however, had explained the name of the gland by analogy between its shape and that of a pine-cone.

34   For the notion of engram, see [392].

35   "Which shows how the recollection of one thing can be excited by that of another which was imprinted in the memory at the same time" (Descartes [99d], p. 90).

36   Niels Stensen, or Steno (1638-1687) studied under Thomas Bartholin, and worked with Silvius and Blasius.

37   Melchisedec Thévenot (1620-1694).

38   The basic ideas on which contemporary speculation relied were borrowed from Antiquity. The great anatomists of the preceding centuries had only added details that made interpretation of the overall picture that much more complex. Descartes had not just failed to transcend the speculative tradition; he gave himself over to it in the very name of reason. See [74b].

39   Mention should be made of Bartholius the Elder and the Younger (see [20]); Gaspard Bauhin (see [22]); J. Riolan the Younger, and J. Vesling (see [344]); and last but not least Sylvius, who directly influenced Steno.

40   Chapelain (1595-1674).

41   Graindorge writing to Huet: "This Monsieur Steno is a sensation". And the *Journal des Sçavans*, 25th March 1665, states: "He has the particular gift of making most things so concrete that one is forcibly convinced of them, and astonished that they could have escaped previous anatomists."

42   Silvius' modest and cautious nature was no doubt shown in his teaching. His personal remarks are inserted in the works of Bartholin in the form of notes [387].

43   Willis' localization of the common sense in the *corpus striatum*, imagination in the *corpus callosum* and memory in the grey matter was purely hypothetical. See [423b].

44   It must be noted that Silvius had an approach to dissection that revealed the anatomical reality of the brain to an extent little known before him and dissipated some of the illusions created by manipulation.

45 Imaginary, that is, in the function which Descartes attributes to it: "What Descartes says, that the Glandula Pinealis may perform its Functions, though it sometimes inclines to one side, sometimes to another, Experience shows to be groundless; because it is so hedged in between all the Parts of the Brain, and so fixed to them on all sides, that it cannot be moved in the least without violence, and without breaking the Fibres by which it is connected" ([384], p. 15).

46 "Besides, the greatest number of these terms are so low and so unworthy of the most noble part of the Body of Man, that I am at a loss whether I ought most to wonder at the bad turn of thought of those who first made use of them, or at the Indolence of their Successors who continue still to return them. What necessity could there be to imploy the words Nates, Testes, Anus, Vulva and Penis, which in their common Signification have no relation at all to the Parts expressed by them in the Anatomy of the Brain? And accordingly what one Author calls Nates, another calls Testes, &c." ([384], p.21).

3. LANGUAGE AS A PHYSICAL OBJECT

THE SEARCH FOR A PHYSICAL THEORY OF SPEECH

> One could not do with a million machines what we do with our
> mouths. After that, one can boast all one likes about [artificial] talking
> heads... Only those who have not paid attention to the way we speak
> believe that one can simulate such an admirable work as the head of
> man.
> Lamy ([218], p. 191)

It has been said that the stock phrases of a period reveal its underlying
ideological premises. If so, the frequency with which we encounter the
terms "physics" and "mechanics" in discussions of language from the late
seventeenth century through the eighteenth is perhaps not without significance.
Making use of the definitions in Richelet's Dictionary,[1] one might canvass
the proposition that, physics being the science of natural things, speech as
a natural phenomenon belongs to that science.

Steno had unambiguously localized the faculties of the soul in the brain,
thereby establishing their relation to physical science:

> It is very certain that it is the principal Organ of the Soul, and the
> Instrument by which it works its very wonderful Effects[2]... The Soul
> which imagines it can penetrate into every thing without it; and that
> nothing in the World can set bounds to its Knowledge, is nevertheless
> utterly at a loss to describe its own Habitation, and is nowhere more to
> seek than at home. ([384], p. 2)

The problem was, therefore, that the soul expresses its imperceptible
thoughts in the perceptible elements of speech, but that the nature of that
operation remained a mystery. One way of dealing with the problem was to
start at the other end, with language, considered as a tangible, natural
phenomenon. This was the approach taken by the Cartesian philosopher
Géraud de Cordemoy[3] in his *Physical Discourse on Speech* [79b].

That speech could be explained in physical terms still counted as a rather
bold claim in the second half of the seventeenth century. The dichotomy
between speech as a process of sound production and speech as the expression
of thought (and therefore communicative medium of the soul) suggested the possibility of a middle way that a cautiously conservative thinker
of Cordemoy's type was glad to take. At the same time, his philosophizing
opened up new and much more radical horizons.[4]

By the time Cordemoy came around to this difficult intellectual problem he had already shown his mettle as a philosopher in six preceding Discourses [79a]. In the preface to his major work, we find the different strands of Cordemoy's thought pulled together in the following way (the words given here are those of the seventeenth century English translator):

> I proposed in the six discourses, which preceded this, the means to know Ourselves... Now I propose the means of knowing Others, and that is Speech. I explain as far as I am able, What it is; and poursuant to my first dessein, I endeavour in this Discourse exactly to distinguish what it borrows of the Soul, from what it holds of the Body. ([79b], p. 13)

Cordemoy's approach is resolutely Cartesian in the sense that it relies solely on the precise analysis of the contents of consciousness to achieve the self-evidence of truth. Here again, it is the rigour of philosophical statement itself that is believed to underwrite the correctness of speculative thought. Noting that the speech act ensures effective communication between human beings - he sees the proof of the action of the soul in this behaviour - Cordemoy proposes a definition of speaking strongly reminiscent of the Port-Royal grammarians:[5]

> Hitherto I have discours'd of it but in general, and said only, that to speak was to give signs of one's thought... (p.42)

Cordemoy observes that these signs have no correlation with thought, but are linked to it by convention, and he sees in this linking a mirror-image of the body-soul relation:

> But what is most admirable herein, is, that this vast difference between those Signs and our Thoughts, doth by marking to us that, which is between our Body and Soul, teach us at the same time the whole Secret of their Union. (p. 44)

The model which Cordemoy has in mind for explaining this "Secret" is Descartes', but he retains only the outline of it:

> For, seeing the Soul can have no thought, but at the occasion whereof there will be made a motion in the Body, and that also she cannot receive any Idea of what is without but by the motions excited in the Body, which she animateth, it must needs be, that two Souls united to two different Bodies do express their thoughts by Motions, or, if you will, by outward signs. (p. 45)

The agent of these motions is defined in terms of the speech mechanism:

Lastly, I am to take notice, that there is so great a communication and correspondency between the Nerves of the Ear and those of the Larynx, that whensoever any sound agitates the Brain, there flow immediately spirits towards the muscles of the Larynx, which duly dispose them to form a sound altogether like that which was just now striking the Brain. (p. 32f.)

The movements of the soul are artlessly expressed by bodily gestures: facial expression, hand and arm movements, exclamations, tears and laughter, and so on. This gestural inventory constitutes the natural signs of a spontaneous "language".

Descartes' influence is still noticeable.[6] According to Cordemoy, there is in fact a close relationship between the soul and thought on the one hand and facial and bodily movements on the other. Speech and writing are two further means for the soul to express itself, but, in contrast to natural signs, the signs of speech and writing are conventional.

This conventional character of linguistic signs raises an additional question: how are those signs acquired? Cordemoy proceeds to investigate the learning of foreign languages and child language acquisition. He proposes an associationist model to explain both cases. The identification of word meaning arises from the juxtaposition of word and object. Cordemoy's view of child language development to some extent recapitulates statements of St Augustine, however, Cordemoy's gift for independent observation is unmistakable:

But in the taking pains to teach them certain things, we often perceive, that they know the names of a thousand other things, which we designed not to shew them: And what is most surprising therein, is, to see, when they are two or three years of age, that by the sole force of their attention they are capable to find out in all the constructions which are made in speaking of one and the same thing, the name we give to that thing. (p. 52f.)

In his progress from acquiring names of objects (nouns) to acquiring qualities of objects (adjectives), the child points the way to the grammarian, whose analytical procedure is in all respects similar. Here again the influence of the Port-Royal thinkers is detectable. Cordemoy remarks that a person who speaks several languages may recall the topic of a conversation without being able to recall what language it was in. He takes this as a clear indication of the validity of the distinction between our thoughts and the words we use to express them.

One interesting postulate of Cordemoy's would receive manifold developments at the hands of the philosopher-grammarians of the following century:

> But if the Soul were not distinct from the Body, and if Thoughts were
> not distinct from Motions, it would happen, that when the Brain of
> many persons should be affected in the same manner, they would all
> think the same thing at the same time, because they have equally what
> in that matter depends from the Ear and Brain. (p. 218)

There would, in other words, be congruence if not identity between the
soul, thoughts and signs; signs in this case would enjoy the transparent
quality peculiar to the mythical origin of language, which would again be of
central importance to eighteenth century thinkers.

Having clarified the distinction between thought and language, Cordemoy proceeds to define the physical aspect of speech: in the first place, the
formation of voice. The anatomical and physiological mechanism of human
phonation is compared to a wind instrument. This metaphor would be strongly
developed by eighteenth century writers.[7]

There follows a description of the formation of articulate sounds, vowels
and consonants, which shows the sophistication of seventeenth-century phonetics.[8] This description has many points in common with the description
penned by Cordemoy's contemporary, the churchman and educator Bernard Lamy. A course of lectures given by Lamy in 1667 forms the basis of
his *Art de Parler*, published in 1675. One might conjecture that Cordemoy
and Lamy, both avowed Cartesians, had some contact with one another,
but they may just have been drawing on a common source of ideas.

Oddly enough, Cordemoy next proceeds to discuss the effect of sounds
on animals. This discussion in fact serves to reinforce the view that the
speech production process can be purely mechanical, and therefore constitutes only the material aspect of human language. The skill shown by
some species of animals in reproducing speech sounds does not indicate
the presence of a soul in them.[9] In contrast, the way humans use their language
capacity shows that they do have a soul.

Beyond the physical mechanism of speech and the assumed dynamics of
"spirits" underlying it, consciousness of speaking and the will to speak both
belong to a higher level of mental life proper to man:

> We are therefore to consider two things in that we call Sound; one is
> the manner in which the Air, striking the nerve of our ear, shakes our
> Brain, and the other is the sensation of our Soul on the occasion of that
> agitation of the brain. The former belongs necessarily to the Body, be-
> cause 'tis nothing but a Motion; and the latter belongs necessarily to the
> Soul, because 'tis a Perception. So likewise in speech there are two
> things, viz. the Formation of the Voice, which cannot come but from the
> Body, according to what we have already discours'd; and the signification
> joyn'd with it, which cannot be but from the Soul. ([79b], p. 98f.)

Here Cordemoy's views are quite close to those of some of his French contemporaries, such as de la Forge, Chanet and de la Chambre.[10] In the remainder of his *Discourse*, Cordemoy turns to an investigation of what he calls "the physical causes of eloquence". As a conclusion, he develops over several pages the postulate that "we do not have a clear idea of the soul" - echoing Steno's statement quoted at the start of this chapter.

Cordemoy's *Discourse* represents a significant milestone in thinking on the relationship between physical and mental life, between body and mind. Time and again he appeals to language as the human activity that, by virtue of its twofold nature, best illustrates the connection between the two levels.

In order to appreciate Cordemoy's originality of approach at its true value, we must also appreciate the depth of intellectual background on which his philosophizing is based. Cordemoy reflects a dominant preoccupation of the second half of the seventeenth century in his discussion of the body-mind problem through the first six *Discourses*.[11]

This was the problem that Descartes had set himself to solve; he had written his *Treatise on Man* to establish the correct line of demarcation of the mechanical or physical aspect of man from his soul - to define what is uniquely human about man. This philosophical preoccupation explains the intense interest shown by Descartes and his contemporaries in automata.[12] Cordemoy's *Third Discourse* is entitled "on natural and artificial machines."[13] Recall, too, the quotation from Lamy at the head of this chapter, which shows something of the interest aroused by the topic. It is to be found in other minor authors of the period such as Dilly[14] and de la Forge.[15] G. Rodis Lewis[16] in his article "Le domaine propre de l'homme chez les cartésiens"(1964), along with Chomsky in *Cartesian Linguistics* (1966) point out the importance of automata for seventeenth-century thinking on language and mind. Of Cordemoy Chomsky says:

> For our purpose what is important in this is the emphasis on the creative aspect of language use and on the fundamental distinction between human language and the purely functional and stimulus-bound animal communication system, rather than the Cartesian attempts to account for human abilities. ([72b], p. 9)

In the eighteenth century, this line of thinking would make philosophers increasingly attentive to the physical and mechanical aspects of speech, to the detriment of the abstract, "moral" aspect. Indeed, the debate continues today. Leaving aside the terms and ideas of contemporary philosophizing, we can see that the concept of language as meeting-point of the mental and the physical is still central to the problems discussed in the literature.

That concept goes back to the primal contrasts of figure-ground, form-content, visible-invisible, and so on. The descriptions of *homo loquens* that emerge from this long debate vary, of course, in the type of solutions they offer. While in exile in New York in 1942, some European scientists started the Ecole libre des hautes études. There, Roman Jakobson was invited to teach a linguistics course entitled "Six Lectures on Sound and Meaning", another version of this debate. In his last lecture, he provided a well-known and fruitful statement of the problem. To quote his conclusion:

> The systematic investigation of the way in which phonological re- sources are put to use in the construction of grammatical forms, which was initiated by Baudouin's school and by the Prague Circle under the name of "morphonology", promises to construct an indispensable bridge between the study of sound and that of meaning, as long as one takes into account the range of linguistic levels and what is specifically funda- mental to each of them. ([198b], p. 116)

It is hardly an exaggeration to say that Géraud de Cordemoy, contempo- rary of the Port-Royal grammarians, was aiming at nothing less than the construction of such a bridge between the sound and meaning of language.

THE SEARCH FOR A PHYSICAL THEORY OF LANGUAGE

> God having designed man for a sociable creature, made him not only with an inclination, and under a necessity to have fellowship with those of his own kind, but furnished him also with language, which was to be the great instrument and common tie of society.
> Locke [241], III, 1

The theme of language as a gift of God, or of the gods, is one that recurs down through the ages.[17] In Leibniz [229a] we find a statement modelled on Locke's - despite the differences between these two thinkers.[18] Bernard Lamy[19] [218] rejects the theories of such historians as Diodorus Sicilus who see in human language the fruit of human ingenuity and social living only; he cites Genesis to affirm a unique creation of man and God's gift of language. In 1678, however, in the second edition of his book, Lamy stressed that there would be no society among men "if they could not give one another sensible signs of what they think and what they want" ([218], p. 1).

In 1703, this reasoning was repeated almost step for step by Frain du Tremblai[20] [134], who also emphasized the social imperative of language. God having created man for society, and

> speech being the first and most necessary bond of that society, he must have had the faculty of speech from the moment he was formed. ([134], p. 30)

In 1765, Charles de Brosses[21] began the first chapter of his *Treatise on the Mechanical Formation of Languages* with these words:

> The principal aim of this treatise is to examine the material of speech; this great privilege of humanity, which contributes to raising man above the other animals, so far did it please the Creator to endow the human species more than any other with this important natural faculty.
> ([58], p. 3)

The notion of "gift of God" is still very much in evidence here; but note also the phrase "natural faculty", which defines the nature of the gift.

In 1776, Court de Gébelin[22] entitled the fourth chapter of his work [81] "Speech is of divine origin". However, the opening paragraph qualifies this claim somewhat:

> Although language is the application of sounds to objects that have some relation to them, it is nonetheless of Divine origin. It was not men who formed these sounds and relations; it was God who made man a speaking creature. ([81], p. 15)

God's gift to man consisted of the organs required for speech. The notion of language as a gift of God thus undergoes a gradual shift in meaning during the course of the century. The interpretation that eventually crystallizes is that God did not give language ready-made to man, but gave him the capacity to generate it; in other words, man was equipped at the outset with a language faculty which has developed through social life so as to give rise to a particular language in each human community. A new view of innateness is emerging.

Echoing his compatriot Montaigne, who at the end of the sixteenth century had reiterated the proposition that a child left to himself would find his way to language unaided, Montesquieu shows in his *Pensées* that he too believed in the innateness of language:

> A prince could make a fine experiment. Raise three or four children as animals with goats or deaf and dumb nurses. They would construct a language. Examine this language. See Nature by itself, removed from the prejudices of education...[23]
> (Pléiade edition, I, p. 1213)

Similarly, Charles de Brosses entitled one section of his treatise "A number of children raised together would certainly make themselves a language," and recalling the various historical anecdotes on the subject which point to the social nature of language, he remarked that:

the little need that a man alone has to make himself understood
would do a great deal of harm to the progress of development of his
vocal organs. ([58], II, p. 9).

This interpretation was widespread in Enlightenment Europe, and Adam
Smith, in his *Essay on the First Formation of Languages* ([371b], p. 2),[24]
states that two savages who had never learned to speak and had been raised
away from human society would invent a language to communicate their
needs to one another.

The notion of "gift of God" has been supplanted in all of these statements by a notion of "natural faculty". Condillac[25] makes reference to Adam
and Eve, "who did not owe the exercise of the operations of their minds to
experience", and goes on to say that two children left to themselves (after
the Flood, for example) would have progressed naturally through successive stages, from the language of action to the discovery of sign values, to
the development of conventional articulate language making use of their
sound-producing apparatus. There is, however, some evidence of a refinement of Condillac's views between 1746, the date of the *Essay on the Origins of Human Knowledge*, and 1755, the date of writing of the *Course of
Studies* prepared for the young Prince of Parma, to whom Condillac had
been appointed tutor:

> We call articulate sounds those which are modified by the movement
> of the tongue when it strikes against the palate, and those which are
> modified by the movement of the lips when they strike against one
> another. Thus you see, my Lord, that if we are made to speak the lan-
> guage of action, we are also made to speak the language of articulate
> sounds. But here Nature leaves us with almost everything to do our-
> selves. However, it still guides us. From its impulsion we select the first
> articulate sounds, and by analogy we invent others, in so far as we need
> them. ([78c], p.431)

Innateness is thus reduced to a kind of natural inclination to motor activity
upon which man has built language, conditioned both by social stimulus
and by the nature of his intelligence. Such a view does not exclude the
intervention of a Creator,[26] but limits it considerably.

This conception of a gift disguised as an innate property which is itself
regarded as a natural faculty opens the way to an increasingly materialistic
interpretation of the faculty of language. In this, the eighteenth century
prepares the century that follows. Nevertheless, the development of these
ideas was slow, and did not proceed linearly, but through a series of de-
tours that turned out to be necessary for coming to grips with the physical
reality of language.

Philosophers had first to grapple with a significant problem: the diversity of human languages. This was studied by Bernard Lamy among others.[27] If man is endowed with a natural capacity for language, why did that capacity not give rise to a universal language common to all humanity? "On the primitive language, and onomatopeia" is the title of chapter VI of Charles de Brosses' treatise. In his inquiry into the characteristics of this primitive language, De Brosses focusses his attention on the child. Section 63 of the chapter is headed "Observations on the primitive language, as it is spoken by children", and in it we find an idea recalling similar statements by previous writers:

> In order to know how human language began to be formed, it has first been necessary to turn our attention to those who are beginning to speak it.

The argument concludes with a justification of the hypothesis of a single original language, thought by some to be the perfect language, spoken by Adam in the earthly paradise: *lingua adamica.*

Such a notion had, of course, been current since the Renaissance. We recall that for Juan Luis Vives[28] the order of language was a natural one; the speaker can neither determine it nor modify it. Languages evolve over time in the direction of increasing complexity. The more simple ones are likely the most ancient. According to Vives, going back in time we would arrive at the perfect, original language - which is not necessarily to be identified with Hebrew. However, in the course of the sixteenth century the theologically-inspired theory of monogenesis with Hebrew as the primitive language was subscribed to by such scholars as Bibliander, Nebrija, Lefèvre d'Etaples, Calepin, Postel, Goropius and Gesner.[29]

Frain du Tremblai, writing at the beginning of the eighteenth century, entitled chapter V of his treatise *On the Perfection of the First Language.* The first language referred to is, of course, Adam's, conjectured as the original Hebrew, of which Biblical Hebrew is a sort of degenerate descendant.[30] Apparently without much personal conviction he reports:

> Some have thought that this language had such great energy that names expressed the nature of things and were, so to speak, abbreviated definitions of them. ([134], p. 46)

For the Christian thinker of the Renaissance or the Age of Reason, it was the sinful state of man exiled from Paradise that ultimately determined the qualitative regression to Babel. To account for this regression, Frain du Tremblai puts forward an interesting physiological hypothesis - interesting in that it reduces Divine intervention to a slight modification of the innate faculty:

> My thinking is that God so arranged those men's organs that when they tried to pronounce the words they customarily used, they pronounced completely different words to signify the things they wished to speak of.
> ([134], p. 58)

Thus was the immemorial pact between word and object undone, and words, once transparent, became no more than opaque symbols.

Leibniz had come up with a somewhat more sophisticated interpretation of the problem: according to him, languages (note the plural) arose from a kind of natural human drive to adapt sounds to feelings and emotions.[31] Making language a plurality right from its origin disposed of the difficulties; and Leibniz' point of view gradually became the predominant one.

However, this approach complicated the question of the word-object relationship. A whole tradition weighed on the chances of solving that question in the eighteenth century. First, there was the assumption of priority of the concept over the word. That assumption dominated the thinking of the Port-Royal grammarians; for them, words are only the mirror of our ideas. At the close of Antiquity, Boethius[32] had used this distinction to contrast the universality of natural signs with the particularity of conventional signs. Secondly, there was the heritage of Augustine: for him, the articulate sounds that make up speech are *vox verbi* ("the voice of the word"), not "the word" itself which belongs wholly to the sphere of mind, because - as Frain du Tremblai put it - it is "nothing but thought" ([134], p. 18). That is why sensible signs of speech are to be regarded as conventional signs as opposed to natural signs. However, Frain du Tremblai qualified his position somewhat when he declared that conventional signs

> ...if they are not truly natural signs... are neither purely conventional signs; and it can be said that they in fact belong both to nature and convention.[33] ([134], p. 19)

At a later date Charles De Brosses would express a point of view that sums up the problems of the sound-meaning relationship as they were seen in the eighteenth century.[34] De Brosses notes that languages are based on the inflections of the human voice, the form of which depends on the form of the organs producing them, and that the organs of speech are few in number. As a result,

> the number of vocal articulations should be no greater, since that is the total of what the machine can produce. ([58], pp. x-xi)

It follows that:

> Intelligence can do no more than repeat, assemble and combine [the articulations or "germs" of speech] in every possible manner, so as to produce both primitive and derived words and the entire apparatus of language. ([58], pp. xi-xii)

However, the choice of combinations is not arbitrary:

> it is physically determined by the nature and the quality of the object itself, in such a way as to depict the object as it is as far as possible, without which the word would not give any idea of it.[35] ([58], p. xii)

There is thus at the outset a kind of correspondence between word and object that is harmonic rather than symbolic. This view leads De Brosses to claim that,

> there exists a primitive, organic, physical and necessary language, common to the entire human race, which no people on earth knows or uses in its pristine simplicity; that all men now speak nonetheless, and that constitutes the basic mold of all languages in all countries - a mold which the immense range of accessories it carries with it scarcely allows to be seen. ([58], p. xvi)

The same claim was made by Court de Gébelin writing ten years later:

> To know a word is in fact to know the causes which made it take on the meaning attached to it, the language it originated from, the family it belongs to, and the changes it has undergone. ([81], p. 25)

In the course of his argument, De Brosses discusses some interesting phenomena that he was the first to address. He emphasizes the material constraints weighing on "the manufacture of words". He realized intuitively that the development of languages from an innate basis conforms to a hierarchy of implicational necessity, which curtails the scope of the theory of imposition of meaning. He saw that languages contain the principle of their evolution in their nature and their structural ground-plan.[36]

In England, following Locke, a movement of ideas had developed which affected both native grammarians and philosophers and their French counterparts in the second half of the eighteenth century.

Homo loquens corresponds to the intention of his Creator, who endowed him with language so that he might be a social being - thus Locke.[37] But at the same time Locke casts a suspicion on language that is not felt in De Brosses or in the Cartesians. Since the role of the Creator was limited to

giving man the means to speak, Locke believed that languages as the creation of social man were imperfect like everything else in his nature. Languages have meaning (incompletely) by convention alone, and they reflect
only feebly the iconic power of a natural sign.

In 1751, James Harris published his *Hermes, or a Philosophical Enquiry
Concerning Language and Universal Grammar*.[38] As much a work of philosophy as a grammar, Harris' book is noteworthy for the topics absent
from its table of contents as well as for those discussed. There is practically
no discussion of the origin of language, apart from a brief mention at the
beginning of the book [39]. Again, the nature of the word-object relationship
is considered from a viewpoint that goes beyond the conventional debate
about necessary versus arbitrary meaning. For Harris, the relationship arises
from the close association of a sound chain, which he calls "the matter of
language" (i.e. a physical entity), with representations that constitute its
form, without there being any motivation between matter and form (Saussure's
signifiant and *signifié*).

What is striking in Harris, though, is his manner of stating the problems
around the relationship of language and thought. If we go back to the *Port-
Royal Grammar*, we find that thought preexists language:

> Speaking is to explain our thoughts by signs, which men have invented
> for that purpose. ([12], p. 1)

and Part II chapter 1 states the proposition:

> That the knowledge of what passes in the mind is necessary to com-
> prehend the foundation of grammar; and on this depends the diversity
> of words which compose discourse. (p. 21)

But for Harris language no longer has the function of revealing previously organised thought-content. It is the faithful mirror, not of reality, but
of the mental operations by which man grasps reality and reconstructs it at
the level of consciousness. Leibniz had called language "the mirror of the
understanding".

There is in fact a great intellectual gap between Port-Royal and Harris,
in spite of the similarity of titles. The dynamic conception of language
favoured by Harris has its roots in Antiquity (Aristotle in particular), but it
looks forward to the developments of modern linguistic thought in the work
of Saussure and his successors.[40] A friend of Harris', James Burnett, Lord
Monboddo,[41] put forward original ideas while still being clearly influenced
by Harris. In [274], he set out to show that language is not natural to man,
but that it has determined all of his intellectual progress. It is the social,
political environment that, by engendering the need for language, has led

man to mastery of abstract thought. Unlike Harris, Monboddo remained unknown to the French Enlightenment; but both of them, through Herder,[42] deeply influenced German thought.

Throughout eighteenth-century Europe, such ideas were taken up and discussed in quite similar ways by authors often unfamiliar with each other's work. Frain du Tremblai, for example, set out in 1703 to establish rules for judging the merit and excellence of any language. With hindsight, this may seem a rather sterile undertaking, but the discussion led Frain du Tremblai to the idea that there is a necessary relationship between intellectual evolution and the evolution of language.[43] The same idea was expressed by Harris with his novel use of the term "genius" (of the language). Several years previous to that, however, we find Condillac using the title *On the Genius of Languages* for Part II, chapter 15 of [78a]. There Condillac deals with the very same problem: the structural originality of any given language in relation to its creative capabilities. Harris does not seem to have known Condillac's work; he would surely have cited him had he known how close they were on this point.

The basic idea informing these different approaches is language as the creative, or at least the organizing instrument of thought. In the final analysis, this is perhaps the really original element in Enlightenment thinking on language and languages.

De Brosses in his *Treatise* notes that the growth of languages accompanies the growth of civilization (chapter IX, props. 157-159) and that thought ultimately depends on the clarity of the language it uses:

> The truth or falsity of ideas depends to a great extent on the truth or falsity of expressions, i.e. of the exact correspondence of the first notions contained in each of the terms used with the new ideas one wishes to put across or with the opinion one wishes to establish. ([58], p.ii)

Condillac provides the fullest and most authoritative treatment of the idea. His *Essay* [78a] bases human knowledge on sensation transformed by signs, and points out that ideas are connected with one another by the medium of these signs alone. The sign came to have increasing importance in Condillac's thinking. Though admitting the existence of pre-discursive thought, he held that it could only grasp the totality of phenomena projected into consciousness. The language act imposes a linear structure on that undifferentiated perception - the structure of discourse. Locke had ascribed two functions to language: communicating, and assisting memory. Condillac adds a third: organising thought. Language had now become the essential underpinning of thought; its task, not merely to reflect thought, but to construct it.[44]

For Condillac, therefore, General Grammar is also an "Art of Thinking" (as logic had been defined by the Port-Royal thinkers). For the rest of the eighteenth century, philosopher grammarians - notably the Revolutionary French school known as the Ideologues - would define the subject in this way. Michel Foucault has given the following definition of General Grammar, it is:

> the study of verbal order in its relation to the simultaneity which it has the task of representing. ([132b], p. 97)

This philosophical discipline studied language in the construction of discourse through the combination of thought and sign.

Harris is probably one of the first to have sensed the more complex reality obscured by the various attempts to force language into a classificatory straitjacket, at a time when the identities of particular languages were poorly distinguished from language in general:

> We can thus, in the final analysis, define language as a system of articulate sounds, signs or symbols of our ideas, but principally of those that are general or universal. ([174], p. 337)

But what does Harris understand by "system"? From the explanation he provides, it would seem that he is still quite close to Condillac, who defines the term at the beginning of his *Traité des Systèmes* (1749):

> A system is nothing other than the arrangement of he various parts of an art or science in an order in which they each supports the other, and where the last are explained by the first. ([78b], p. 121)

"System", "structure" (some authors were already using the latter term);[45] late eighteenth-century thought was focussing on concepts that had still not freed themselves from the shackles of tradition but that nonetheless indicate a new way of perceiving the object. Beauzée,[46] in the preface to his *Grammaire générale*, wrote:

> Language, based everywhere on the uniform analysis [of discourse] which is, as it were, its intellectual mechanism, also becomes the common instrument of the manifestation of thought and human reason, the interpreter of feeling and affect... ([25], p. viii)

Here we find brought together the various aspects of man's relationship with language as perceived towards the end of the eighteenth century. As a social fact, language is the instrument whereby thought is embodied in discourse, and without which no intellectual progress would have been possible. But language obeys laws which are amenable to analysis and which

indicate the universal foundations of discursive thinking.[47] It is the object
of General Grammar to explain them.[48]

Again, the discipline known to Enlightenment authors as etymology projected onto language a mechanistic vision in which language is organised
on principles determined by the nature of the physiological processes of
speech. Cordemoy had emphasized the physical aspect of these processes.

Language, languages were losing their sacred aura. Mechanism, instrument, tool, structure, system - the terminology is indicative of the new
perception of language as a physical object influenced by environment, climate and race, as Rousseau sought to show.[49]

Language thus became an object reducible to scientific observation in
space. Soon it became the domain of typology, and of an emerging historical grammar.[50] But through Universal Grammar (which, according to Dumar-
sais,[51] constructs statements that apply to all languages) it also revealed
the deep level mechanism of thought, and thus provided an avenue for a
better knowledge of man.

In the space of a century, language had become a human phenomenon
fully dependent on its somatic foundation. The importance of that foundation was revealed by observation of disordered verbal behaviour.

On the other hand, language as a twofold system of sounds and meanings indicated the extent to which thinking itself depended on a somatic
foundation. The study of thinking was also now being transformed from
logic to psychology.

Man with disordered language now ceased to be regarded as a victim of
the gods and became merely a case of pathology. And pathology, from the
beginning of the nineteenth century on, would be regarded as the key to
language in the ordered edifice of the human body.

THE PHYSICAL REALITY OF THE SPEAKER

> The knowledge of an art always depends on the elements that com-
> pose it; one could not therefore get a correct idea of the origin of lan-
> guage and of the relations between languages without knowing their first
> causes, especially the nature and effects of the vocal instrument from
> which all the elements of speech are drawn - these sounds without which
> there would be no speech, and no painting of ideas.
> Court de Gébelin ([81], p. 53)

Court de Gébelin's metaphor is a coherent one. Language is the instrument of thought, but the human voice is also an instrument used to trans-
form the prime matter of speech, the sound chain, into utterance. Anatomists studying the organs involved in voice production chose musical in-

struments as explanatory models. Speculative and experimental science had
by now reduced every aspect of human anatomy and physiology to mechanistic modelling. Soon this would affect man in his entirety, the soul being
dismissed as a fiction. Descartes' *Treatise on Man*, which inaugurated the
trend, has as its logical consequence La Mettrie's *Man-Machine*.

Study of the phenomena of voice production at the close of the seventeenth century was based on a long tradition.[53] The use of the musical instrument model now became quite regular, as is exemplified in the work of
Denis Dodart, [54] who was a physician and a Regent of the Paris Medical
Faculty. It was, among other things, Dodart's interest in music that led him
to study the human voice in the later years of his life. In 1700, he read a
paper at the Académie Royale des Sciences [102a], with two supplements
in 1706 and 1707.

Like Galen, Dodart held that the principal organ of voice is the glottis.[55]
He studied the functioning of the components of the phonatory system,
comparing them to various kinds of musical instruments. In the end, he
found that wind instruments provided the most suitable model to elucidate
the mechanism of the human voice, but noted that the glottis is not a reed:

> The whole tone-producing effect of the glottis depends on the tension
> of its lips and its various degrees of opening; this manifestly represents
> the greatest miracle that there is among voluntary movements, and ac-
> cordingly one of the strongest proofs that physics can offer to natural
> theology so as to make appreciable and (as it were) palpable the infinite
> power and knowledge of the Creator. ([102a], p.280)

The 1706 paper extends this exposition. In it Dodart deals with the question
of the difference between speaking voice and singing voice. The difference,
Dodart claimed, has to do with a change in position of the larynx. The
1707 supplement was to have a continuation which death prevented Dodart
from completing. Here his attention was drawn to what he called the "labial
glottis",[56] which made him think that the model of stringed instrument also
applied to the human voice. It is the quantity and movement of air that
produce voice and modulate its tones.

In 1741, Antoine Ferrein,[57] another French anatomist, read his paper on
the human voice at the Académie Royale des Sciences. In it he cites Dodart,
and explains that although there are no musical instruments that are both
wind and stringed, this very type of instrument is to be found in the human
body - the voice.

Anatomically speaking, Ferrein's approach represented a step forward,
because, contrary to the teaching of the Ancients, and latterly of Perrault[58]
and Dodart, "shrinking of the glottis and speed of air movement are neither of them adequate to explain the variety of tones produced by the voice,

even in [Dodart's] system" ([122], p. 414). Now, he continues, looking for more satisfactory explanations,

> ...I looked for a theory that could better explain the admirable mechanism which produces all the various sounds that charm our ears. Examining the larynx first gave me the idea. I thought I had found in the lips of the glottis strings that could vibrate and sound like the strings of a viol, and I regarded the air as the bow that sets them going, and the chest and lungs as the hand that draws the bow. I used this principle to explain the loudness of the voice, the variety of tones and many other phenomena the cause of which had previously eluded understanding. I even felt justified in taking away from the glottis its title of organ of voice and assigning it to the strings I have spoken of. ([122], p. 416)

Ferrein supports his theory by detailing the results of experiments he had carried out on human and animal larynxes. This procedure implies a new approach to scientific research. Proof is no longer founded on axiomatic statements but on experiment incorporating real-world conditions.[59] After Ferrein, the mechanism of voice production seems to have been considerably clarified.[60] On the other hand, while the voice was studied as the prime matter of language, articulation was still regarded as its distinguishing feature. As Bernard Lamy remarked,

> Voice would be something we had in common with a number of the animals, were it not for the fact that it assumes other forms than the one it takes leaving the larynx. ([218] 1, iii, chapter I, p. 188)

It is in fact this "form" assumed by the human voice that harnesses it to carry the sounds of language. Here the will to meaning enters the process. As a result, there was a desire on the part of scholars at this period to find out the physiological mechanisms by which the "form" is brought into being. Answering this question would in fact mean pinpointing the area of contact between body and soul which - according to Cordemoy - is indicated by the phenomenon of language. Frain du Tremblai had grasped the importance of this issue:

> It is no small mystery, the connection between purely spiritual and intelligible ideas and these corporal and sensible sounds; and how it can be that a particular sound can have first excited a particular sound in the soul. ([134], p. 36)

The search for answers necessarily led back from the readily accessible domain of vocal anatomy to the motor centre organising and controlling vocal movements - the brain. An overall model was emerging. Court de Gébelin states:

All the fibres making up these nerves and muscles are hollow and
filled with cells in which there floats a fluid having the ability to move
about and inflate by an effect of will; thus the vessels containing it necessarily enlarge; as a result, they shorten, and by shortening they pull
and move all the parts connected to them, whence derives the movement of the parts of the body. ([81], p. 56)

However, the apparent explanatory rigour of this mechanistic model cannot
conceal the fact that the problem is merely being evaded - the problem
being "the connection between... ideas and... sounds" as Frain du Tremblai
put it.

The issue is still, as always, the relationship between the spiritual and
the material, between soul and body. In the meantime, the language in which
supporters of the dualistic thesis couched their arguments was becoming
more and more materialistic as the searched for the elusive somatic point
of contact. The philosopher Charles Bonnet,[61] writing in 1760, reveals the
driving force behind this approach:

We are made in such a way that we believe ourselves the authors of
our actions; and, were that not so, were that motive power which our
inner feeling makes us attribute to our soul non-existent, it would suffice
that action follow the decision of the will constantly, as the will follows
the decision of the intellect constantly, and the human system would be
no different. To attribute action to the Machine alone is still to attribute
it to ourselves, because this machine is ourselves - the soul is not the
whole man. ([45], p. 17f.)

Bonnet goes on to say:

Anatomy reveals to us one of the principal instruments of union in
the nerves. This science, today so advanced, shows us that the soul only
feels and moves by means of the nerves.

As a result,

The discovery of the point of origin of the nerves leads one to situate
the soul in the brain. ([45], p. 18)

It seems hardly necessary to dwell on the wanderings of the soul through
the various parts of the brain. One of Bonnet's eighteenth-century contemporaries, La Peyronie,[62] situated it in the corpus callosum. The author of
the article "Soul" in the *Encyclopédie* remarks:

So there is the soul, settled in the corpus callosum until some new
experiment moves it out of there and leaves the physiologists in the
position of not knowing where to put it. ([C], vol. I, p. 342)

From Pico della Mirandola[63] and Bodin[64] to La Mettrie or Bonnet, we see that from the Renaissance to the Enlightenment philosophizing about the body-soul relationship moves towards a reduced role for the soul and an expanded role for the body. At the same time, the bodily space assigned to the soul shrinks till it is no more than a junction point between the two hemispheres, the corpus callosum. Its imagined localization almost follows by necessity from the conceptualization of its function.

In concluding his *Physical Discourse on Language*, Cordemoy had claimed that "we have no clear idea of the soul". La Mettrie, after having done his utmost to show that the notion of soul adds nothing to the understanding of the brain's complex machinery, observes that "the soul is therefore but an empty word, of which no-one has any idea, and which an enlightened man should use only to signify the part in us that thinks" ([264b], p. 128). Before making this claim, La Mettrie had first demonstrated the interdependence of the movements of body and soul, and had emphasized the degree of difficulty there was in reconciling the medical man's practical experience with the theoretical views of philosophers. There is a close interdependence between the physical life and the consciousness of human beings. "The soul and the body fall asleep together" ([264b], p. 65). For La Mettrie, this interdependence shows that:

> The human body is a machine which winds its own springs. It is the living image of perpetual movement. Nourishment keeps up the movements which fever excites. Without food, the soul pines away, goes mad, and dies exhausted. ([264b], p. 93)

If one compares human and animal anatomy, La Mettrie goes on, the only observable difference between the two is that man is "the one whose brain is largest, and, in proportion to its mass, more convoluted than the brain of any other animal" ([264b], p. 98). This man-animal comparison next leads La Mettrie to consider the problem of language in animals. He states that the reason why some do not speak while others are very skilled at imitating the human voice is probably to be found in "some defect in the organs of speech" ([264b], p. 100). Given this author's Cartesian perspective, the admission of the possibility of some speech in the animal, an actual machine, implies that speech has no need of the action of a soul to come into being. If one used the techniques of those who, like Amman,[65] have succeeded in making the deaf speak, in order to train a great ape, which is close to man, to pronounce and thus to know a language, "then he would no longer be a wild man, nor a defective man, but he would be a perfect man." ([264b], p. 103)

It is language that makes man; man before language was only an animal. The tendency of the age, which was to see language not merely as the mirror of thought but as its instrument, is here developed to an extreme.

> Words, languages, laws, sciences and the fine arts have come, and by
> them finally the rough diamond of our mind has been polished.
> ([264b], p. 103)

The problem is how such a miracle could have come about. La Mettrie's explanation is rather vague:

> Everything was done by signs; every species understood what it could;
> and in this way men attained symbolic knowledge...

As for the origin of that knowledge, a question which fascinated the scholarly world of his age with such little result, La Mettrie's explanation is really a poetical one, in which the musical instrument metaphor is transferred from the voice to the brain:

> As a violin string or a harpsichord key vibrates and gives forth sound,
> so the cerebral fibres, struck by waves of sound, are stimulated to render
> or repeat the words that strike them. ([264b], p.105)

Thus human knowledge is reduced to words and the images brought forth by them, which "are so connected in the brain that it is comparatively rare to imagine a thing without the name or sign that is attached to it" ([264b], p. 107). Man owes everything to the faculty of imagination by which "the cold skeleton of reason takes on living and ruddy flesh"(p. 108). The organization of man's brain, along with his education, has made him what he is. To account for this development, there is no need to bring in the theory of innate ideas, on which La Mettrie strongly attacks Descartes.[66]

However, the Man-Machine (La Mettrie cheerfully accepts this designation for himself) at least has the virtue of humility:

> Let us not lose ourselves in the infinite, for we are not made to have
> the least idea thereof, and are absolutely unable to get back to the origin
> of things. (p. 122)

This acceptance of man's limitations, which brings La Mettrie's thought close to that of the Cynics, as also the implicit hedonism in his philosophy (he held that man's goal was "enjoyment")[67] aroused the ire of his contemporaries. Even the more open-minded ignored the flashes of insight[68] in this rather garbled philosophy, and could see in the Man-Machine only a crude perversion of their own ideas.

Admittedly, La Mettrie had few qualms about overstating his case, and proceeded to push the mechanistic thesis to its limit. In the light of such intellectual curiosities, one can understand the fascination that Vaucanson's[69] automata must have exercised. Citing these as an example, La Mettrie claims:

> To be a machine, to feel, to think, to know how to distinguish good from bad, as well as blue from yellow, in a word, to be born with an intelligence and a sure moral instinct, and to be but an animal, are therefore characters which are no more contradictory than to be an ape or a parrot and to be able to give oneself pleasure. (p. 143)

That leads him to a final profession of faith:

> Let us then conclude boldly that man is a machine, and that in the whole universe there is but a single substance, variously modified. (p. 148)

If we look up the headings "Automaton" and "Android" in the *Encyclopédie*, we see that La Mettrie's tone is in accord with contemporary fads. The notion that machines could take over human roles would take on a new lease of life in the nineteenth century. Having first attracted scientists and philosophers, it would capture the imagination of novelists. *L'Eve Future* is only one of many examples.[70]

Materialism, which would reach its apogee in the nineteenth century and reign supreme in the sciences of man, finds its epistemological basis in La Mettrie's paradoxes, greeted at the time by a wave of indignation that took long to subside. Whatever the book's excesses in the way of gratuitous claims of the undemonstrable, its radically materialistic outlook was perhaps necessary, after all, in order to free the scientist's essential capacity to see from its ancient taboos, and to reveal the human speaker both as an object and as a topic that could be discussed with objective detachment, as the physicist discussed matter. It is at the price of this dehumanization of the body object that the anatomist's scalpel would be able to explore the inert substance of the brain with cool detachment, a brain in which the soul no longer had a place. As a first step in this intellectual process, La Mettrie's thought, by its very excesses, freed brain science from a pseudo-problem: the soul's place in the body.

The Enlightenment encouraged this bold attempt to deduce the body's secrets, following Steno and his contemporaries. Philosophical commentary now tended to free that attempt from the metaphysical outlook that had weighed upon it for so long. Having studied perception in relation to the instrument at some length, we now turn from the preoccupation with words to the new preoccupation with objects.

NOTES

1   "Physics: it is the science of natural things. It is a science that teaches
    us the reasons and causes of all the effects of nature. Speech also means
    the natural faculty of speaking. Only man possesses speech."
2   On the following page Steno remarks, on the appearance of the brain:
    "If the substance is everywhere fibrous, as indeed it seems in several
    places, you must admit that the disposition of these fibres must be
    arranged with great art, since all the diversity of our feelings and our
    movements depends on it."
3   Géraud de Cordemoy (1636-1684).
4   Reflexion on the nature of language is not new: see p. 22. Through the
    ages, the exclusively human character of language is reaffirmed in the
    wake of Epicurus and Lucretius by Fabius Claudius Cordianus Fulgen-
    tius (480-550), much later by Abelard who saw the result of it in the
    man of reason.
5   "To speak is to explain one's thoughts by signs which men have in-
    vented to that end" [12].
6   In a letter to Mersenne (December 18, 1629) Descartes writes: "For
    utterances which signify naturally, I find it a reasonable explanation,
    that what strikes our senses so much it forces us to put forth some
    sounds: as, if we are struck, it makes us cry out; if something funny
    happens, it makes us laugh; and the sounds put forth in crying out or
    laughing are similar in all languages."
7   Aristotle is the first model. But Cordemoy also knows the moderns,
    particularly Riolan and Steno. See p. 53.
8   Grammont ([160], p. 13): "One must not think that between the Greek
    and Latin grammarians and the nineteenth century no-one was inter-
    ested in the study of phonemes and their articulation. For instance, the
    Discourse on Speech of G. de Cordemoy, printed in Paris in 1668, in
    which the articulations of a number of French phonemes are described
    with remarkable precision and accuracy. These descriptions were re-
    produced word for word by Molière in Le Bourgeois Gentilhomme Act
    II, Scene 6 (1670). Also the De corpore animato of J.B. du Hamel
    (1673)." It should be mentioned that like du Hamel and Lamy, Corde-
    moy may have known the work of Wallis. See p. 119.
9   [79b], p. 231.
10 LaForge was a great supporter of Descartes and made numerous notes
    on the Treatise on Man published along with the work itself in Amster-
    dam in 1677. See p. 65. Pierre Chanet (born c. 1603): his thoughts
    [67a] were criticized by Cureau de la Chambre in vol. II of [87a].
11 Noam Chomsky, in [72b], gives an interesting modern interpretation
    of Cordemoy's thought.

1 2 With Descartes, the theme of automata does not just appear in the *Treatise on Man*, but in many passages of his work, especially in his letters. It is interesting to look at his "Letter to · · ·" of March 1638, p. 1000 of the Pléiade edition. See pp. 76 ff.

13 To quote a passage early in the text: "We are convinced well enough that the arrangement of the parts of a watch is the cause of all its effects, and whether it marks the hours or sounds them, whether it identifies days, months or years, or whether it does even more difficult and unusual things - we seek no form, no faculties, occult virtues or qualities in it. We are sure that it is not animate, because we can account for all it does, by the movement and shape of its parts."

14 Dilly [100]. Chapter xv is entitled "On admirable machines made by men" (p. 178ff.).

15 See note 10 above.

16 Cf. [346a].

17 See p. 22.

18 "Philalethe: God having formed man to be a sociable creature, He not only inspired in him the desire and placed him in the necessity of living with those of his kind, but gave him the faculty of speaking" ([229a], p. 221).

19 See p. 64 and [218].

20 Frain du Tremblai (1641-1724).

21 Charles de Brosses (1709-1777).

22 Antoine Court de Gébelin (1725-1784).

23 Presumably Montesquieu knew Herodotus; see the ancient author's account of the experiment of the Pharaoh Psammeticus [184].

24 Adam Smith (1713-1790).

25 Condillac (1715-1780), Part II, *On Language and Method* [98a], Section 1, *On the Origin and Progress of Language*, chapter 1, "The language of action and the language of articulate sounds considered in their origin".

26 "It is nature and imitation that teach children the use they have to make of their organs for the pronunciation of their native language; and it is again from imitation and not knowledge of the organs and principles of grammar that the older man learns to imitate articulations alien to the language of the country where he was born" (pp. iii-iv).

27 This concern already appears in the 1675 edition of [218]: "In languages - as in all other things - there are insensible changes which bring it about that after some time they appear to be something quite different from what they were at the outset."

28 Of Vives (1490-1540) must be mentioned 7, Book XII, and *Epistola de*

ratione studii puerilis, cum rudimentis grammaticae, 1536, composed for the use of the Princess Mary, daughter of Henry VIII.

29 Mention must be made of the *De originibus seu de Hebraicae linguae et gentis antiquitate atque variarum linguarum affinitate* of Guillaume Postel, Paris, 1538; and the *De ratione communi omnium linguarum et litterarum commentarius of Bibliander*, Zurich, 1548.

30 "We should also be assured, that there was nothing lacking in the language that he [Adam] spoke... His language could provide him with all necessary terms and expressions to speak with eloquence" ([134], p. 42).

31 G.W. Leibniz: "Languages were not sacrificed by virtue of a decree nor created by any law" [229b].

32 Boethius (480-525).

33 "These signs are positive or by institution, in that a term is different by itself to all sorts of meanings, and they are natural, in that they are established without the prudence and counsel of man"([134], p.20).

34 This presentation figures in the "Preliminary Discourse" to the *Treatise on the Mechanical Formation of Languages*, 1765 edition.

35 In support of his claims, De Brosses gives the following example: "Let us suppose a Carib who wants to name 'a cannon-shot' to an Algonquin, a new object for these two men who do not understand each other; he will not call it Nizalie, but Poutou." This leads the author to believe "that the system of the first manufacture of human language and of the attachment of names to things is thus not arbitrary and conventional as is commonly imagined."

36 [58], p. 215f.

37 Locke [241], Book III.

38 See [174].

39 "If nature had destined men to live in isolation, they would never have felt that urge that led them to communicate with one another" (from Thurot's French translation).

40 André Joly, in [201a], sums up the Port-Royal position (somewhat pedantically) as follows: "The whole Port-Royal theory, both in the Grammar and the Logic, is in fact based on the ectopy of language in comparison with thought."

41 James Burnett, Lord Monboddo (1744-1799).

42 J. G. Herder (1744-1803).

43 Indeed, it is only by cultivation of the Arts and Sciences that languages can reach their perfection [134], (p. 69).

44 This new conception had a profound effect on the Ideologues. "Language" said Thurot following Destutt de Tracy, "is not only a means of expressing our ideas, but an instrument with whose help the faculty of thinking gains more flexibility and activity, more force and range" ([201a], pp. 32f.).

45 Joly notes: "In parallel, we see developing, from the 17th century on, the usage 'structure'... In 1708, Morhof speaks of the 'structure' of Sanskrit" ([201b], p. 53).
46 Nicholas Beauzée (1717-1789).
47 Beauzée writes in his preface: "I thought I should deal with the principles of language, as one deals with those of physics, geometry, and all the sciences" [25].
48 "Since discourse connects its parts like representation its elements, General Grammar must study the representative functioning of words in relation to one another; which presupposes, to begin with, an analysis of the bond that links words together (theory of the proposition and, singularly, of the verb), then an analysis of the various types of words and of the way in which they divide up representation and are distinguished from one another (theory of articulation)..." ([132b], p. 107).
49 [350], pp. 61f.
50 The groundwork was laid by La Curne de Sainte-Palaye (1687- 1781), Court de Gébelin, Charles de Brosses and also by Turgot (1727-1781). Reference should also be made here to G. B. Vico (1668-1744), author of the *Scienza nuova*, published in 1725 and revised until his death. Finally, we must include Leibniz and Monboddo.
51 César Chesneau du Marsais (1676-1756).
52 Julien Offray de La Mettrie (1709-1751).
53 Aristotle: [11a], Book IV, chap. 9. Galen, who took great interest in the function of the recurrent nerves of the voice, and who, by successive experiments, came to believe that the brain was the true seat of the vocal faculty (see Souques [374a], p. 210; cf. also p.26f.).
54 Denis Dodart (1634-1707).
55 [102b].
56 "...It is the glottis which makes the human whistle, and which I will call for short 'labial'" ([102b], pp. 66f.).
57 Antoine Ferrein (1693-1769).
58 Charles Perrault (1613-1707).
59 "I reflected afterwards that voice requires not only a stronger breath, but also a new degree of contraction of the larynx: I took that of a dog, put the lips of the glottis together and blew hard into the trachea; at this point the organ seemed to come alive and produced, I say not only a sound but a ringing voice, more pleasing to me than the most touching concerts" ([122], p. 417).
60 Vicq d'Azyr (1748-1794) corroborated Ferrein's work. See [412a].
61 Charles Bonnet (1720-1793).
62 François Gigot de la Peyronie (1678-1747), see [309], p. 19.

63 Giovanni Pico della Mirandola (1463-1494).
64 Jean Bodin (1529-1596). In [41a] he studies the problem of the body-
    soul relation. According to Bodin, the soul is "the form of the body";
    the soul should be defined differently depending on whether it is an
    element of the animate body or whether it is separate from the body. It
    then has the character of a hypostasis, because it is the "human intel-
    lect". These self-mirroring phrases reflect the fugitive image of a soul
    which is in turn defined as "quickening substantial form", "a hierarchy
    of separate and different principles", and whose "powers" are numer-
    ous: from motor activity to will, by way of memory and sensation.
65 Amman: see p. 130, n. 21.
66 "The Cartesians would here in vain make an onset upon me with their
    innate ideas. I certainly would not give myself a quarter of the trouble
    that Mr Locke took, to attack such chimeras. In truth, what is the use
    of writing a ponderous volume to prove a doctrine which became an
    axiom three thousand years ago?" ([264b], p. 111).
67 See [264c].
68 "There you have many more facts than are necessary to prove beyond
    all doubt that every little fibre or part of organized bodies moves by a
    principle peculiar to it whose action does not at all depend on nerves,
    like voluntary movements, since the movements in question operate
    without the parts that manifest them having any commerce with the
    circulation. Now if this force is to be noticed right down to pieces of
    fibres, the heart, which is composed of singularly interlaced fibres, must
    have the same property" ([264b], pp. 115f.)
69 Jacques de Vaucanson (1709-1782). His automata imitated life, and his
    goal was to understand its mysteries by the artifice of mechanics. With
    the support of Louis XV, he actually undertook the construction of an
    automaton inside which the entire mechanism   of the circulation of
    the blood was to operate! In an activity which some considered a frivo-
    lous game many 18th-century thinkers perceived a fascinating search
    whose tacit aim was to reproduce nature by means of technology. It is
    enough to read the articles "Automata" and "Androids" in the *Ency-
    clopédie* to get a sense of the fascination that such undertakings held
    for the 18th-century mind.
70 Villiers de l'Isle Adam's novel *L'Eve Future* dates from 1886. A scien-
    tist (Edison), using electricity, makes a "woman", and a young English-
    man falls in love with her. Jules Verne was another author fascinated
    by imitations of humanity by the marvel of electricity: see his novel *A
    Castle in the Carpathians*. The 20th century imagination has not proved
    immune to this illusion either.

III
FROM THE REALM OF WORDS
TO THE REALM OF OBJECTS

1. The Body as an Object of Knowledge

Eye and Instrument

> The entire conduct of our life depends on our senses, among which sight being the most universal and the most noble, there is no doubt that inventions which serve to augment its power are the most useful that can be imagined. And it is difficult to find any that augment it more than these marvelous lenses...
> Descartes ([99], p. 180)

In the course of the seventeenth century, optical instruments became the necessary mediator between the eye and the object, the hand and the human body. Two technical fields illustrate at this point the evolution of the instrumental function in research: the emerging field of optics, with the development of the magnifying glass; and dissection, which by exploiting the new possibilities of instrumentation as well as physics and chemistry, assisted and guided the hand of the anatomist.

Using a lens whose magnifying power was still slight and which was as difficult to use as the preparations were imperfect, Robert Hooke succeeded in identifying vegetable cells around 1665.[1] At about the same time several anatomists used this new tool in an attempt to define the nature of cerebral tissue. Between the eye - whose power is increased by the instrument - and the object, however, speculative imagination and ideology often intruded. In many cases the role of the instrument was limited to validating the initial hypothesis with an appearance of greater scientific objectivity.

Marcello Malpighi,[2] one of the most notable biologists of his time, believed along with many of his contemporaries that the brain, as the Hippocratic writers had taught, was a gland. Under the microscope he therefore saw a brain composed of glandular cells.

Use of the microscope again about a quarter-century later led Ruysch[3] to observe (1699) that the cortical substance is not glandular in nature but vascular.

The best illustration of the difficulty in seeing what is real is provided by the approach taken by Leeuwenhoek,[4] chronologically half-way between the two preceding cases. It was in Holland that Descartes busied himself with anatomy and devoted his thinking to a speculative physiology in which imagination won out over real-world data; and it was in Holland that the exacting discipline of lens-cutting developed, giving rise to the avocation of a very talented amateur, Leeuwenhoek. Between Descartes and Leeuwenhoek there is the gap of little more than a generation;[5] but this can hardly justify even in part the tremendous difference in mental attitudes towards the percep-

89

tion of reality. Descartes believed in the value of direct information from the senses guided by reason; Leeuwenhoek believed in microscopes. But did he believe in them enough?[6]

In 1674, Leeuwenhoek identified what he called red blood cells. Observation of cortical tissue taken from the cerebellum of a turkey led him to believe that it was made up of cells which he called "globules."[7]

What did Leeuwenhoek actually see? Was it the magnified image of fatty cells, or was it some optical illusion caused by the treatment of the preparation or even the instrument itself? Specialists agree with a fair degree of certainty that he could not have seen actual nerve cells.

The same year, Leeuwenhoek observed in nerve tissue what he called the nervous fibre. It must be pointed out that nerve fibre, as it is now thought of, was not identified till Fontana[8] (1781). Before that time the term should therefore be taken in a less specific sense. Leeuwenhoek's initial observations led him to the surprising conclusion that the nerves were not hollow:

> ...but I could find no hollowness in them; I only took notice that they were made up of many filamentous particles, of a very soft substance... ([227a], p. 180)

In 1664, Willis[9] had observed almost the same thing, and had conjectured some kind of porosity allowing the circulation of the animal spirits. A century earlier, Vesalius had encountered the same difficulty.[10] For Leeuwenhoek, the apparent absence of a "hollow" did not cast doubt on the theory of the animal spirits. The data of the experiment were instead called into question by the experimenter himself. The following year he published further observations on the subject,[11] and he now found an apparent hollowness in the fibres composing the nerves. Leeuwenhoek returned to the question of nerve fibre at regular intervals: in 1677, in 1685, in 1693, and finally in 1717, more than forty years after his first communication on the subject. Aged 85 at the time, he presents what may be regarded as the first attempt at diagramming a cross-section of a peripheral nerve.

Henceforth Leeuwenhoek believed that he had clear proof that the fibres composing the nerves are hollow, and the nerves themselves also:[12]

> I saw that the single nerves, as far as they extended lengthwise, were hollow or pervious like a kind of channel. [227b]

In this way, the eye aided by the instrument sees what it wants to see of reality as preempted by thought. What was it that Leeuwenhoek saw in the core of the tissue? It has been speculated that he might have noticed the myelin sheath, whose appearance would have convinced him that the nerves were indeed hollow as they were supposed to be if the spirits were to circulate. The inadequacy of the instrument and the quality of the preparation may both have been sources of error. The most difficult obstacle to overcome, however, must have been the very limits of imagination. A very gradual forward movement of thought and observation would have to occur in the Enlightenment period for scientists to come to the realization that, in spite of the undoubted power of the microscope, what the eye discovered was still only appearance, in comparison with the extraordinary complexity of the structures of matter to be found in the realm of infinitely small objects.[13] Only with the invention of the achromatic microscope around 1820 would a surer observation of matter begin.

The salient feature of these first efforts is the change in mental attitude on the part of the researcher which they indicate: the desire that the object impinge directly on perception. An identical change was taking place in anatomical procedure with the exemplary approach of Steno. In spite of the controversies that inevitably arose during and after his stay in Paris,[14] the impact of Steno's example was felt all through the eighteenth century.

J. B. Denis,[15] the advocate of blood transfusion, recommended Steno's technique for studying the structure of the heart; F. Bernier[16] quoted Steno with reference to the arrangement of fibres in the muscles, and Verduc[17] with reference to their movements. It was J. B. Winslow,[18] however, Steno's grand-nephew, who was principally responsible for the transmission of the great anatomist's teaching in France and beyond.

Tarin,[19] who perfected the technique of dissecting the brain, and who was himself commended by Portal at the end of the century,[20] wrote:

> We can never praise Steno enough, Steno who, inspired by the god of anatomy... opened a new and distinct path. [388c]

F. D. Hérissaut,[21] a pupil of Winslow and of R. A. Ferchault de Réaumur,[22] drew a practical application from Steno's teaching. He produced an acid which, in accordance with the recommendations of the great anatomist, "could dissolve bones in a short time, or soften them" ([384], p. 46). In this way he obtained surprising results, finding that he could keep the parts of the brain in a very different state from what had previously been the case. Thanks to this softening process, Hérissault adds, he had succeeded in following the path of several nerves previously unknown, again in accordance with Steno's method.[23] Twenty years later, Hérissault's findings seemed still of sufficient interest to be worthy of mention by S. A. Tissot.[24]

At the same period, J. R. Tenon[25] [389] based his entire argumentation on the *Discourse of the Illustrious Steno*, referring to the latter's thoughts on the social condition of the anatomist. Portal stressed that Steno on the anatomy of the brain destroyed the most accepted opinions by facts "incontrovertible by reason of their self-evidence" [384].

He recognizes the fruitfulness of Steno's techniques as attested by the findings of those who have followed his teaching. Again, in the nineteenth century, Flourens[26] still sings his praises in 1845 and then in 1849:

> I call him the first real anatomist of the brain, for he was the first truly to see the brain's fibres, that is to say, what is most important to see in the structure of that organ.[27]

This citation of Steno and reference to a fundamental change in anatomical procedure points to the development, over the course of the eighteenth century, of an approach more closely tied to experimental data, increasingly emancipated from the mirages of axiomatic discourse, and willing to submit to the rigour of instrumental technique.

Pourfour du Petit[28] illustrates this new orientation. His first medical communications were published in 1710, and presented his thesis as follows:

> I am sending you some observations I have made on the structure of the parts composing the brain, together with observations and experiments that prove that the animal spirits filtered into the right side of the brain are used for the movements of the left side of the body, and that those filtered into the left side of the brain are used for the right-hand parts of the body, at least as regards the arms and legs. ([325], p. 1)

After recalling that the Ancients, Cassius and Aretaeus[29] in particular, believed that the nerves,

> were laced together at their origin and crossed in such a way that those of the right side passed over to the left side, and those of the left side passed over to the right side,

he expresses surprise at the fact that anatomists,

> who have come after have not noticed that this idea was probable...
> ([325], p. 1)

Following this preamble, Pourfour du Petit relates the clinical observations he has made, which all converge on the same finding of a chiasmus.[30] On the way, he notes a correlation, in the light of cases observed, between lesions of the left side of the brain and loss of the language faculty:

> Some time after I made the experiments I have just reported, a

> cavalry officer of 35 years of age was brought to our hospital. He had a
> paralysis of the whole right side the day before... He could not move his
> tongue without great difficulty and could not stick it out of his mouth or
> pronounce a single word...

A month later,

> ...he could move his tongue fairly easily... but he could not say any-
> thing except *non*."([325], p. 7)

An attack of scurvy and a "stomach flow" caused the death of this patient two months after entering the hospital. Pourfour du Petit now conducted an autopsy:

> I found, in the left side, the entire frontal protuberance, which con-
> tains the internal and upper, the middle and external or lower cannelate
> bodies, completely dissolved and reduced to a substance rather like wine
> dregs. ([325], p. 7)

A basic anatomical fact had been brought to light. Although more than
a century would go by before that finding was generally accepted, the approach taken by the anatomist and the practitioner nonetheless attest the
efficacy of a new technique based on clinical observation and anatomical
verification. Adherence to factual evidence was the new element in the
intellectual attitude of researchers who were now refusing the attractions
of dialectic exposition.

The ground had been prepared for a new orientation, and only the direction was still lacking. The discovery of electricity would soon provide it.

THE BRAIN EXPLORED

> Brain, n. The inner part of the head contained in the skull, which is the prin-
> ciple of movement and feeling.
> *Dictionnaire de l'Académie* (1695)

Does the above definition from a major contemporary reference work
reflect what an educated person knew about the brain on the eve of the
eighteenth century? It at least affirms the triumph of the cerebrocentrist
thesis and the localization of motor activity as well as sensation in the brain.[31]

There are other sources, however, that give a better idea of the knowledge at the disposal of non- specialists. We shall compare two other French
works, Furetière's *Dictionnaire Universel* (1690) and Thomas Corneille's *Dictionnaire des Arts et des Sciences*, first published in 1665 (the revised edition

of 1694 deals with the heading "brain" in some detail). Similarities are apparent between the two dictionaries, but the articles differ somewhat in the information presented.

With Furetière, the brain is "...a marrowy and white, cold and moist substance..." (The last two adjectives reflect an ancient conception of the brain as cold and moist in comparison with the hot and dry heart.) Thomas Corneille, on the other hand, establishes the distinction between two objectively visible aspects: "the brain is made up of two substances, one grey and the other white." This contrast, according to the author of the article, stems from the fact that blood vessels are more numerous in the grey matter than in the white matter.[32]

The technical detail provided reveals the involvement of a specialist:

> ...All this is taken from the description of the brain made by M. Drouin,[33] master surgeon of the General Hospital.

The glandular nature of the brain is mentioned by Thomas Corneille only as a hypothesis about the grey matter. In Furetière's dictionary, the glandular nature of the brain comes in a historical connection:

> Galen calls its substance glandular because it is white and flaky, and brings the same materials to the head as the other glands elsewhere. It is certain, however, that it is a true marrow which spreads out and continues into the spine...

The ventricles and the pineal gland are mentioned by both editors. Thomas Corneille:

> The pineal gland, which is composed of a hard and yellowish substance, covered with a very fine and loose membrane, has its place at the entrance to the channel leading from the third to the fourth ventricle.

Furetière is the only one to cite Descartes:

> The second pipe of the third ventricle leads straight to the fourth, where there appears a gland which looks rather like a pine cone. This is why it is called conoid, or the conarium. M. Descartes calls it the pineal gland, and claims that it is the seat of the reasonable soul; but Steno gives it a different site.

As regards the function of the brain, Furetière is both cautious and precise in presenting the man's brain as the place: "where all the sense organs end, and where it is believed his soul principally resides," whereas Corneille's definition has a more modern ring, with the seat of the soul not even being

mentioned in it: the brain "is the principle of movement and feeling..."
As evidence of the persistence of old mythologies, both articles deal with the internal structure of the brain, the ventricles, and mention the florid imaginary toponymy so vigorously criticized by Steno[34] - especially Furetière:

> Underneath we see two conduits called pelvis and infundibulum, that is to say, the basin and the funnel... behind the conarium are two small and rather hard bodies in contact with one another which are called nates, that is, buttocks, because of their shape, and lower down we see two others that are called *orchis* and *didymoi*, that is to say, testicles.

Though Corneille says nothing about the role of the spirits, Furetière is quite explicit:

> [The brain] has a systolic and diastolic movement, that is to say, it restrains or dilates its capacities [ventricles] so as to push the animal spirit into the sense organs.

Very clearly, the representation of the brain is still being modelled on the representation of the heart, a hollow muscle. While the brain is regarded as having an important role in affective and cognitive life as well as in motor activity, both authors (in the article "cerebellum") agree in recognizing in almost identical terms the importance of this latter organ for vegetative life.

> Corneille: The slightest injury to the cerebellum or the spine causes the immediate death of the animal.

> Furetière: One cannot injure the cerebellum or the spine without the animal immediately dying.

Comparison of the articles on "spirit" in both dictionaries shows that the editors have identical views on the matter.[35] This is corroborated by the article "nerve," where in both dictionaries we find echoes of the same certainty.

> Corneille: Nerve... part which enters into the makeup of the animal and which serves to carry the animal spirits to the whole body and to give it movement and sensation.

> Furetière: Nerve... This, according to medical men, is a spermatic[36] part of the animal's body, which derives from the brain or the spine... it carries the animal spirit for feeling and movement.

Now let us consult the article "nerve" in the *Encyclopédie*:

> ...a round, white, long body, like a string made out of different threads
> or fibres, which has its origin from the brain or the cerebellum via the
> medulla oblongata and the spine, which is distributed to all parts of the
> body, which serves to carry thereto a particular juice which some schol-
> ars call animal spirits...

What was being presented as a certainty at the end of the seventeenth
century had, by the second half of the eighteenth, become a hypothesis to
be mentioned with caution. The structure of the nerve calls forth this remark:

> It was supposed a long time ago that nerves are small tubes, but it has
> been very difficult to discover the cavities; at last it was thought that M.
> Lewenhock [sic] had succeeded in demonstrating the cavities inside the
> nerves, but this discovery still suffers from some difficulty.

A remark opening the way to a further consideration, which is perhaps
the newest and the most fruitful direction:

> There does not seem to be the slightest probability in this opinion
> (which nonetheless enjoys support) that the nerves carry out their opera-
> tions by the vibration of stretched fibres; indeed, it is a thought contrary
> to the nature of the nerves, whose substance is soft, limp and flat,
> crossed and wavy...

The article "Spirit" in fact puts forth the most widely accepted viewpoint at the time:

> ...These spirits, which are thought to flow rapidly in the nerves, are
> probably a subtle fire. Dr Mead[37] is seemingly the first to have provided
> evidence for this in the preface to his treatise on poisons.

The "liquor" spoken of by Thomas Corneille in the article "Brain",[38] the
"subtle substance" that he mentions in the article "Spirit"[39] has thus become fire. From fire to electricity, the distance is at least somewhat less-
ened.

Another French dictionary, the *Grand Vocabulaire français* (1767), expresses the same uncertainty as the *Encyclopédie* with regard to the nature
of the animal spirits, and mentions the contradictory opinions regarding
their existence:

> These bodies which are also called vital spirits... are... an extremely
> mobile fluid which separates from the blood in the cortical substance of
> the brain, whence it passes into the medullary substance, and from there

to the nerves which carry it from the head to all parts of the body, and carry it back from all parts of the body to the head... There are nevertheless philosophers who deny the existence of the animal spirits. They think that the nerves are stretched strings rather like those of instruments, and our actions are carried out by the various vibrations we give them.

In the same reference work, the article "Nerve" is treated with a wealth of anatomical detail, without the term "spirits" even being mentioned. There is talk (with accompanying citation of Haller)[40] of "irritated nerve," of "muscles... agitated on the spot by a convulsive movement," and the correlations that exist between the tensing of a nerve and the contraction of a muscle are noted. At the end of this long article, the writer only says:

That being given, it does not seem that one can doubt that it is in the brain, the cerebellum and the medulla united to it, that the cause of all bodily movement resides, and that from there it extends into all the muscles and all the parts of the human body.

The same resistance to obscuring the object with traditional categories of discourse is to be seen in the major article on the brain in the *Encyclopédie*, written by Tarin.[41] The brain is there described as: "a soft mass, part greyish and part whitish," and portrayed as: "the source of our senses."

The membranes protecting the brain are correctly identified, and the author's attention is attracted to its outer surface.

One sees there the substance of the brain which forms countless deep folds whose convolutions almost imitate those of the intestines.

But, two centuries after Vesalius, the reference to the intestines is still obligatory, and two thousand years after Erasistratus the rediscovered convolutions do not hold the writer's attention for too long. The word "cortex," which was first used in anatomy around 1741,[42] does not occur here. The fissure of Sylvius[43] is mentioned, as is the resulting separation into "lobes." The internal structure of the organ is still the main focus of attention:

Behind the third ventricle is a small glandular body, called the pineal gland, and below this gland the quadrigeminate bodies, of which the upper ones have been called nates and the lower ones testes.

Study of the anatomical plates confirms this impression. A remarkable work of craftsmanship, they constantly direct the eye to the interior.

This condensed account of knowledge of the brain for the general public does not reveal any differences from knowledge created by and for the scientists themselves. Vesalius[44] had noted the difference in colour between the grey matter of the brain's surface and the white matter of the interior; but he seemed to pay no attention to the outer surface. Piccolomini[45] was perhaps the first to establish this colour difference, but even more importantly he had the originality to observe "certain lines" on the outer surface, and to enshrine his perceptual distinction in his terminology, proposing *cerebrum* to designate the grey matter and *medulla* the white matter. Among the anatomists of the Age of Reason, Willis is the one who seems to have ascribed the most importance to observation of the brain's outer surface.

Struck by its complexity of organization, he sought to justify this by identifying functional specializations in it. Returning to Erasistratus' viewpoint, he suggested a direct correlation between the complexity of the convolutions and the degree of intelligence; and in accordance with his theory of the localization of brain functions, he situated memory in the cortex, also assigning to this anatomical terra incognita the production of animal spirits. Why did he thus oppose Galen's teachings, respected up till his time, which ascribed that very function to the white matter? Willis was an iatrochemist[46] and wished to assign the production of spirits to a chemical process, for which the cortex seemed to him an appropriate place. Perhaps because of all these accumulated assumptions, Willis' teaching in this regard found no continuation.

In fact, at the end of the seventeenth century the cortex had still to be invented. The tool which would enable exploration of the cortex, the achromatic microscope, was not yet available. In Willis' time, the eye could not get very far beyond the immediate appearance of the object.

Gaspard Bartholin[47] noticed the fissure at the base of the brain, attributed first mention of it to Silvius, and named it after him. As dissection techniques developed, it was the inside of the organ that was most regularly described. Tarin first identified the transverse bundle uniting the two optic layers and the two upper extensions of the cerebellum. It was hoped to dismantle the entire complex machine like the mechanism of a clock. Chanet[48] believed that the brain was composed a large number of small organs which we see dispersed in different parts of the cerebral mass without knowing their exact purpose. He worked towards discovering a "language of the brain" the signs of which would be decoded by scientists. An identical viewpoint is expressed by Hartley.[49]

Steno had proposed investigation of the cerebral mass of the white matter by means of a technique in which the anatomist's scalpel should try to follow the fibres through the complexity of forms. Operating in this manner, Vieussens[50] recognized the independence of the spine in relation to the brain, contrary to tradition.[51] By a kind of intuition not fully appreciated till much later, his careful examination of the cortex convinced him, like Willis, that the extensive development of the surface in folds must have some functional cause; and the greater the complexity, the greater the power of sensory integration and analysis of the organ, and of its motor response. Santorini,[52] who left brain drawings of perfect technique but lacking in realism, illustrates the same growth of perception.

Rolando[53] was interested in the internal fibres, and postulated their importance for the formation of voluntary motor functions. Vicq d'Azyr[54] in 1777 gave a description of the nerves of the second and third pairs, and in 1781 read four papers at the Académie des Sciences on the structure of the brain and spinal cord and the origin of nerves. His *Treatise* [412c], which his short life did not allow him to finish, clearly shows his interest in the brain's internal structure. The captions to the excellent accompanying illustrations also bear witness to the close attention he paid to the brain surface. He seems to have observed the presence of separate cortical layers in remarking on the existence of a white line in the occipital cortex. The same observation was made, almost at the same time, by Gennari[55] and Soemmering.[56] Vicq d'Azyr thought that the two hemispheres were not symmetrical, and paused to compare the sizes of convolutions rather than to study their arrangement. He weighed, measured, and established proportions. Now observation was being subjected to the constraints of mathematical objectivity.

As Cabanis[57] explains:

> Anatomy, too often cultivated by dissectors rather than by minds worthy of considering it in its true light, is perhaps to an extent greater than any other part of medicine confused and obscured by this vice of words and which in the long run deforms objects themselves.
> ([66] p. 162 T.II)

Vicq d'Azyr was particularly aware of this problem. He called for the establishment of a rigorous anatomical nomenclature, on the model of the chemical nomenclature developed and successfully promoted by Lavoisier. He returns several times to this matter, more fully developed in [412d]. Here again, he reflects a new but profound growth in the late eighteenth century.[58]

From the seventeenth to the eighteenth centuries, the anatomist's eye had searched the inner structure of the brain by refining techniques and instruments, gaining more and more objectivity, and ridding himself of many a prejudice. But the effectiveness of this progressive approach was limited by three factors:

First, a technical factor: the inadequacy of the microscope.

Second, a psychological factor: the orientation of inquiry, which brings the anatomist back constantly to the interior of the brain, where he puzzles over the inscrutable clockwork mechanism.

Third, a conceptual factor: the use of a model of functioning based on the theory of fluids to drive this mechanism, whether the agent is thought to be spirits or any other representation of a fluid.

In this way, scientific reasoning was always being brought back to the inherited mythology of soul-body relations, whose fascination was still to be felt at the dawn of the nineteenth century, as is seen with Soemmering.[59] There needed to be change in these three related factors for anatomy to gain any new ground.

Those changes would take place almost simultaneously in the first thirty years of the new century: technically, by the appearance of the achromatic microscope. This tool would at last give the eye sufficient power to examine a structure with infinitely small components; psychologically, by a reorientation of perception. Under the influence of Gall[60] and Spurzheim,[61] anatomists began to believe that the cerebral convolutions are not a random arrangement, but that they should be carefully studied like any other anatomical structure. Under this heading, the first to continue the work of Willis, assisted by the contribution of Gall and Spurzheim, was Tiedemann,[62] though Leuret[63] also deserves mention; and conceptually, by the emergence of the electrical model. This would consign to the museum the hoary doctrine of pneuma which had come down through the centuries. The electrical model, because it was totally new, gave knowledge tempting new vistas, but also tempted imagination to create new will-o'-the-wisps.

THE ELECTRICAL MODEL

> Since Franklin's fine experiments drew scientists' attention to the phenomena of electricity, it has not been difficult to see that living bodies have the faculty of producing those condensations of the electrical fluid, by which its existence manifests itself...
> It even seems that the nervous organ is a kind of condenser, or rather an actual storehouse of electricity as well as phosphorus.
> P. J. G. Cabanis, *Mémoire VI*, ([66], p. 325f.)

In the course of the seventeenth and eighteenth centuries, the doctrine of animal spirits was doubted, and then eliminated. Its disappearance left a vacuum which various hypotheses on the nature of the transmitting agent circulating inside the nerves tried to fill. Differences in vocabulary illustrate the variety of opinions: "nervous fluid," "igneous substance," "vibrations".[64] Observation and experiment had established some facts, however: the cerebral and spinal origin of motor commands, the cerebral destination of sensory information, the correlation now established between particular pathological states of the brain and particular muscular disorders, the excitation of particular nerves and the contraction of specific muscles.

With the progress of perceptual objectivity, natural scientists became more demanding and tried to verify and demonstrate theory:

> ...They make ligatures to see if the [animal spirits] would inflate the nerves above the obstacle. ([256], p. 8).

Such experimentation regularly produced negative results, in the case both of Swammerdamm,[65] operating for the first time on sciatic-gastrocentric preparations from frogs,[66] and Glisson.[67] Because of this finding, Glisson developed a new interpretation of motor command. In 1672 [153b][68] and in 1677, the year of his death, ([153c] - the first work containing conjectures on the nature of simple fibre), Glisson advanced the theory of an innate principle of irritability of simple fibre, wherein he distinguished irritability from sensibility. Willis,[69] as we know, had already declared - without being heard by his contemporaries - that the nerves were not hollow.

The principle of irritability opened up a new speculative avenue for all those who recognized its anatomical validity; but, in the context of the period, Glisson's contribution was mainly regarded as a kind of reaction to Descartes. To the mechanistic model of the French philosopher he opposed a vitalist model, which laboured under the disadvantage of appearing to be a throwback to Scholastic philosophy, a belated postscript to the thinking of Aristotle.[70]

The fact that Glisson did not base his theory on any experimental test at a time when experiment was becoming the rule for every scientific undertaking explains (along with the Aristotelian colouring of his ideas) why his work met with little interest from his contemporaries. Boerhaave,[71] however, regarded him as the most exact of all anatomists, and Haller[72] considered his work excellent.

In his paper [172], he ascribes the credit for the irritability idea to Glisson, but then develops the implications of the theory in the light of his own extensive experimental work. Whereas sensibility seems to him the privilege of the nerve, irritability and contractibility are in his view the privilege of muscle. He prefers, to the coherence of a general theory, the exactness of experimental data which make it possible for the concepts in question to be refined and verified. However, the nature of the agent in the nerves that makes the connection between the central organ and the periphery remains as much a mystery as ever, and Haller cares to say little on this subject.

At the same time as Haller was preparing his paper, the work of David

Hartley[73] appeared in London in 1749. On the basis of Newtonian principles and vocabulary:

> Sir Isaac Newton supposes that a very subtle and elastic fluid, which
> he calls Aether... is diffused through the pores of gross bodies as well as
> through the open spaces which are void of gross matter.[74]

Hartley constructed a theory of vibrations[75] complemented by an Associationist approach derived from the use Locke himself had made of this concept in his theory of knowledge.[76] By uniting the two phenomena, association and vibration, Hartley believed he could show the close interdependence of the spiritual or mental and the material which the unity of man presupposes.

Many interesting views are developed in the first part of the book. Hartley distinguishes automatic and voluntary movements. In accordance with the principle that all actions - such as hand movements in the newborn - develop by dint of regular repetition from automatic to voluntary until becoming automatic again at another level, Hartley explains how the child acquires speech gestures beginning with automatic movements produced accidentally, then learning to reproduce them voluntarily and finally re-automatizing them.

This attempt to explain motor activity and sensation by the combination of association and vibration obviously assumes an electrical model. Hartley says so explicitly:

> The effluvia of electrical bodies seem to have vibrating motions. For
> they are excited by friction, patting, and heat, and excite light, sound,
> and a pricking sensation... so that electricity is also connected in various
> ways with the doctrine of vibrations. ([175], p. 28)

Himself a physician by profession, Hartley was aware of his own period's ignorance about the articulation of the nervous system. He notes that it is reasonable to assume that nerves coming from different parts of the body have countless connections with one another in the brain; he also knows that anatomically this is practically impossible to prove. Again, speaking of this seeming identity between electrical phenomena, he remains cautious, given the uncertainty around this completely new area of investigation.

To get an idea of the knowledge then available on the subject, it is useful to look at the article "Electricity" in the *Encyclopédie*. Note firstly the phrasing of the introduction:

> This word signifies in general the effects of a very fluid and very subtle
> matter, differing by its properties from all the other kinds of fluid matter

we know of; which has been found capable of being joined to almost any body, but preferably to some rather than to others; which appears to move with very great speed, following laws peculiar to itself, and which, by its movements, produces very singular phenomena which this article will attempt to describe.

And then the following admission:

Since we do not yet know the essence of electrical matter, it is impossible to define it otherwise than by its chief properties.

Reference is also made to the existence of *succin*, known by all naturalists.[77]

Electricity remained an anecdotal affair, a matter for entertaining drawing-room experiments. The experimenters were playing with fire without understanding its nature. The therapeutic virtues of electricity were divined from a heuristic approach. The notoriety surrounding Mesmer's[78] experiments are a case in point, and illustrate the credulity of which the Age of Enlightenment, at its close was capable. "Mesmerism" had been preceded by the more serious investigations of the Abbé Nollet.[79]

The electrical model of nervous transmission depended on experiments which, because of the element of charlatanism involved, immediately undermined its credibility.[80] A physical phenomenon, but one which seemed to manifest itself at the surface of things, electricity hardly seemed able to account for the invisible and mysterious exchanges between the brain and the peripheral nerve endings. Hartley's theories were accordingly greeted with skepticism.

For Haller, the properties Hartley attributed to the medullary substance of the brain were absolutely incompatible with nature. Hartley's doctrine appeared to court materialism, as was noted by Priestley in a paper published in 1775, where he wittily attempts to show that Hartley is no less a materialist than himself.[81]

Alexander Monro primus[82] was particularly aware of the evidence against the idea of a fluid transmitting agent between the brain and the periphery. In [276], he therefore examined the electrical hypothesis. The basic concept in an electrical model, the concept of nerve as conducting agent, had surely been available since Antiquity. Hales,[83] Haller and others had not rejected such a possibility outright. But Monro primus remarks:

We are not sufficiently acquainted with the properties of an Aether (or electrical effluvia) pervading everything to apply it (them) justly in the animal oeconomy, and it is as difficult to conceive how it (they) should be retained (or conducted) in a long nervous cord as it is to have any idea how it should act. These are difficulties not to be surmounted.[84] ([277a], p. 333)

Whytt[85] goes from cautious skepticism to rejection:

> Upon the whole, then, we may fairly conclude that the contraction of
> an irritated muscle cannot be owing to any effervescence, explosion,
> ethereal oscillation, or electrical energy excited in its fibres or mem-
> branes, by the mechanical action of stimuli upon them.

Twenty years later, in 1783, Alexander Monro secundus[86] took up the
whole question again in [277b]. The chapter is entitled: "Of the Nature of
the Energy of the Nerves." The hypothesis of a conducting fluid is excluded
on the basis of the inertia of such an agent, and the hypothesis of electricity is clearly posited. Two main arguments militate in favour of this second hypothesis, according to Monro secundus: first, the extraordinary velocity of nervous energy, estimated by Haller at 9,000 feet per minute[87], and
second, the finding that some animals such as the eel and the electric fish
have the power to give off electrical discharges. Note that this observation
goes back to the beginning of the century. In 1715 Réaumur[88] described the
singular action of the eel. Despite these facts, Monro secundus does not
disguise his skepticism. Does electricity, seemingly revealed by such phenomena, come from the animal, or have the nerves just the property of
capturing it?

The work of Charles Bonnet[89] brings home to us the difficulty his contemporaries had in understanding the electrical model. He repeats Haller's
criticism of Hartley.[90] The term "vibration," often used by supporters of the
electrical model and associated with the term "cord" or "string," also used
in reference to the nerves, lent itself to a metaphorical representation little
in keeping with reality:

> But nerves are soft, they are not taut like the strings of an instrument:
> would objects therefore excite vibrations in them like those of a plucked
> string? Would these vibrations communicate instantly with the seat of
> the soul? The idea seems difficult to conceive. But if we claim that in
> the nerves there is a fluid whose subtlety and mobility approach that of
> light, we can easily explain with the help of this fluid both the speed with
> which impressions are communicated to the soul and the speed with
> which the soul carries out so many different operations. ([45], pp. 20f.)

It was ignorance of the nature of electrical phenomena and inability to
experience them in any other than a spectacular but superficial way[91] that
kept contemporaries from accepting the addition of an electrical model to
the map of the nervous system.

Towards the end of the century, the electrical model began to encounter further problems of interpretation, particularly the finding that a ligature stopped nervous conduction but not the flow of electricity. In the meantime, various experiments had led scientists to claim the existence of "animal electricity," though none of them could demonstrate its origin. This was the context in which Luigi Galvani[92] worked. In 1786, he investigated the action on nerve and muscle of artificial electricity produced by machines and natural electricity whose existence had been brilliantly demonstrated by Benjamin Franklin.

According to the legend, love was the motive: Lucia Galeazzi, Galvani's wife, was in poor health, and Galvani used to cook medicinal frog broth for her. One of the skinned frogs called for by the recipe had been left on a table near an electricity machine. One of Galvani's assistants unwittingly touched the internal crural nerve with a scalpel, and immediately all the muscles in the limbs appeared to go into convulsions. Galvani's wife, who witnessed the incident, was struck by the peculiarity of this phenomenon, and thought it had occurred at the release of the electric spark. Galvani himself immediately set about replicating the experiment. Seeing as the contractions might be attributed simply to contact with the scalpel acting as a stimulus rather than to transmission of the spark, he touched the nerves of some other frogs when the machine was turned off. The contractions failed to occur.

There is another version of this chance discovery, but it may be just a continuation of the foregoing. Galvani, who was working with frogs, observed contractions in the feet of an animal he had hung up on an iron frame with a brass hook in the spinal cord. Investigating this phenomenon, he found that the contractions were not due to atmospheric electricity. It is this observation that Galvani reported in [145], published in 1791. Galvani there claimed that there exists in the animal's body what may be called (as Nicholas Bertholon[93] proposed) "animal electricity." This electricity, inherent throughout the body, is concentrated in the muscles and in the nervous system. Muscular fibres were thus miniature Leyden jars. At the moment when the metallic arc establishes contact with the nerve and the surface of the muscle, it discharges the Leyden jar, which produces the contraction.

Reaction to Galvani's work was considerable. Physiologists now thought they could put their finger on the "vital force," and medical men saw a new road to infallible cures.

The opposition came from a man who had at first subscribed to Galvani's conclusions, only to reject them after more stringent testing, Alessandro Volta.[94] Galvani was more medical man than physicist, and his rather limited theoretical knowledge of electricity perhaps explains the rapidity with which he had drawn his conclusions. Volta was a physicist. He had built the electrophore in 1775, and the electric condenser in 1782. He quickly observed that the contractions also occurred when the two extremities of the arc only touched the nerve.

To sum up the protracted debate, while Galvani was for animal electricity, Volta championed the idea of metallic electricity that appears in different conductors. Volta's opposition to Galvani's ideas induced the latter to devise the experiment which, fifty years later, Du Bois-Reymond[95] still regarded as basic in electrophysiology. Seeking to eliminate the metallic arc on which the whole opposing argument was based, Galvani conducted his experiment as follows - again on frogs:

> I bent the nerve in one of the feet in the shape of a small arc, then I raised the nerve of the other with the usual glass ring, dropped it on this nerve arc, taking care that the nerve in its fall touched the other nerve in two places, and that the sectioned extremity of that other nerve was one of the two points. I saw the foot whose nerve I dropped on the other contract. [145]

Galvani exclaims:

> What heterogeneity could be invoked in the case of these contractions when only the nerves are in contact with one another?

Indeed, the experiment demonstrated the production of electricity by a living tissue.

However, Galvani was imprudent enough to present too systematic a view of his discovery. He proposed a model whereby the electrical fluid is produced by the brain, which extracts it from the blood. This was unfortunately reminiscent of the model of the animal spirits, and it led back to a kind of speculation based more on words than real-world objects. Volta's objective mathematical rigour stood in contrast, and for a time physics seemed to be winning against physiology. In fact, progress would bring benefits to both disciplines.

Giovanni Aldini,[96] Galvani's nephew, in trying to preserve the doctrine of animal electricity so dear to his uncle, probably did him more harm than good. On the other hand, the experiments of Nobili[97] in 1828, measured by galvanometer; those of Matteucci[98] later in the century and finally the research of Du Bois-Reymond, would shed light on the positive contribution Galvani had made to electrophysiology, while illustrating what it also owed to the physicists. In the meantime, Rolando was carrying out the first experimental research on the effects of electricity on the brain.[99] The way was a long one, but the path was now open for an electrical model of the central nervous system. We shall now return to consideration of the human speaker.

NOTES

1   Robert Hooke (1635-1703).
2   Marcello Malpighi (1628-1694) was not the first to examine a cerebral cortex under the microscope, but the first to give a detailed account: *De cerebri cortice*, [252].
3   Frederick Ruysch (1638-1731): see [353].
4   Antony van Leeuwenhoek (1632-1723). An able lens-cutter, his curiosity drew him to make observations on animal tissues. His scientific observations would make this amateur known as a true scientist.
5   Leeuwenhoek was only 18 years old when Descartes died in Stockholm on February 11, 1650.
6   Bradbury ([53], p. 79) provides this information: "Leeuwenhoek's lenses were of surprisingly good quality. Van der Star has measured the resolving power and the magnification of several examples. Two of these, now in the Leyden Museum, magnified 79x and 126x respectively and had a resolving power of 3-5 microns..."
7   A letter written to the Royal Society of London, July 25, 1675. Leeuwenhoek's work was translated into English from originals in Dutch; see [227c].
8   Felice G. F. Fontana (1730-1805).
9   Thomas Willis (1621-1675) (see also n. 12, p. 60) [423a]: "The passages of the nerves are not hollowed out like those of the arteries and veins because their substance is not only impervious to any stylus, but the use of a lens or microscope confirms that there is no cavity present in them" (chap. XIX).
10 Vesalius (see p. 42, n. 12) refused to discuss the question of the way in which the animal spirits are transmitted. He in fact avoided claiming that the nerves were hollow.
11 [227a].
12 Letter to Abraham van Bleisuyk of Delft, March 1717, Epistola XXXII, in [227b]. See also XXXIV, March 6, 1717, and XXXVI, May 26, 1717.
13 In this respect Leeuwenhoek illustrates rather well in his approach as an observer the difficulty there can be in remaining objective toward the data of perception. There has been much discussion of his discovery of animalcula which he noticed in sperm. These observations are detailed in Buffon's *Histoire naturelle*.
14 See p. 53.
15 J. Denis (?-1704), *Journal des Sçavans*, March 1673, p. 213, note 1.
16 F. Bernier (1620-1688): [36], vol. V, p. 387.
17 J. P. Verduc (1662-1693): [406]
18 Jacques-Bénigne Winslow (1669-1760): see [424]. He came from Denmark to study medicine in Holland and later in France, where he settled.

19   Pierre Tarin (170?-1761).
20   Antoine Portal (1742-1832) says: "Tarin's manner of dissecting the brain is very good" - it was the method propounded by Steno - "and I use it to considerable advantage" in [324], vol. V, p. 442.
21   F. D. Hérissant (1714-1773), a member of the *Académie des Sciences.*
22   René Antoine Ferchault de Réaumur (1683-1757).
23   [182], p. 329.
24   Simon René Tissot (1728-1797): [394], vol. I, p. 31.
25   Jacques René Tenon (1724-1816).
26   Pierre Flourens (1794-1867).
27   *Journal des Savants*, August 1845, p. 462; and July 1849, p. 422.
28   François Pourfour du Petit (1664-1741).
29   Aretaeus: see p. 16, note 4.
30   Note that Domenico Mistichelli (1675-1715) in [271] describes the decussation of the fibres of the meninges covering the medulla oblongata.
31   In Richelet's (1679) dictionary the word "Sensation" is defined as follows:"term used in philosophical discussion which means power or faculty of feeling, sentiment."
     A century later, the Grand Vocabulaire Français (1773) defines "Feeling (sentiment)" as: "perception which the soul has of objects by means of sense organs." Later in the article, the writer notes that: "feeling also means the awareness we have of what occurs in our soul witout any aid of the senses."
32   "The large number of vessels and the fluid they contain cause this grey colour" (art. "Brain" [80]).
33   Vincent-Denis Drouin (1660-1722).
34   See p. 53, and particularly note 36, p. 69.
35   In Furetière's dictionary we find: " 'Spirit' in medical terms is used of the light and volatile atoms, which are the most subtle part of bodies, which give them movement and which are media between the body and the faculties of the soul, which enable it to perform all its operations."
     In Thomas Corneille's dictionary, it is specified that: "...Physicians mean by this word nothing other than blood broken down into a very subtle substance and volatilised precisely in the heart and lungs, both by continual fermentation of the blood and by the air that is unceasingly being breathed."
36   The medullary substance was for a long time identified with sperm.
37   Richard Mead (1673-1754).
38   "The white substance, which has this colour because it has few vessels, and the fluid they contain is transparent and clear."
39   See above, note 35.

40 Albrecht von Haller (1708-1777). It is to him that La Mettrie (see p. 76ff.) had impertinently dedicated his *Man Machine.*

41 On Tarin, see note 19 above.

42 On the word "cortex," see note 16, p. 58. It should be pointed out that the word is used in the sense of envelope or outer covering in 1677 in English, then as an anatomical term with reference to the brain in 1741.

43 See n. 42, p. 59.

44 See n. 12, p. 42.

45 See n. 15, p. 58.

46 I.e., an advocate of chemistry being used in medicine.

47 See n. 39, p. 59.

48 See n. 10, p. 82.

49 Hartley (1705-1757), English physician and philosopher.

50 Raymond Vieussens (1641-1716?).

51 Willis had worked mainly with animals. Vieussens' main work [413] is distinguished by its exclusive empirical basis in the human brain.

52 Giovanni Domenico Santorini (1681-1736).

53 Lodovico Rolando (1773-1831).

54 Félix Vicq d'Azyr: see n. 60, p. 83.

55 Francesco Gennari (1752-1797): on February 2, 1776, Gennari sectioned a frozen human brain and with the naked eye observed a white line in the cortex (lineola albidior) particularly visible in the occipital region. Vicq d'Azyr, who also mentions this line, does not seem to have known of Gennari's work.

56 Samuel Thomas Soemmering (1755-1830) also described this white line, but referring to Gennari.

57 Pierre-Jean Georges Cabanis (1757-1808), French philosopher of the Ideologue school.

58 Among others, Johann Christian Reil (1759-1813) must be mentioned, a German anatomist who devised new procedures for preparing brains for study, and expressed his conviction that the brain had specific functions. The name of Jiri Procháska (1749-1820) also deserves mention here.

59 He devotes the fourth volume of his treatise [373b] to the study of the brain and nerves. He divides the brain into four parts: "the ashen," "the marrowy," "the intermediate part, which is slightly yellow," and finally "the black part." He describes the five ventricles of the brain and indicates that the pineal gland is bigger in men than in women. Finally, in [373c] (1796), he assigned as the place for this immaterial part of man's being the watery humour that bathes the surface of the ventricles.

60 Franz Joseph Gall (1758-1828): see p. 124ff.

61 G. Spurzheim (1776-1832): see p. 125ff.

62 Friedrich Tiedemann (1781-1861): see [393]. It was he who showed the variations in organisation of the cerebral convolutions across species.

63 F. Leuret (1797-1851): see [234]. He could only write the first volume; the second was completed by Gratiolet (n. 28 p. 149).

64 A more important place should perhaps be given to Giovanni Alfonso Borelli (1608-1679), who illustrated this tendency in proposing a new label for the animal spirits that hints at an intuition of a model of transmission prefiguring the electrical model. See [46], where he expounds his theory of nervous transmission. He posits the existence of a new transmitting agent, the *succus nerveus*, which although it bears a name that seems to be a mere substitute for the term "animal spirits" is presented as having properties strictly obedient to physical laws. When the *succus* reached the muscle, a chemical process rather like the one posited by Willis was triggered. Some of Borelli's statements evoke present-day conceptions of nervous transmission, albeit somewhat vaguely and distantly.

65 Jan Swammerdam (1637-1680). He moved from the study of man to the study of insects, and made outstanding contributions to both fields.

66 An experiment of 1664, published only in 1738.

67 Francis Glisson (1597-1677). He held a chair of medicine at Cambridge. He was the first to attribute the contraction of the heart and other muscles to the action of a stimulus on their irritable principle. Glisson thereby contributed a new statement of the problem of nervous transmission and introduced into the discussion the principle of irritability, an innate property of simple fibre. This *robur insitus* was mentioned by Glisson for the first time in 1654, in [153a].

68 See [153b], and [153c].

69 See n. 9 above.

70 M. Vervorn in [407] speaks of the "wilderness of Scholastic phraseology," p. 3.

71 Hermann Boerhaave (1668-1738). One of the most illustrious medical figures of his time, he pursued his entire career at the University of Leyden.

72 See n. 40 above.

73 See n. 49 above. We are referring here to [175].

74 Proposition 5, from which this quotation is taken, states: "The vibrations mentioned in the last proposition are excited, propagated and kept up, partly by the Aether, i.e. by a very subtle and elastic Fluid, and partly by the Uniformity, Continuity, Softness and active Powers of the medullary Substance of the Brain, spinal Marrows and Nerves." ([175], p. 13).

75 "These vibrations are Motions backwards and forwards of the small

Particles... of the same kind with the oscillations of Pendulums and the Trembling of Particles of sounding Bodies" ([175], p. 11).

76   The title of Proposition 10 is: "Any sensation A, B, C, etc., by being associated with one another a sufficient Number of Times, get such a Power over the corresponding Ideas a, b, c, etc., that any one of the sensations A, when impressed alone, shall be able to excite in the Mind b, c, etc., the Ideas of the rest." ([175], p. 65).

77   Amber: "A yellowish translucent fossil resin, found chiefly along the southern shores of the Baltic. It is used for ornaments; burns with an agreeable odour; often entombs the bodies of insects, etc., and when rubbed becomes notably electric (so called from its Greek name élektron)." (*O. E. D.*)

78   Anton Mesmer (1733-1815). A German doctor, his career in Paris caused a great stir because of the miraculous cures he claimed to make by "mesmerizing" his patients.

79   Jean Antoine Nollet (1700-1770). See [290], where he explains Newton's theories and records his own electrical experiments.

80   The article "Electricity" in the *Encyclopédie* is instructive in this regard. Under the heading "Medicinal Electricity," an account is given of the first applications of electricity to man, by use of the Leyden jar. There is talk of luminous saliva issuing from the mouth of a person being electrified, and luminous blood spurting from an open vein. There is also mention of the application of the electric globe to the treatment of paralysis. The late eighteenth-century mind was indeed mesmerized!

81   Joseph Priestley (1733-1804): see [326a, b].

82   Alexander Monro primus (1697-1767), Scottish physician and anatomist. See [276].

83   Stephen Hales (1677-1761), physician and scientist. See [171].

84   Note that the words or phrases in parentheses were changed or added in the later editions, for example, the sixth edition, Edinburgh, 1758; and *The Works of Alexander Monro, M.D.*, published by his son Alexander Monro secundus, Edinburgh, 1781.

85   Robert Whytt (1714-1766). In 1736, he became professor of medical theory in Edinburgh.

86   Alexander Monro secundus (1733-1817), a physician like his father. His son, Alexander Monro tertius, continued their work.

87   "Thus Dr Haller observes how often a muscle of any part could act in a minute; and supposing that previous to every contraction, the nervous fluid moved from the brain to that part has attempted to calculate its velocity [footnote:] not less than 9,000 feet in the first minute" ([277b], p. 74).

88   See n. 22 above.

89   See n. 61, p. 85.

90   Charles Bonnet writes: "I am here using expressions one can tell are not to be taken literally. We do not know the nature of the Animal Spirits; they are even more outside the reach of our senses and our instruments than the vessels that filter or prepare them. It is only by way of reasoning that we are led to claim their existence and to suspect some similarity between these spirits and electrical fluid. The similarity rests principally on certain very singular properties of this fluid, in particular, on the rapidity and the freedom with which it moves along one or several strings, and through a mass of water, even moving water" ([45], p. 21f).

91   The *Encyclopédie*, again under the heading of "Medicinal Electricity," reports the experiments of Jallabert, a clever physics professor in Geneva who brought about the almost total cure of an arm that had been paralysed and atrophied for ten years. "He strongly electrified his paralytic; and from each of the parts of the skin that correspond to the different motor muscles of the forearm and arm he drew successively a large number of sparks. From these first days the patient began to move his fingers and to make some other movement. The experiments having been continued every day in the same manner, the freedom and extent of the movements of the whole paralytic arm increased by degrees and rather quickly; but what was most surprising was to see this arm that had for long been atrophied and partly withered getting more healthy, fatter and becoming almost like the healthy arm; then it was observed that by drawing the sparks on the different muscles of this paralytic arm, there appeared there at the same time an involuntary agitation of the fibres, a sort of snaking movement, or like a small convulsive movement. Finally the patient was electrified to the point where he could raise his hand to his hat, take it off his head and put it back on, and lift certain heavy bodies as well."

92   Lodovico Galvani (1737-1798), Italian physician and scientist. See [145].

93   Nicolas Bertholon, known also as Bertholon de Saint-Lazare because he belonged to the religious community of that name (1742-1799).

94   Alessandro Volta (1745-1826), Italian physicist whose fame is especially due to his invention of the electromotor apparatus.

95   Emil Du Bois-Reymond (1818-1896), German physician, born in Berlin of French-Swiss origin. At the request of Johannes Müller, with whom he was working in Berlin, he verified Matteucci's experiments in 1841, concluding that the latter had been right to defend the existence of an electrical current in the nerves and muscles, but that he had been wrong about the current's direction.

96   Giovanni Aldini (1762-1834), a doctor of the University of Bologna

and Galvani's nephew. He was one of his most ardent supporters. See [5].

97 L. Nobili (1784-1835) found, with the aid of the compass galvanometer which he had helped to develop, the existence of a current which he called "current proper to the frog," but which he did not venture to interpret as a current produced by living tissue.

98 Carlo Matteucci (1811-1868).

99 See n. 53 above. Rolando carried out these experiments in the years 1823-24. Flourens (see n. 26 above), who had been doing the same experiments, published an annotated translation of Rolando's account. Rolando's method was rudimentary and his results doubtful because of the disturbances produced by the strength of the electrical current he used. His merit as a pioneer should not, however, be discounted.

2. INSTITUTIONALIZING DEVIANCE

ABNORMAL OR ABSENT SPEECH

> And there appeared unto him an angel of the Lord... and when Zacharias saw him, he was troubled, and fear fell upon him. But the angel said unto him, Fear not, Zacharias; for thy prayer is heard; and thy wife Elisabeth shall bear thee a son... And Zacharias said unto the angel, Whereby shall I know this? for I am an old man, and my wife well stricken in years. And the angel answering said unto him, I am Gabriel ... and am sent to speak unto thee and to shew thee these glad tidings. And behold, thou shalt be dumb, and not able to speak, until the day that these things shall be performed, because thou believest not my words...
> Luke 1, xi-xx

The prejudice would remain a long time. Impaired speech was regarded as the punishment of a hidden misdeed that the punishment itself exposes. It is an object of scandal, for the misdeed is disruption of an order which only supernatural intervention can restore.

A cursory look at the order and succession of things would seem to lend weight to the thesis that language abnormality was not "institutionalized" until the eighteenth century, at least in the West. Thus in the monumental *Biographie Michaud*, the biographer of the Abbé de l'Epée[1] states:

> One could not deny, however, that several deaf-mute teachers preceded the Abbé de l'Epée in his career by a greater or lesser period of time, but no-one has been able to bring to such perfection the art of metamorphosing (as it were) these poor creatures hitherto confined in the sterile regions of death.

This presentation gives a highly simplified view of the facts. Abnormal or absent speech has been the object of continuous attention from Antiquity to the modern period.

Impairments of speech were at first attributed to the tongue.[2] Hippocrates and Aristotle concerned themselves with appropriate treatments to prevent an excess of moisture in the tongue, regarded as the cause of speech defects. We find in some authors like Cornelius Celsus[3] details of the operation in which the ligament of the tongue was cut so as to free it and thus facilitate articulatory movements.

Hippocrates probably mentions stuttering in a few obscure passages.[4] For many centuries, very different defects of speech with a confused nosology were grouped under the common name of stuttering.

115

Mercurialis,[5] commenting on Aristotle in the late sixteenth century, explains that stutterers are melancholy because all melancholy persons have a prompt imagination and that, as a result, the rapidity of their thinking requires an equal rapidity in speech. Stutterers have spastic movements of the tongue because, due to its muscular weakness, it cannot keep up with the flow of ideas.

A quarter-century after Mercurialis, Sir Francis Bacon,[6] in his *Silva Silvarum*, catalogues similarly obscure observations. People stutter, he says, because their tongue is cold, and stutterers are less affected when they have drunk some wine, which heats the tongue. We must wait till the eighteenth century until progress is made under several headings:

·nosology
·psychology
·pathological anatomy, and
·the nature of the tongue.

David Hartley put forward his theory of vibrations and associations as a conceptual framework to explain the origin of stuttering. It is, he says, the consequence of violent emotional states which prevent the child from making the necessary effort of muscular coordination to produce speech.

The accuracy of Hartley's purely empirical statements explains the influence he had on those who studied disorders of language after him.[7] The work of Spalding,[8] Moses Mendelssohn[9] and Erasmus Darwin[10] continued Hartley's line of investigation without exhausting its inherent interest. In another direction, the efforts of several observers, from Felix Platter[11] to Boissier de Sauvages,[12] led to the identification and classification of these defects, so diverse that they had been written about only in a general way. The most important contribution to nosology is represented by the work of Morgagni,[13] who emphasised the truly pathological character of these defects. To classify them, he adopted topographical criteria which benefited by the progress made around the same time in the knowledge of articulatory mechanisms. In [279] he describes numerous cases of language impairment. His theory of stuttering is based on a putative relationship with abnormalities of the hyoid bone. His error was to link an anatomical defect with a language deficit, using some questionable data.[14]

Trying to bring together the different tendencies emerging down through the centuries with regard to this type of impairment, we find three main directions of thought:

The first expresses the theme of deficiency or debility of an organ. To some extent Morgagni represents this viewpoint in the eighteenth century. However, the organ most often held responsible for the impairment is the tongue itself. Even in the *Encyclopédie* there is talk of atrophied or missing or double tongues.[15]

The second approach is psychophysiological. It expresses the theme of conflict between two tendencies, two opposing systems. This interpretation provides supporters of the theory of humours with the basis of their argumentation, from Aristotle to Mercurialis. It receives a new lease of life with Hartley, and continues into the nineteenth century, with Erasmus Darwin's idea of inner conflicts of will and with the Phrenologists speaking of conflicts of active faculties (namely intellect and language). Finally, among the various conflict theories of the twentieth century, two in particular should be mentioned: one, anatomically and physiologically based, which identifies conflict between the two hemispheres; and another, psychologically based, in which desire to speak is opposed to fear of the act.[16]

The third approach is taken by the observers closest to the impairment. It is a recurrent view, expressed by the finding that impaired children think faster than they can speak. A modern restatement of this frequently made observation would be to say that there is "dyssynchronisation" between the conceptual act of thinking and the speech production program.

Although the progress of knowledge usually happens in leaps and bounds, we often find motifs recurring from one period to the next. What changes by spontaneous mutation in such cases is not the knowledge of a particular problem so much as the community's attitude to a deficit and thus to its victims.

Vives,[17] who mentions the need for systematic correction of poor speakers, includes in his criticism deviances of a geographical and social nature (dialects) as well as those resulting from pathological deficits.

Increasing knowledge of the factors causing impairments, and ways of reducing their effects by appropriate reeducation, gradually brought about a change of attitude with regard to the victim of language deficit. He ceases to be an object of scandal and instead becomes a patient to be treated. This development is particularly noticeable from the sixteenth to the eighteenth centuries in the case of the most striking impairment, deaf-mutism.

The deaf-mute is cut off by his impairment from the hearing, speaking community. From contact with other deaf-mutes, when such contact is established, the child acquires some sort of sign language, a gestural code that puts him in a ghetto outside of which he cannot function socially. The first known efforts to try to help deaf-mutes were aimed at providing them with a compensatory system to allow them access to speech and thus to the normal world. The objective here was not to accept deviance, but to hide it.

The techniques to overcome deaf-mutism were created in contexts that often appealed to the notion of the miraculous, thus reinforcing the mysterious, almost sacred character of the affliction. Thus Van Helmont[18] attempts to prove that the very shape of the letters of the Hebrew alphabet is an enigmatic representation of the articulatory configuration required for the pronunciation of each letter. The writing system, he believed, expressed the nature of audible sounds in a visible manner. He therefore regarded it as a model to help the deaf to pronounce sounds that they could not hear by teaching them how to articulate them through sight.

Leaving aside the quaintness of such theories, they do contain interesting assumptions that illuminate the problem-situation of the deaf-mute.

Firstly, the close relationship that exists between the ear and the voice, a relationship long recognised, as we are reminded by Alberti[19] at the end of the sixteenth century and by Holder[20] in the middle of the seventeenth, and as the *Encyclopédie* stresses in its article on "Deafness", and in another on "Hearing", where we find this comment:

> Whence comes the great degree of communication that exists between hearing and speech? By the correspondence of the hard portion of the auditory nerve with the branches of the fifth pair, which is distributed to the parts which serve to form and modify the voice.

Secondly, with Alberti and then with many others, the recognition of the fact that the mute, because he is deaf, is not necessarily a simpleton - as is confirmed by successes in re-education. And finally, the idea that in any reeducative procedure the best way is to make use of the intact sensory resources - in this case sight, to make up for the sense that is lacking, hearing.

On the other hand, there is a close relationship between sounds pronounced and the movements of the mouth and facial muscles which produce the sounds. Amman[21] remarks:

> For Human speech as it appears to anyone who observes it with attention is a combination of diversified types of sounds whose variety results, I think, from the different movements of particular organs; movements which, if they were visible enough, I believe, would be sufficient for the deaf man to discern sounds by sight just as others perceive them by hearing. Thus with time the deaf should learn to speak.
> ([8d], p. 4)

Amman recounts that he then proceeded to experiment on himself before a mirror. His experiments revealed the constant relationship between the sound and the facial expression that occurs in producing it, and the relative ease of identifying the sound from the movement. In this way Amman reaccomplished the progress made thirty years before by Holder.[22] He seems, however, to have had more confidence in his success, whereas Holder perhaps showed more clear-sightedness in understanding the difficulties of the undertaking.[23]

Amman went on to identify a very important problem: the nature of the voice itself, and the difficulty of eliciting and controlling it in the deaf-mute. In Amman's view, the origin of the voice is to be found in the communication of a vital force which, starting from the heart and the brain, propagates itself to the muscles of the larynx, which act directly on the cartilages attached to them. Though the detail is wrong, the explanation is basically valid.

What is perhaps most striking in this period of initiatives and experiments in the area of deaf-mutism is the lack of communication. Every one of these pioneers seems to have been isolated within the narrow confines of his own experience, and their errors as well as their achievements seem to have reached only sporadically beyond their immediate audiences. When Amman published his first book, *Surdus loquens* [8a], he was quite unaware of the work of such predecessors as the mathematician Wallis,[24] who continued the work of Holder. An exception that proves the rule is that Amman and Van Helmont knew of one another. None of them seem to have been aware of the efforts of still earlier forerunners.

In Italy, we find that a theory on the instruction of deaf-mutes was part of the voluminous writings of Hieronymus Cardanus.[25]

The Spaniard Pedro de Ponce[26] is often cited as the first known inventor of the art of teaching the deaf; but nothing is known of his method except what can be gathered from Valles [399], Bonet [43] and Morales in his *Antiquities of Spain* (1575). The method seems to have been a purely empirical one, lacking any theory of sounds like those developed by Holder or Amman, for example. From Bonet[27] we also hear of the initiative of another Spaniard, Emmanuel Ramirez de Carrion.[28] He is spoken of by Nicholas Antonio as the first man to discover the art of teaching the letters and their pronunciation to the deaf.

In London in 1648 a treatise by John Bulwer[29] had appeared, who, like Holder a little later, showed an especial interest in the study of sounds, their articulation and classification.

All these early teachers of the deaf took on individual cases in which their success, which is impossible to verify, involved factors beyond any analysis. We are dealing with isolated events rather than programs of intervention. Nevertheless, the importance of their contribution cannot be denied. All these efforts served to demonstrate the possibility of reintegrating such a deviant population into the normal community. This was the lesson that would be learned by the next generation. As they learned it, their discussions, assisted by the eighteenth-century philosophers of language such as De Brosses, gave rise to serious attempts at analysis of sounds and the processes of articulation. Here we see the beginnings of a descriptive phonetics, which, though based on a purely empirical approach, would open the way for later research efforts. The nineteenth century would benefit greatly.

The man who is regarded as the first teacher of the deaf in France, Jacob Rodrigue Pereire,[30] seems to have had a broad background, derived from his travels and experience, which included the work of Amman, the Spanish school, and the English school. Reeducation as practised by Pereire was not confined to lip-reading and the production of oral sounds, but also involved the use of a manual alphabet and other aids invented by him, including an arithmetic machine. Pereire was, however, highly secretive about his method and divulged next to nothing about it - which did not prevent him being plagiarized by Ernault.[31] He showed himself quite hostile to the theory of methodical sign language developed by the Abbé de l'Epée. No doubt he found the Abbé a threatening rival. Indeed, before the Abbé de l'Epée, Pereire had started group teaching, which went beyond the attempts with one or more individuals that were the rule with his predecessors.

Up till this point, the deaf-mute had an ambiguous role: he was both experimental guinea-pig and victim in need of deliverance. With Pereire and the Abbé de l'Epée, the move towards institutionalization of deviance begins. The objective shifts from proving the well-foundedness of a particular method to doing everything possible to rehabilitate as many individuals as possible, in an institutional setting.

In this perspective, the originality of the efforts of the Abbé de l'Epée, continued by the Abbé Sicard,[32] becomes quite apparent. Theoretical statement is sparse in the writing of the Abbé de l'Epée. He is convinced, he writes, that the relationship between ideas and articulate sounds is no more natural than the relationship between ideas and written characters. That is a notion that contemporaries of Condillac could accept easily. What is in fact crucial in the Abbé de l'Epée's approach is the pragmatic development of an entire educational system in which all means are good provided they work. The deaf-mute is to be accepted with his handicap, and it is his education that counts rather than an apparent (and often transitory) reeducation intended to make him a pseudo-speaker-hearer.

DEFECTIVE DISCOURSE

> Aphonia is an inability to produce sounds, which is always accompanied by loss of speech, a rather common accident in hysterical suffocations; or, in a more restricted sense, it is an inability to produce articulate sounds originating from some fault in the tongue or other speech organs.
> Encyclopédie p. 524

The observation of loss of speech has a repetitive character that regularly accompanies descriptions of stroke, epilepsy or cranial trauma. Observations on impairment of discourse, however, are almost totally lacking.

Pliny the Elder[33] [320] notes the vulnerability of memory. No other human faculty is so fragile. He cites the case of a man struck on the head by a stone who loses the ability to read and write, or another who, having fallen from a high roof, forgets his mother, his relatives and friends. Messala Corvinus, the famous orator and grammarian, even forgot his own name. There is every reason to believe that Pliny has gathered under the heading of loss of memory widely differing cases of traumatic aphasia according to our present-day criteria, and perhaps even insanity in the case of Messala Corvinus. In the nineteenth century there would be talk of "amnesic aphasia", and Trousseau,[34] in Book II of his *Cliniques* , devoting a chapter to loss of speech, does not fail to mention Pliny, remarking that the physiological conditions of aphasia had long been recognized.

Valerius Maximus[35] reports the case of a cultured Athenian who, having been struck on the head by a stone, completely lost his memory for reading, but recovered it for all other mental activities subsequently. This is perhaps the earliest mention of the impairment which the nineteenth century would call *alexia*.

Islamic tradition is oddly silent as regards the observation of these impairments. Avicenna[36] himself does not provide a single observation on the subject.

In the seventh century, the Venerable Bede[37] mentions the case of a man who was mute but then recovered speech. Aulus Gellius the grammarian seems to have recorded a similar case in Antiquity.[38] About six hundred years later, Opicinus[39] reports the case of a man whose writing was disturbed by repetitive and self-critical expressions. Could it have been a case of schizophrenia?

Guainerio[40] mentions two cases of loss of speech which could be regarded, in modern perspective, as cases of aphasia. In the first, the patient could no longer pronounce more than three or four words; in the second, the patient could no longer find names for things. Guainerio comments:

> When humours accumulate in the posterior ventricle,[41] the organ of memory can hold little or nothing.

Baverius de Baveriis[42] mentioning a "good young man" who suffered from an inability to move one side of his body or to speak, suggests another interpretation for the deficit. Noting the patient's apathy and his continual drowsiness, he attributes this state to a "debility of the seventh pair of nerves, by which the tongue moves". He also notes the concurrence in a woman patient of a cramp of the neck vertebrae which prevented her from getting up and a cramp of the tongue that prevented her from speaking. Holding the tongue responsible for a loss or obstruction of speech is quite ancient, and would enjoy a long development.[43]

Paracelsus[44] may have guessed the nature of the relationship between insults to the brain and disorders in discourse production; this is at least the claim of Ebstein [115].

The case described by Niccolo Massa[45] seems to have been what we would today call traumatic aphasia. Young Marcus Goro had been struck by a halberd, and sustained a skull fracture with protrusion of cerebral matter. The unfortunate patient had been deprived of speech for a week when Massa was called in. He concluded that the loss of speech was due to the presence of bone fragments embedded in the brain. He immediately proceeded to extract these, and the patient began to speak, saying "Thank God, I am cured". Along with Massa, we may hope that the young man survived this terrible injury. Francisco Arceo[46] mentions a similar case. Like Massa, he pulled bone fragments from the brain substance, observing inflammation of the meninges. Three days later, the patient was speaking.

Could there be a common explanation for traumatic shock causing temporary blocking of speech, and cases of permanent speech loss? Two themes crop up again and again: the impairment of memory, and the weakening of the tongue. Johann Schenck von Graffenberg,[47] finding that in many cases of apoplexy, lethargy and other infirmities of the brain the patient cannot speak although the tongue is not paralysed, concluded that the deficit could only be attributed to an impairment of memory. Half a century later, Chanet[48] says the same thing in his precise description of a rather complex case:

> I have a relative whose memory was injured at the siege of Hulst. He did not just forget his name like Messala Corvinus, but also many kinds of words, so that he no longer knew the letters of the alphabet. He did not, however, forget how to write: that is to say, when he was given an example and signs were made that he was to copy it, he did it quite well. [67]

On the other hand, when William Harvey[49] was dying in 1657 and his speech was paralysed, the apothecary Sambroke treated it by making a small incision in the frenum.

There are repeated observations of right-side paralysis accompanying a more or less total inability to produce or perceive speech, to perform writing movements or recognise written characters, during the seventeenth and eighteenth centuries. Johann Schmidt[50] in 1673 describes the case of Nicolas Cambier, aged 65 years, who after suffering a stroke found himself paralysed on the right side, with a severe speech impairment.[51] Thomas Willis also reports two right-sided paralyses accompanied by partial loss of speech; the two patients seems to have retained some form of understanding - they could recognise their friends and were aware of their condition. Around the same time, Hobbes[52] is known to have died after losing the use of the right side of his body and his speech. In 1683, Peter Rommel[53] reported a case of paralysis of the right side accompanied by partial loss of the speech faculty in a woman of 52. She could say only "yes" and "no", but she was still able to recite the Our Father and the Apostles' Creed if she was prompted with the first few syllables. Here Rommel was observing the difference between automatic and voluntary speech.

Giovanni Battista Morgagni,[54] in [279], mentions several cases of loss of speech accompanied by paralysis, as a result of a stroke. The autopsies he carried out enabled him to establish that various types of cerebral lesions are complicated by paralyses and motor disorders of language. He notes the frequency of cases in which the verbal impairment is associated with right hemiplegia. To conclude, however, with Ebstein[55] that Morgagni and his teacher Valsalva[56] established the connection between aphasia, right hemiplegia and lesion of the left cerebral hemisphere is perhaps reading too much into the text.

Some years before the publication of Morgagni's work, Olaf Dalin,[57] a Swedish scholar, told the strange story of "the dumb man who could sing". A man, born in 1703, had suffered a severe stroke in 1736, following which he was paralysed on the right side and totally deprived of the use of speech. Some motor activity slowly returned, but he could only utter one word: "yes". However, he could still sing hymns he had known before his illness if someone sang the first words for him.

In the course of the century, remarks on the retention of mental faculties in cases of speech loss become quite frequent. Gerard van Swieten[58] writes, around 1745, that he had seen many stroke victims affected by a severe deficit of verbal memory nonetheless keeping intact their mental faculties. Similar features occur in Linnaeus'[59] account of a professor at the University of Uppsala affected by paraphasic disturbances who spoke as if he were trying to express himself in a foreign language.

Van Goens[60] mentions the wife of a mathematics professor at the University of Utrecht, herself a mathematician and astronomer. This woman was suffering from severe amnesic disturbances revealed by her inability to name things, and particularly by the fact that she regularly used one word for another. However, she retained mastery of her mental faculties and could even show her husband the position of the stars on a chart. Afterwards, she made an almost complete recovery.

William Falconer[61] is to be credited with noting this apparent preservation of mental faculties in the case of impairments which would now be called aphasias - while expressing some doubts.

Several other observers noted the irremediable character of the deficit in the most severe cases, especially with the elderly. Goethe describes such a condition in Wilhelm Meister , based on his own grandfather. J. W. Ogle,[62] and later MacDonald Critchley, have studied the case of Samuel Johnson, who suffered a stroke on the 17th of June 1783, and recounted the experience in writing on the 19th. Johnson was 73 years of age at the time. The loss of speech seems to have lasted only a few hours, like the difficulty he at first experienced in writing. However, careful examination of his writing, as MacDonald Critchley has shown ([84b], p. 90), reveals that the deficit was permanent.

Clinical practice thus already constituted an important sum of pathological data. However, linguistic description of the deficits was still only sketchy. One exception that requires mention is Gessner,[63] who in 1770 provided the first serious study of a case of jargonaphasia. This early case would be cited later in the century by Crichton,[64] and Falret[65] mentioned it again in 1864. It concerns a man of 73 years of age who was affected by severe muscular pains in his mouth. Two weeks later, he suddenly began to show signs of a confused state accompanied by a rather specific disorder of speech. He could articulate with ease, but formulated incomprehensible neologisms. He wrote down the things he said in a phonetic spelling. However, he could neither write his name nor read. The common denominator in all these deficits, Gessner found, was difficulty in associating the image or idea with the linguistic sign. This general conception would be the basis of the discussion of aphasia throughout the nineteenth century.

At the end of the eighteenth century, then, well-informed patients were able to be the best judges in providing nosology with the most detailed data.

In 1783, Jean-Paul Grandjean de Fouchy[66] wrote an account of the peculiar accident that happened to him. After a fall the day before, having completely recovered consciousness and being of sound mind, he noticed that:

> although the vocal organs which had been impeded for some time had become free again, they no longer obeyed his will.

Thus, when he wanted to utter a particular word, his mouth produced another,

> with the result that at the very time when he had clear ideas, the words were without continuity.

His report on this experience was published in the *Mémoires de l'Académie*. In the same year, Johann Joachim Spalding[67] describes in similar detail his experience of an episode of paraphasia and dysgraphia. After an initial panic reaction, he tried speaking to see if he was still able to express his thoughts. To his chagrin, he found that he had no control over his own language. His thoughts were incoherent, and the words coming out of his mouth were not the ones he had intended to utter. This crisis lasted about half an hour, and was followed by a period of trying to speak slowly with the control of his will. By evening, his recovery was sufficient for him to begin writing an account of what had happened. Moses Mendelssohn[68] attempted to provide an interpretation of this impairment, but without much success.

Marcus Herz,[69] a Berlin doctor, in 1791 recounted a case which is interesting by virtue of the therapeutic approach used. In 1785, he was called to the bedside of a 40-year-old artillery officer struck by paralysis following a violent fit of rage. The physician in charge asked him about the possibility of electrical treatment. Mesmerism had by this time spread all over Europe.[70] The treatment was accordingly tried, but Herz did not see the patient again for a year. Herz was called back for consultation, at which time he noted a definite improvement. The patient could use his hands and feet, but his language had scarcely progressed. He attempted to speak, but could only mutter unintelligibly. However, he was able to read with some facility, but could not afterwards repeat what he had read.

At the end of the eighteenth century, nosology provided a rich and varied range of cases whose clinical analysis was becoming more and more precise. The various disorders that would compose the clinical picture of aphasia at the end of the nineteenth century were already recognised. No general view had yet emerged, however. As for the etiology of these disorders, it was still beyond the level of the immediate observations. The basic role of the brain, though already intuited, still remained vague. Therapeutic intervention remained at the empirical level, and the rehabilitation of patients had as much to do with miracles as it had with a favourable disposition. By virtue of some aspects of the deficit, the patient seems close to the idiot or the lunatic; in other cases, his intact intelligence is demonstrated. Beyond immediate clinical observation, nonetheless, there now existed a body of knowledge about pathology; and on this knowledge, the age of Broca would base its theoretical claims.

EMERGING CONCEPTS OF PATHOLOGY

Up to the first quarter of the nineteenth century... aphasia was not recognised as such, not distinguished from dysarthria, delirium or schizophrenia.
MacDonald Critchley ([84], p. 23)

Observation results in reflective thinking, and reflective thinking results in concepts. The minting of concepts is modelled on the ideology of the epoch, and almost any generalisation is liable to lead to incorrect interpretation of experimental data.

Since Antiquity, the practitioner has tended to become a theorist. Take Soranus of Ephesus,[71] a physician of the methodist school,[72] whose views are known through the writings of Caelius Aurelianus.[73] In his study of paralysis, he establishes a distinction between deterioration, sensory or motor, and paralysis, spastic or athetosic. Caelius says that while paralysis of the tongue leads to an articulatory deficit, this form of paralysis should be distinguished from other instances of language loss resulting from other kinds of illness.

It would seem, according to Creutz,[74] that the majority of medical theorists of the period operated with a similar distinction.

Theoretical enlightenment sometimes emerges from a single fact. Riccobaldo da Ferrara[75] reports the case of a dumb man who recovered speech, a phenomenon which he regards as miraculous - though that is not the point: what is remarkable is his interpretation of the facts. He notes that the deaf-mute acquired hearing and speech but did not grasp the meaning of utterances that he heard and could repeat. He concludes that a distinction must be made between language aptitude, the gift of God to his creatures, and knowledge of a particular language, the socially given code that must be acquired. This is a highly interesting indication of the emergence of the innateness-learning dichotomy, though expressed in the ideological currency of the time.

From the sixteenth century on, a slow movement began that would culminate, during the eighteenth century, in a demystification of language. Laurent Joubert[76] establishes a relationship between verbal deficits and those of hearing. The hearing deficits cause the verbal deficits, and they may be explained by accidental circumstances, such as cranial trauma which results in loss of memory. Memory has an essential role in the progression from perception of sound to transmission of speech. That such disorders can be the object of medical treatment and reeducation shows that they are indeed natural phenomena.

At the same period, Mexia,[77] relating the story of Croesus and his sons,[78] searches for natural causes for the phenomenon of recovery of speech. He sees in this phenomenon an act of will triumphing over physiological inhibitions. He borrows the foundation of his argument from Aristotle, for whom the child, born without language, and thus to some extent in the same situation as the deaf-mute, must win his linguistic birthright by a series of conquests.

Nevertheless, at the end of the seventeenth century, the understanding of pathological anomalies was still not yet free of the fascination of the miraculous and even the grotesque. Boerhaave[79] describes the case of a beggar who used his *calvarium* (the top of his skull) as a begging-bowl. For a few coins, he allowed people to perform tricks and experiments on him. Finger pressure on the dura mater made him *see* a myriad sparks before his eyes; heavier pressure caused complete loss of vision; pressure with the hand put him to sleep. This case, which might have suggested the cerebral localization of some sensory functions, does not in fact seem to have interested contemporary observers as more than a freak of nature. Very much later, Archibald[80] mentions the story in his *American Practice of Surgery*.

The natural philosopher Robert Boyle,[81] confirming the view of Schenckius[82] and the observations of Chanet,[83] seems to have grasped concretely the determining relationship between the brain and higher intellectual functions.

An accident quite similar to the one related by Massa[84] prompted him to hypothesize a precise relationship between paralysis and a very localized area of the brain. A young man was left paralysed on the right side following a skull fracture that had required trepanation. One of the surgeons in charge concluded that this persistent paralysis could only be explained by the presence of bone splinters in the surface of the dura mater. Some hours later, the patient recovered sensation and the use of his limbs.

Note here that the covering of the brain, the meninges, are thought to be the cause of the disturbance, not the deep cerebral tissue. The whole of the eighteenth century reflects this kind of perception in its procedures of pathological anatomy. Attention lingers only on the surface or the internal cavities, not on the substance of the brain itself.

Thus Pourfour du Petit[85] believes that destruction of nerves interrupts the flow of spirits and thereby prevents motor activity. His mistaken theorizing nonetheless contains a correct anatomical perception, the chiasmus or crossed arrangement of nervous pathways, a principle which he had guessed when he concluded that movements of the limbs depend on the opposite side of the brain.

Later, in the eighteenth century, we find in Hartley's[86] work a real effort of systematization which goes beyond empirical pragmatism. He believes that paralysis of the speech organs may be due to causes common to other forms of paralysis. He finds, however, that paralysis of the speech organs does not necessarily entail paralysis of the muscles of the lips, cheeks, tongue and back of the mouth [175], p. 260). Hartley further points out as a cause of language loss weakening of memory, even where the organs are not affected by an onset of paralysis.

The notion of memory loss itself became more refined in the course of the eighteenth century. Boissier de Sauvages,[87] in [42a], used the term "amnesia". However, neither the term nor the concept occur in the *Ency-*

clopédie (vol. I, 1751), where the article "Memory" does not even deal with the pathological aspect of the loss of memory and its consequences for language in particular. On the other hand, the article "Paralysis", after giving a precise definition of the term ("an illness characterised by a more or less complete privation of movement and feeling, or one of the two"), states specifically that "paralysis of the tongue muscles produces aphonia". This terminology cross-references with the article on "Aphonia".

Eighteenth-century thinking in this area leaves an impression of some incoherence probably because of the lack of information exchange between researchers. Precise observations such as those of H. F. Delius,[88] who in 1757 proposed a distinction between *aphonia* (loss of voice) and *alalia* (loss of articulate speech), for lack of integration into a broader context, remain only the fragments of a clinical picture. The observation - made over and over again - that paralysis of the right side was often complicated by severe loss of speech does not seem to have triggered any new line of thought.

The recursive character of discussion on language pathology is also illustrated by the repeated use of the theme of memory loss. Still in 1797, Sir Alexander Crichton was mentioning it and adapting it to Gesner's viewpoint. For Crichton, verbal deficit has to do with the erasure of associative relations between ideas and the particular expressions that denote them.

The etiology of pathological phenomena was attached to statements that attempted to avoid error by their very generality. The concept of an undifferentiated brain, where the only question is whether it functions as a whole or as a juxtaposition of parts, in fact prevented any attempt at precise localization of a given disorder. Duverney[89] criticizes Willis for proposing in his system a functional distinction of parts in a homogeneous brain, and he himself favours the idea of identity of structure as well as physiology of the whole of the brain, suggesting the principle of a hierarchy between superior (cerebral) functions and natural (cerebellar) functions.

Nevertheless, throughout the century there was a current of thinking that opposed this conception of a global, homogeneous physiology of the brain. This current of thinking is represented by Haller, Soemmering, and especially Bonnet. The latter saw the likelihood of specialization of cerebral regions in terms of sensory and motor pathways, and the different functions indicated by those pathways:

> If all our ideas, even the most intellectual ones, originally depend on the movements that occur in the brain, there is reason to wonder if every idea has its particular fibre designed to produce it, or if the same fibre moved in different ways produces different ideas. ([45], p. 51)

The concepts were now in place for the development of a true pathological anatomy and physiology.

The procedure of observation had gradually, over a very long period, overcome the ancient fear aroused by anything to do with speech, and rid its mental image of the aura of the sacred, the marvellous or the magical. Nevertheless, the effort to integrate pathology into the framework of natural phenomena did not reach its fulfillment until everything having to do with the language act, speech as well as language and discourse, could be situated at the purely physical level. Eighteenth century discussion provides evidence of this development; it also served to delimit the respective domains of exact science and speculative philosophy, of instrumental technique and research in which hypothesis is dominant. In so doing, it gave investigators a better framework for their activities. Even on the threshold of the nineteenth century, however, the confusion of those two domains still dominated the mental habits of the "man of science", and Gall, to whom we now turn, is the prime example.

NOTES

1   Charles-Michel de l'Epée (1712-1789).
2   In the *Enclycopédie*, we find, in the article "Tongue" (*langue*): "Such is this marvellous instrument, without which men would be deprived of the pleasure and advantage of society".
3   Cornelius Celsus, a physician of the first century.
4   The Book *Epidemics* uses the term *traulos*, but it is impossible to say whether this word refers to a particular defect of speech or if it is a generic term.
5   Hieronymus Mercurialis (1530-1606).
6   Francis Bacon, Lord Verulam (1561-1626): see [17]. Quoted by Rieber & Wollock [341].
7   at the end of the 19th century, Charcot writes, in one of his *Leçons du Mardi* (1-362; see p. 160, n. 15), that he considers Hartley a remarkable analyst and a forerunner in the study of speech disorders.
8   1714-1804 [376].
9   1729-1786 [263].
10 1731-1802 [93].
11 Felix II Plat(t)er (1605-1671).
12 François Boissier de la Croix de Sauvages (1706-1767).
13 Giovanni Battista Morgagni (1682-1771).
14 See [29a].
15 Quoted there is the case reported by Jussien who lived in Portugal in 1717: "A poor girl then 17 years of age, born without a tongue", and

who nonetheless succeeded in being able to speak. Also mentioned is the case: "of a pleasant girl who came into the world with two tongues".

16 Interpretation in terms of conflict between the two hemispheres: see [296]; psychological conflict: see [367].

17 See p. 83, n. 28.

18 Franciscus Mercurius Van Helmont (1618-1699). He published in Germany claiming that he had found the language that every man spoke naturally before the corruption of society. He went so far as to claim that a man born dumb would articulate its characters at sight. Fabre d'Olivet (1786-1825) a century later had the idea of renewing Van Helmont's bizarre quest. He had previously been interested in deaf-mutism.

19 S. Alberti (1560-1600), *Oratio de surditate et mutitate*, Nuremberg, 1591.

20 William Holder (1616-1698), an English churchman who acquired considerable fame in 1659 by teaching speech to a young man of distinction, born deaf and dumb, the son of Admiral Alexander Popham. Afterwards deprived of his teacher, the young man seems to have lost the skills he had learned. He was again taken in hand by Dr Wallis, who gave him back the use of speech. This was the subject of a public dispute between the two scholars.

21 Johann Konrad Amman (1669-1730) was interested in the case of a little girl, Esther Kolard, born deaf and dumb, to whom he taught reading, writing and speaking.

22 Holder explains: "Finding then a person in his condition, not capable of hearing; if we would endeavour to make use of the organs of speech (supposed to be of sufficient constitution), there is no way but to have recourse to the other learning sense, which is seeing..." ([189], pp. 115f.).

23 Holder, indeed, notes: "Some of the consonants and most of the vowels, being articulated by so obscure motions and figures that the most learned can hardly agree to describe them, it may well be doubted how they can be described to the eye of deaf persons" ([189], pp. 118f.).

24 See note 20 of this chapter. John Wallis (1616-1703).

25 Hieronymus Cardanus (1501?-1576?).

26 Pedro de Ponce (15??-1584).

27 J. P. Bonet (late 16th, early 17th century).

28 Emmanuel Ramirez de Carrion. Born towards the end of the 16th century.

29 John Bulwer (17th century).

30 Jacob-Rodrigue Pereire (1716-1780). He opened a school for deaf-mutes in Cadiz. Later he appeared in France. D'Azy d'Etavigny asked him to take on the education of his son, a deaf-mute. The pupil was presented to Louis XV, who questioned him by signs and in writing, and rewarded his teacher.

31   Pereire kept his technique a secret. As for Ernault, he made his public, and claimed credit as inventor for a report of the Académie des Sciences. The two rivals were eclipsed when the Abbé de l'Epée devised his "methodical signs".

32   Roch-Ambroise Cucurron Sicard (1742-1822) deserves credit for continuing and developing the work of the Abbé de l'Epée both in its material aspect and in its methods, because he succeeded in raising to the level of abstract mental operations the procedure that the Abbé de l'Epée had used for concrete objects.

33   23-79 A.D. Book VII, 24.

34   Armand Trousseau (1801-1867).

35   Valerius Maximus (c. 30 A.D.): [206].

36   Avicenna: see p. 30, note 31; [166].

37   The Venerable Bede (673-735).

38   Aulus Gellius lived in the 2nd century; see [15]: Book V, chapter ix.

39   Opicinus de Canistris (1296-1350).

40   Antonio Guainerio (died 1440).

41   See pp. 42ff.

42   Baverius de Baveriis, or Bavierus, or Baverio: see [23].

43   It is found in 1725 with Richard Blackmore, who assigns the patient's inability to pronounce words correctly to the state of the tongue; and in 1743 R. James speaks of a "hesitation of the tongue".

44   Paracelsus, Philippus Aureolus Theophrastus Bombastus von Hohenheim (1493-1541): [298].

45   Nicolas Massa (died 1563 or 1569).

46   Francisco Arceo (1493-1573?).

47   Johann Schenck von Graffenberg (1531-1598). Trousseau cites him in his *Clinique médicale*.

48   Pierre Chanet (see note 10, p. 82).

49   William Harvey (1578-1657).

50   Johann Schmidt (1624-1690): see [364], 4: 195-197.

51   The patient was able to write a word or sentence that he could not read.

52   Thomas Hobbes of Malmesbury (1588-1679).

53   Peter Rommel (1643-1708): ([348], 222-227).

54   See note 13 above.

55   See E. Ebstein [115].

56   Antonio Maria Valsalva (1689-1723): [400].

57   Olof Dalin (1708-1763): ([89], 114-115).

58   Gerard Van Swieten (1700-1772).

59   Karl von Linné (1707-1778), known as Linnaeus ([239], 6:116-117).

60   Rykof M. Van Goens (1748-1810).

61 William Falconer (1741-1824).
62 J. W. Ogle, in [291b] (1: 163-165, 1874).
63 Johann Gesner (1738-1801).
64 See [83].
65 J. Falret [121].
66 Jean-Paul Grandjean de Fouchy (1707-1788). He was 76 years old [161].
67 Johann Joachim Spalding (1714-1804).
68 See note 9 above.
69 Marcus Herz (1747-1803).
70 See p. 111, note 78.
71 Soranus of Ephesus (98-135).
72 On *Methodism*, see note 22, p. 17.
73 Little is known of Caelius Aurelianus. Conrad Amman made an edition of his works in 1709. Cf. [103].
74 See [82].
75 [48], p. 864. Riccobaldo da Ferrara (1243-1312).
76 Laurent Joubert (1529-1583). The text that concerns us here is [202a]. The Lyons edition of 1608 contains a treatise entitled: *Question vulgaire: quel langage parleroit un enfant qui n'auroit jamais ouï parler?*
77 Peter Mexia (end of 15th cent.-1522?).
78 See [184], p. 86.
79 See p. 110, note 71.
80 W. C. Gibson [152]. He also notes that W. Heberden, in works published posthumously in 1802, provides some very precise cases of aphasia, while T. de Bordeu (1722-1776) expressed the idea that each part of the body had its representation in the brain.
81 Robert Boyle (1621-1691): see [52].
82 See above, note 47.
83 See p. 82, note 10.
84 See above, note 45.
85 See note 28, p. 108.
86 See note 49, p. 109.
87 See note 12 above.
88 H. F. Delius (1720-1791).
89 Joseph-Guichard Du Verney or Duverney (1643-1730).

3. Illusions of Science

The search for localizations

> Even if Gall had claimed to owe nothing to any of his predecessors, even if he had thought that he was starting from scratch, we would still have to place his work in the context of works near to his own time and a few decades previous to that, in order to be able to read him with any understanding.
>
> Lanteri-Laura ([220b], p. 13)

In 1784, Procháska,[1] taking up the ideas of Willis,[2] divided the nervous system into *sensorium commune* (brain stem, spinal cord and nerves), and the rest of the brain as seat of the intellect. Since the brain was composed of such differently fashioned parts, he reasoned, it seemed that nature, which never acts in vain, chose, in differentiating these parts, to give them different functions as well.

In 1798 still, Soemmering[3] thought that the seat of the soul resides in the "fluid" that fills the ventricles! At the dawn of the nineteenth century, no relationship had as yet been proposed that could define - other than at a speculative level - the close interdependence between the intellectual and emotional faculties and their somatic basis. The path of knowledge is uncertain, however; and, as it turned out, physiognomy provided the imaginary elements whereby the study of the brain could find new direction.

The eighteenth-century anatomist still knew little about the actual structure of the brain, though brains had been weighed, measured and subjected to cross-species comparisons. On the other hand, he had a very good knowledge of the osteology of the skull. Eighteenth-century physiognomy would make use of this contemporary knowledge while resting on a very ancient tradition that extended from Aristotle to Porta[4] and Ghirardelli.[5] The abiding theme of this speculative discipline with a very practical aim[6] was that there is a logical relationship between the physical characteristics of an individual and his personality. What is new in Lavater's[7] *Physiognomical Essays* is not the subject but the fact that the author was by training a theologian rather than a medical man.

In the eighteenth century, nonetheless, a pragmatic approach in keeping with the emergence of sensualist theories brought a change in perceptions, and the brain, formerly thought of as the container of something innate, was transformed into a receptacle for something acquired. It is the senses that bring it the essential information from which (and therein lies the innateness) it has the ability to construct knowledge of the world.

133

Under the impulse of physiognomical research, Gall[8] transformed anatomists' perceptions yet again. Gall began from the outside, ascribing semiological value to the irregularities of the surface of the skull, and attempting to deduce from these the structure of the cerebral masses formerly perceived only in their amorphous, enteroid softness. Gall, whose own memory was always rather weak, though his mind enjoyed a remarkable gift for integration and analysis, had been struck while still a youth by the observation that those of his schoolmates with the best memories had a wide forehead and protruding eyes:

> Two years later, I went to a university. My attention at first was drawn to those of my new fellow-students who had big, protruding eyes. Usually, their excellent memory was spoken of...([142d], I, p.3)

(When Pierre Marie[9] studied the bases of Broca's[10] theory of aphasia, he bluntly referred to Gall's ideas as "nonsense".) These observations led Gall to believe that there could be a logical relationship between the shape of the face and skull and the mental faculties. Of course, this meant that there must be constant action of the brain, as it developed, on the shape of the bones in the skull. He was able to assume such action on the basis of a long tradition in embryological studies according to which the bones of the crown of the head were closely modelled on the underlying cerebral cortex.[11] This view was shared by Lavater.

These ideas determined the whole direction of Gall's thinking.[12] From observations on living subjects as well as study of biographies in conjunction with palpation of skulls, he developed a semiology of bony prominences that implied a particular kind of organisation in the substance of the brain itself. As a result, he was able to lay out the basic points of his doctrine. The highest mental functions are strictly localized in the brain according to a three-part hierarchy somewhat reminiscent of Aristotle.

The faculty of language, although distinguished from the faculty of memory, is connected to it. He assigns both a localization in the frontal zone of the brain.[13]

Gall believed that a bilateral lesion of this cortical area leads, in the child, to an inability to learn to speak, and, in the adult, to various disorders including mutism. In 1819, Gall described two cases of language loss whose origin he believed could be localized in an insult to that zone.

Localization thus came to mean associating specific and clearly differentiated functions with certain precisely circumscribed zones of the cortical territory. What had been a hypothesis for Charles Bonnet became a postulate for Gall. However, as Lanteri-Laura points out,

we must wait for Rolando,[14] Longet[15] and Foville[16] before the learned world will hold that man's cerebral cortex can be the object of any kind of systematization. ([220b], p. 37).

In the early years of the century, the systematization Gall was proposing must have appeared quite arbitrary, and the modern reader should not be led astray by the terminology used. For example, Gall's use of the word "physiology" in the title of his work *Anatomy and Physiology of the Brain* is not to be understood in quite its modern sense. The philosopher gourmet Brillat-Savarin,[17] who had at one time taken a fancy to medicine, uses this word in a non-metaphorical way in his title *Physiologie du Goût* (Physiology of Taste). Both Gall and Brillat-Savarin reflect the usage of their time.

Gall, however, would react against the idea of an anatomy-based physiology, going so far as to invert the relation of the two disciplines.[18]

Even when these shades of meaning are taken into account, Gall's project was an inordinately ambitious one. The cartography of the cortex established by Gall with the assistance of Spuzheim[19] up till 1813 and then carried on alone till 1820, the date of completion of his magnum opus,[20] aroused great interest and strong objections amongst his contemporaries.

As Lanteri-Laura reminds us, Gall drew forth two responses that deserve special consideration because of their early date and the penetration they show. These are the responses of Hegel[21] and Maine de Biran.[22] Hegel cites Gall's work without mentioning him by name in a brief passage in the *Phenomenology of Mind* where he uses phrenology to buttress his own arguments. The subtitle is quite explicit: "The skull as an effective reality, external to the mind". Hegel's attention is drawn to the relationship thus presupposed:

> With regard to the relation of the interior to this exterior, it is clear, in the first instance, that this relation seems to have been conceived as a relation of causal connection, since the relation of a being-in-itself with another being-in-itself, being a necessary relation, is precisely that relation. ([178], I)

According to Hegel, this means that mental individuality, to have an effect on the body, must itself be bodily. What is then the semiological value of a mapping of the skull?

> The skull is by no means an organ of activity, neither is it an expressive movement; one does not steal, one does not commit murder with the skull, and, by such phenomena, it does not change in the least bit and does not thereby become an expressive gesture. ([178], I)

Without actually rejecting Gall's hypothesis, Hegel stops at the preliminary questions that would need to be resolved in order for the hypothesis to be sustained; as Lanteri-Laura states,[23] his view is that we must know how far we are prepared to go when we undertake something like phrenology.

Though he takes a different approach, Maine de Biran[24] is concerned with the same difficulty. In his address to the medical society of Bergerac, "Remarks on the organic divisions of the brain", which dates from 1808, he brings out his various objections to Gall's doctrine. In keeping with his own philosophical ideas, Maine de Biran claimed other locations in the body - the medulla and the heart - as being the seat of some of the faculties of the soul, particularly the passions; but it is the very legitimacy of Gall's approach that he questions.

That sort of criticism would tend to recur with Gall's critics, particularly Cruveilher,[25] Cuvier,[26] Flourens[27] and Gratiolet.[28]

What is perhaps more serious, and is also brought out by Hegel, is the objection to the procedure whereby Gall listed the faculties and assigned them each a cerebral location. Except for the sensory faculties, this assignation owed nothing to anatomical exploration (as Maine de Biran observed), and is based in the end on a psychological a priori.[29]

Gall seems to have been well aware of the kind of opposition his theory met with. His 1825 work [142d] brings out the basic ideas which, he believed, were most likely to win acceptance for his doctrine in its entirety. Thus he emphasises the concept of organic functional localization:

> I call organ the material condition making possible the manifestation of a faculty. Muscles and bones are the material conditions of movement, but are not the faculty causing the movement... I call organ of the mind a material condition making possible the manifestation of a moral quality or of an intellectual faculty... Man... thinks and wills by means of the brain, but if we conclude that the thinking and willing being is the brain... it is like saying that muscles are the faculty of moving... In both cases we are confusing the faculty with the organs and the organs with the faculty. ([142d], I, p. 232)

Gall reminds us that this error has often been committed. He bolsters his case with the Fathers of the Church, and quotes St. Thomas's explanation to the effect that, although the mind is not a bodily faculty, its functions such as memory, thought and imagination cannot take place without the help of bodily organs, and that when the organs because of some disturbance cannot carry out their activities, the functions of mind are also disturbed, which is shown by "frenzies", "asphyxias", and so on.

As far as the moderns are concerned, Gall notes the position of Boerhaave, to the effect that God himself had so closely united soul with body that its faculties are defective when the organisation is defective, and that they are impaired when the body is sick.

Philosophers like Herder also claim:

> that if man is the most accomplished creature in earthly Creation, it is
> because the most perfect organic faculties we know act in him by means
> of the most perfect instruments... ([142], I, p. 235)

Gall presumably felt that by widening the debate he could drum up much-needed support. Those who hesitated to adopt his doctrine did not reject the very general principles on which it was based, but the highly specific consequences he claimed to derive from those general principles. Excessive detail in the pinpointing of functional specialisation aroused suspicion and set off the liveliest criticisms. Gall's initial intuition was perfectly correct, nonetheless, as were his initial observations and the consequences they implied:

> The division of the brain into two hemispheres, into several lobes and
> several other parts quite distinct in their form, direction, consistency and
> colour, and the very varied but constant distribution of these two sub-
> stances, ought to have prompted anatomists to the suspicion that all
> these variations might be earmarked for different functions... But very
> few physiologists showed any inkling of it. ([142d], III, pp. 147f.)

Without a doubt, Gall deserves credit at this level of his thinking when he compelled medical science to new and attentive observation of the outer surface of the brain. Already in his *Anatomy and Physiology*, he laid down two key concepts:

(1) The mind depends on the structure of the brain;
(2) The cerebral cortex is the site of mind; and an idea that is
     particularly important for the present study, namely that langu-
     age is localized in the frontal lobes of the brain. It was in rela-
     tion to these proposals that the orientations of thought on the
     functionality of the brain would be defined in the nineteenth
     century.

Flourens, like Gall, held that the primary motor and sensory functions were fairly precisely localized in the brain, but he rejected the claim that higher mental functions might depend on some specific area of the cortex. Flourens could nevertheless pay homage to Gall's work by contrasting it with conceptions that were then current - particularly those of Bichat:[30]

> Gall reduced the moral to the intellectual, he reduced the moral
> qualities to the same seat, the same organ as the intellectual faculties; he
> reduced madness to the same seat as reason, of which it is merely the
> disturbance; he took away from the senses what was wrongly attributed

to them; he gave back to the brain what was wrongly taken away from it;
in a word, he restored to the brain its entire domain... but unfortunately,
after having reduced everything to the brain by an admirable generalization, if he had only understood it, he cuts up and breaks down the whole
thing again by the most bizarre system imaginable. ([127e], p. 272)

It is a fact that Gall's concept of "centre" is a concept derived from the
classificatory style of thinking of the eighteenth century, the thinking of
Buffon, Linnaeus and Lavoisier. The thinking of the nineteenth century
gradually adapted these perceptions. In the early stages, they coexisted with
an emerging evolutionism that taught that the organism differentiates itself
as it develops ontogenetically and phylogenetically. Within this kind of model
one could also picture the brain as differentiating itself into increasingly
independent centres while these centres become increasingly specialized. In
later stages, however, when the idea of function suggested the need for a
circuit or transmission to bring it into being, such a conception would seem
much too static to designate the function's organic site. In spite of this
gradual change in ideas, not to mention the imaginary elements in Gall's
doctrine, the Phrenological movement in France, England and the New World
carried on into the nineteenth century long beyond the period when it was
new and controversial. An important focus for the transmission of the doctrine was at first the Société de Phrénologie and then the Société d'Anthropologie, with Bouillaud[31] as high priest of the cult.

PATHOLOGY AS A MEANS OF KNOWLEDGE

But if, on one hand, physiology is the veritable lamp of pathology, it is also certain that pathology is for physiology an inexhaust-
ible source of illumination.
Bouillaud ([50a], p. xxj)

Bouillaud was not an unreserved apologist for Gall. A true scientist, he
proceeded in accordance with a method that had already proved itself, but
which was now guaranteed greater effectiveness because of the improved
communication of information, improved anatomical techniques, and the
emergence of a clinical science. Enunciated in his *Traité Clinique et Physi-
ologique de l'Encéphalite* (1825), it was developed throughout his career.
The initial phase of this approach is clinical observation of the pathological case. The second is post-mortem verification of the hypothesis by
autopsy. In the third phase, correlations are established between all the
cases recorded - in particular, regarding the nature of the impairment, and
the site of the lesion.
In 1827, Bouillaud presented two papers at the Académie Royale de

Médecine on the functions of the cerebellum. The first was called "Experimental researches tending to prove that the cerebellum presides over acts of station and progression, and not over the instinct of propagation". He recalls first that "Monsieur Gall" had stated that the cerebellum was the organ of the instinct of propagation, and mentions opposing views - those of Flourens[32] and Rolando,[33] and the more cautious view of Serres.[34] There follows an account of his own experiments in vivisection of animals and birds. Loss of equilibrium is the common factor, he finds, in disturbances due to lesions of this part of the nervous system. In repeating the experiments of Flourens[35] on the cerebellum,

> I still firmly believed with M. Gall that this nervous centre was the legislative organ of the generative functions. ([50d], p. 225).

This statement leads into the second paper, whose title is "Clinical researches tending to refute the opinion of M. Gall on the functions of the cerebellum, and to prove that this organ presides over acts of equilibration, station and progression". Bouillaud here resumes critical study of the cases presented by Gall in support of his thesis.

Bouillaud's critical stance in these two communications guarantees his objectivity when he supports Gall, as was the case in the paper he read at the Royal Academy on February 21, 1825: "Clinical researches to demonstrate that loss of speech corresponds to lesion of the frontal lobules of the brain and to confirm the opinion of M. Gall on the seat of the organ of articulate language".

Anatomy, he explains, confirms the connections of the brain with the spinal cord and, in consequence, its role in "the various acts which are presided over by muscular contraction." One can go further, however, and show that the various parts of which the brain is composed each command certain movements of particular parts of the body. Bouillaud appeals to various authorities, Saucerotte[36] as well as Serres and Pinel:[37]

> I do not wish to concern myself in this paper other than with the influence of the brain on the movements of the tongue considered as the instrument of speech and on those of the other muscles which collaborate with it in producing this great phenomenon.

Bouillaud presents three well-documented clinical cases of complete or partial loss of speech. After the deaths of two out of three of the patients, autopsies showed that:

> The frontal lobe of the brain, at the part corresponding to the orbital vault, was reduced to a purulent, putrid matter... ([50b], p. 31)

Bouillaud then presents further observations which he discusses in great detail, expunging any fact that he considers doubtful, and proposes the following conclusions:

> The various facts above mentioned each speaks more strongly than the last in favour of the view that the speech organs have the principle of their movements in the frontal lobules of the brain... We have established by experiment and observation: (1) that paralysis of these organs, independently of the other parts of the body, took place in cases of complete disorganisation of the frontal lobules... (2) that the free exercise of speech remained when the brain was affected in other parts besides the frontal lobules. ([50b], p. 40)

Bouillaud then notes that numerous patients who have lost the use of speech:

> nonetheless retain the faculty of expressing their ideas, their feelings, by other languages, such as writing, gesture, etc...

This statement brings him to a revelation of the real distance between his view and Gall's:

> Everyone knows that one of the most illustrious observers of our time has situated a particular type of memory in the front part of the brain; in this M. Gall has manifestly contradicted himself; for having made every effort to show that the general faculties of the mind have no special organs, he assigns a particular organ to memory... ([50b], p. 42)

As Pierre Marie[38] reminds us in his historical article of 1906 in *La Semaine Médicale*, obstinacy was one of Bouillaud's chief characteristics. He would return to this problem again and again throughout his career. From 1825 on, Bouillaud's thesis met with more and more vigorous opposition as Gall's authority was increasingly challenged in the French scientific world of the time. First Cruveilher,[39] then Andral[40] presented several cases that weakened Bouillaud's conclusions. Bouillaud studied these data very closely, and in a paper to the Académie de Médecine of 1839 he wrote:[41]

> ...The eighteen observations that were put forward against me... did not emerge from my tests unscathed. There were even some that, examined with fresh care, came to be for, not against my hypothesis.

He goes on to present thirteen new cases which, he claims, confirm the well-foundedness of his own position.

With opponents unconvinced, Bouillaud dug in and adopted an increasingly dogmatic tone. In 1848, he read yet another paper to the Academy: "Clinical researches tending to show that the sense of articulate language and the coordinating principle of the movements of speech reside in the frontal lobules of the brain"[42] [50e]. Using the same strategy as in his 1839 paper, Bouillaud emphasized the uncertainty of the observations put forward against his theory, and demonstrated their inadequacies.

Bouillaud's attachment to Gall's ideas is understandable in the light of these communications. Bouillaud was convinced that his own work improved Gall's, so he continued to value Gall as an antecedent. To deny Gall would have been to deny himself. He passed on his belief to his followers, particularly his son-in-law Auburtin,[43] who wrote, in 1863:

> The researches of Prof. Bouillaud on the functions of the cerebral lobes in general, and on those of the frontal lobes and the cerebellum, were intended to confirm or disconfirm several of the opinions of Gall. [13]

We may perhaps leave it to Pierre Marie, a severe critic of his predecessors, to put in context this important point in research on brain and language, with the advantage of an extra quarter-century's hindsight:

> Bouillaud, at the time that concerns us, has thus retained such an admiration for Gall that he does not hesitate to put him on the same level as Galileo and Newton. He himself is convinced that the faculty of articulate language has its seat in the frontal lobes of the brain, and in order to signal the firmness of his conviction, he offers a prize of 500 francs to anyone who can contribute a decisive observation against this point of view. ([253a], p. 81)

Into the midst of this scientific but impassioned debate, a new actor would soon make his appearance: Paul Broca.[44]

Let us first, however, look at the wider context of Bouillaud's thinking, so as to follow the direction of contemporary discussions as faithfully as possible. It should be emphasized that, from the beginning, the debate on localization was contaminated by philosophical impurities.

From Lallemand,[45] a longtime opponent of Gall, to Gratiolet[46] and many others,[47] localization theory had met with strong hostility. In the name of a "unity of thought" principle, Flourens rejected the very idea of a "centre" for higher functions, while he accepted it for motor and vital functions. Cruveilher pointed out that if one faculty was localized today, tomorrow people would want to localize all of them. However, he recognized the coincidence of language disturbances with lesions of the corpus striatum.

If ideas often seem confused in this debate, it is because the topic itself was far from clear. Neither in Rostan,[48] nor in Frank,[49] nor in Lordat[50] do we find a precise account of what Trousseau[51] would later name *"aphasia"*. It would appear, from a present-day point of view, that Lordat[52] had a more definite grasp of the phenomena than many of his contemporaries. His contribution to research was known in Paris medical circles even when he was living in the South of France. Already in 1820, he attributed *"ala-lia"* (as he called it) not to a paralysis of the tongue but to an aberration in *"synergies"* of the muscles involved in speech activity. A little later, he seems to have established a distinction between verbal *"amnesia"* or loss of word memory and verbal *"asynergy"* or loss of the ability to pronounce words. Moutier[53] notes that Lordat, in a surprising way that makes him a pioneer, calls *"paramnesia"* the uttering of mistaken words, a syndrome later known as "paraphasia". However, Moutier is probably mistaken (following Dax[54]) about Lordat's bibliography; the first work actually seems to date from 1843.

With Lordat, a new way of using pathological data appears, based on minute clinical observation of the patient's verbal behaviour, whereas with Bouillaud such observation is summary or non-existent, and even with Broca it would remain very superficial.[55] The aims of the two approaches - Bouillaud's and Broca's on the one hand, Lordat's on the other - are teleologically quite different. Bouillaud and Broca both focus on what they believe to be essential: the lesion that the autopsy will enable them to localize as soon as the patient is obliging enough to die. A patient who gets better or who survives leaves an unresolved problem. Lordat, since he does not believe that the higher functions can be strictly localized, is not so curious to get to the lesion that is supposed to explain it all. He thus confines his examination to the outward manifestations of illness as they are expressed in language deficits. In accordance with his avowed intentions, and certainly as far as his conclusions are concerned, Lordat seeks to develop a general theory of the language act. This ambition was confirmed after the attack he suffered in 1825, which deprived him of language almost totally for some time, reducing him to clumsy and incomplete expression and equally limited comprehension of others, with a complete inability to read.[56]

In a course of physiology lectures[57] delivered in 1842 and 1843, Lordat made use of the observations he had accumulated during the long weeks of his illness, and which shed new light on previous observations of other patients.[58] However, the effort of introspection seemed to make him lose his objectivity. He resorted to the vague notion of "vital force" to facilitate what he termed the "corporification" of the constituents of thought.[59] He emphasizes one point which he considers self-evident:

> It was therefore necessary to learn that the internal exercise of thought could do without words, that the corporification of ideas was

something quite distinct from their formation and combination... I
learned that of the complete logos of which I spoke to you before, I
possessed only the internal part and had lost the external part. [243]

This finding opened a discussion which is not yet closed on the relationship between thought and language. Lordat's analysis of language impairments also poses the problem of relations between the faculty of language
and intelligence. Privation of language seems to him a handicap of a social
nature, causing him the humiliation of appearing a mental defective in the
eyes of others while remained a thinking mind, in control of his thoughts.
Lordat's discussion, in spite of its systematizing tendencies, laid the groundwork for a new approach to the problems of language and speech disturbances. As Quercy and Bayle remark:

> Lordat encounters speech as a system of movements... A neuromus-
> cular machine of little complexity, a small group of organs suffice for the
> infinity of movements and oral sounds. ([24], p. 305)

In Lordat's view, this passive executor does not obey the intelligence or
the will. Intelligence invents language, but it is not the direct agent of the
language operation:

> This agent of speech is, between the intelligence and the cerebro-lin-
> gual mechanism, the vital force... the instinct that makes us imitate,
> remake with our mouths, the vocal sounds of others... an instinct which
> will finally endow us with stable oral synergies, almost as solid as the
> innate actions of deglutition or weeping. ([24], p. 305)

Lordat's teaching reveals his indifference to the fashionable concept of
cerebral localization. He does not even indicate which side was paralysed,
as if he were consciously avoiding a pedantic excess of detail.[60]
Lordat's work is based on solid experience as much as on self-observa-
tion. It represents an original attempt to understand the process of thought
into language.[61] However, the work in which Lordat recounted his own
experience of language loss was almost unknown to his contemporaries.
One cannot therefore speak of his influence on the development of thinking in his period. In the middle of the century, however, his example is instructive. In his writings, clinical observation of pathological phenomena is
carried to a high level of accuracy as regards description of the language
deficit, while attention to the possible somatic site of the disorder is totally
absent. Lordat's constructive approach to interpreting the linguistic phenomena unfortunately lacked a theoretical framework that could give it rigour
and explanatory power; it thus became snagged in speculative notions.

Lordat came too late, or too early. Still, his attitude was perhaps wise at a time when so little was known either linguistically or at the level of the anatomy and physiology of the cortex. Cerebral anatomy and physiology would later make giant strides; and a theory of language would develop still later. The clinical work of Paul Broca came between these two points of development. Before discussing Broca, it will be useful to consider the approaches by which the rediscovery of the brain took place.

THE BRAIN REDISCOVERED

> Two substances make up the nervous centres: the white or fibrous substance and the grey substance. The white matter is both sensory and motor: sensory in the posterior bundles of the spinal cord, motor in the frontal. The grey matter is neither sensory nor motor; but it is a conductor of sensation.
> Flourens ([127a], p. 117)

The earliest indication that the cortex might indeed not be uniform in its structure, and that regional differences might be discovered there is to be found in Gennari,[62] whose writings unfortunately did not receive much publicity in their time (1776).

Gall moved the focus of observation to the outermost surface of the cerebral organism, to its bony envelope where (he believed) the peculiarities of its internal organization, both cortical and infracortical, would be readable. In fact, Gall arrived at the position of replacing direct observation with a different exploratory technique in which touch took the place of sight and the hand the place of the eye.[63]

His excesses should perhaps be charitably forgotten. Flourens,[64] who was not kind to Gall, is nonetheless the first to admit his importance:

> Basically I distinguish in Gall the author of the absurd system of phrenology from the profound observer who opened up to us, with genius, the study of the anatomy and physiology of the brain. ([127e], p. 251)

The controversy generated by the doctrines of Gall and Spurzheim had the result of stimulating the line of research started before them by Gennari. In 1821 Tiedemann[65] published his *Icones cerebri simiarum*, where he notes the regularity of the cerebral folds with a single species, the variation in arrangement across species, and the steady increase in complexity during the development of the embryo. In 1839 Leuret[66] published the first volume of his *Comparative Anatomy of the Nervous System, Considered in its Relations with Intelligence*, the second volume being published by Gratiolet[67] fifteen years later. These two volumes corroborated and extended Tiedemann's findings. With the discipline of thinking and perception required by the experimental method as practiced by these anatomists (and as codified later by Claude Bernard),[68] observation was advancing slowly but surely.

With hindsight, we can define the problem-situation that focussed research interests and initiatives at this period.

The first aspect of it is the problem of finding a truly convincing basis in anatomical and physiological fact for the assumption that the cortex contains differentiated areas.

The second is the problem of establishing a precise structural relationship between the inner white matter and the cortical layer of grey matter, to the extent that the two can be differentiated from one another.

The third aspect is the problem of defining the precise nature of the physiological processes of reception and transmission through the circuits of the infinitely complex network of nerves. These three levels of inquiry are clearly interdependent; it seems useful to distinguish them merely for clarity of exposition. Only rarely are observed data significant. Ruysch[69] had begun to explore the surface of the cortex, concluding in 1698 that it is only made up of blood vessels. Later, Gottfried Ehrenberg, [70] with the help of the achromatic microscope,[71] described peripheral and root nerve fibers and at the same time gave the first accurate account of cortical fibre, in 1833.

It was an epoch-making discovery; two years later, Gabriel Gustav Valentin[72] completed it.

Baillarger,[73] who was one of Gall's supporters, attempted to correlate the morphological variations of the cortex with intelligence and mental illnesses. In so doing, he happened to observe in 1840 with the naked eye that this seemingly uniform envelope of grey matter to which Varolio had given the name "cortex"[74] was in fact made up of distinct layers. He identified six of these, and pointed out their connections with the internal white matter. He observed that the fibers of the white matter extended into the grey matter of the cortex. Baillarger thus corroborated Gennari[75] and Malpighi.[76] In 1844, Remak[77] checked and confirmed Baillarger's findings microscopically. He showed that while the white matter is made up of fibers, the grey matter is made up of cell bodies forming the cortex.

In 1852, a new method of observation led Koelliker[78] to describe in greater detail the structure of the different cellular layers of the cortex, while confirming the likelihood of a connection between the nerve cells of the cortex and the underlying fibrous white matter. Fontana,[79] whose observations on nerve fibre had been stimulated by the work of Monro,[80] had used a much cruder microscope to identify the nerve fibre as the simplest structure of the nerve, and had called it the "primitive nerve cylinder". It is not clear what he actually saw, but Remak's[81] observations would later corroborate his. Remak gave the first description of the axon and its myelin sheath.[82]

Science was now on the way to discovering the cellular structural unity that makes up the central nervous system, while noticing its morphological diversity. Physiological research would soon confirm that this morphological diversity corresponded to a functional diversity, which had been claimed previous to that time on the basis of pathological or experimental observations.

After 1850 it became clear that the types of nerve cells, as well as their distribution in the cortex, vary according to the zone considered. The effort to establish a cerebral topography based on the appearance and form of the cells, on the one hand, and the boundaries of their successive layers, on the other, began to crystallize with Rudolf Berlin[83] in 1858, and continued with Meynert.[84] Finally, the pyramidal cell was identified by Betz[85] in 1874. Based on the work of Fritsch and Hitzig,[86] he guessed their functional specialization, since they are abundant in the zones identified as motor by those researchers. Betz thus came to distinguish two kinds of zones on the surface of the cortex: motor zones, where these pyramidal cells predominate, and sensory zones, where they are the minority.

This penetration of vision into the depths of the cortex occurred at the same time as the concept of the fundamental unity of the central nervous system was taking place. We thus come to the second aspect of the problem-situation outlined earlier.

Already guessed at in 1836 by Remak,[87] the structural continuity between the cortical cell and the fibers making up the white matter was attested by Purkyne[88] in 1837. By a different method of observation, Purkyne, only a few months after Remak, described the myelinated and unmyelinated fibers. But most importantly, stimulated by Ehrenberg,[89] he identified similar cells in other areas of the central nervous system, which constituted a significant step in confirming its unity of structure. Schwann[90] laid down the process of myelination of the fibre in 1839, and introduced a very broad notion that all living tissues are uniformly made up of cells. In 1842, Hannover[91] corroborated Schwann's work by means of a technique of preparation which he developed to treat nerve tissues, and he observed the axon. Most importantly, however, he confirmed what Remak, who worked in the same laboratory in Berlin, had guessed, that the nerve fibre originates in the cell itself. In 1845, Koelliker[92] reopened the question of the organic unity of cell and fibre,[93] explaining the difference in colour by the presence of the layer of myelin around the fibre.

In 1865, Deiters[94] confirmed that all fibers are extensions of cells, whether they are dendrites or axons. But one point remained unknown. Were these cells isolated entities relating to one another only by contact, or, with fibers anastomatizing each other, were these cells the nodes of an enormous nervous network?[95] This second point of view (the reticularist theory), had long been held by histologists like Wagner,[96] and seemed to be confirmed by the new techniques of microscopic observation developed by Gerlach[97] in 1871 and especially Golgi[98] in 1885. We will return to this matter.[99]

At the same time, another research orientation was also revealing the organic unity of the cell and its extensions (the neuron of today), and bypassing without further attempt at explanation the problem of the connection and continuity of the basic components of the nervous system.

We thus arrive at the third and final aspect of the problem-situation we spoke of earlier. Research work in physiology would finally lay the foundations of a unified theory of the central nervous system and bring to light the nature of the processes that characterize that system. As Marx[100] explains, around 1840 conceptions of the basic phenomenon of nerve, i.e. the propagation of something that had been called "animal spirits", "nervous force", "nerve influx", had known no progress since Haller.[101] At this point, Johannes Müller[102] commissioned his young assistant Du Bois-Reymond[103] in the Spring of 1841 to check the experiments of Matteucci.[104] The Galvani-Volta debate was still very much a living memory. Du Bois-Reymond subjected all the techniques of investigation to careful scrutiny, and concluded that Matteucci had been right about the existence of an electrical current in the nerves and muscles dissected, but that he had been wrong about the direction of the current. This current actually travelled from the positive intact surface to the negative surface of the section. Since the muscular or nervous current could also be observed in fragments of nerve or muscle, Du Bois-Reymond felt justified in claiming that production of electricity was a property of the very elements of these tissues.[105]

Something that had seemed impossible to Johannes Müller - measurement of the speed of transmission of the nerve impulse - was achieved in 1849-50 by his student H. L. F. von Helmholtz.[106] The repercussions of this fundamental discovery went far beyond the domain of physiology. The average speed of conduction in the motor nerves of man, 30-35 metres per second, was established a little later. As a result, it was now possible to conduct experiments on the human brain with mathematical precision as regards measuring the speed of movement of impulses along the nerves. The influence of this new technique on the development of experimental psychology was immense. However, this discovery had another equally important implication. There was now clear evidence that the phenomenon of nerve conduction could not be compared with the transmission of an electrical current along a wire, in spite of the helpful stimulus of this metaphor. The process, whatever its nature, was slower, and Hermann[107] found particular support in this for his theory of nervous transmission, which was opposed to that of his teacher Du Bois-Reymond.

Within the same time-period another line of research was continuing: electrical stimulation of the cortex. This line of inquiry had been initiated by Rolando. The negative influence of Flourens had retarded its development. With Fritsch and Hitzig, it had demonstrated the existence of motor zones; this in turn linked up with anatomical research, which, as we have seen, discovered the heterogeneous nature of the cortical mantle and hypothesized it to be functionally diverse.

Little by little the pieces of the puzzle were coming together, and a new science was in the making. The representation of the central nervous system that was emerging owed its novelty to the disciplines serving anatomy and physiology: physics, optics, mathematics, and to some extent chemistry and electricity.

We may wonder, at the risk of being irreverent, if all this new knowledge had been absorbed by practitioners contemporary with Broca, or by Broca himself. Judging by their statements, they do not seem to have realized that the cortex was a staggeringly complex structure. We must understand that the clinician first sees the facts, while the laboratory worker explores the hidden depths. It is difficult to imagine one mind synthesizing such different approaches; if such were possible, scientific truth would be very quickly found. Broca tried to find the shortest distance between the facts and their interpretation. In upsetting the course of things, he accelerated the course of history.

NOTES

1   Jiri Procháska (1749-1820).
2   Willis: see [423a].
3   Soemmering: see note 56, p. 109.
4   Giovanni Battista Porta (1550-162?). After establishing the influence of affections of mind on the body, he indicates the signs by which the personalities of individuals can be recognized. Porta was inspired by Aristotle, Polemon and Adamantius.
5   Cornelio Ghirardelli, born towards the end of the 16th century.
6   Broussais recounts the example of the Marchese of Mascardi, Minister for Justice in the Kingdom of Naples, who applied Porta's ideas to decide on the criminality of accused persons, based on an examination of their physiognomy ([220b], p. 24).
7   Johann Kaspar Lavater (1741-1801).
8   Gall: see note 60, p. 110. In spite of his unscientific flights of imagina-

tion, he was a great anatomist: "Gall's research on the formation and structure of the brain has been the starting-point for persevering work which in many ways has brought results of great importance and which has in particular enabled us to know better the conditions of form and structure with regard to the cerebral convolutions." ([300b], p. 685).

9   Pierre Marie (1853-1940).
10 Pierre Paul Broca (1824-1888), founder of the *Société, Journal* and *Ecole d'Anthropologie*.
11 See [220b], p. 194.
12 The essential object is the study of the brain; the skull is only a secondary object ([220b], p. 104).
13 According to Gall and Spurzheim ([143], vol. IV, pp. 68ff.). Note that the essentials of Gall's doctrine are to be found in [142d], which Gall published alone after his break with Spurzheim.
14 Rolando: see p. 109, note 53 ([347b])
15 F.A. Longet (1811-1871).
16 A.L. Foville (1789-1878).
17 Brillat-Savarin (1755-1826). *La Physiologie du Goût* dates from 1825. Balzac (1799-1850) wrote *La Physiologie du Mariage* in 1829.
18 We find in ([142d], vol. III, pp. 145f.): "I owe almost all my anatomical discoveries to my physiological and pathological ideas; and it was only following on these latter that I was able to convince myself of the perfect concordance of moral and intellectual phenomena with the material conditions of their manifestation."
19 Spurzheim, G.: see p. 110, note 61.
20 i.e. [143].
21 Friedrich Hegel (1770-1831).
22 Pierre François Gonthier Maine de Biran (1766-1824).
23 See [220b].
24 See note 22. The paper entitled "Observations on the organic divisions of the brain" originated as the inaugural lecture of the medical society. It was first known under the title "Observations on Dr Gall's system".
25 Jean Cruveilher (1791-1874).
26 Georges Cuvier (1769-1832).
27 Pierre Flourens: p. 108, note 26.
28 Louis Pierre Gratiolet (1815-1865).
29 See [117].
30 Marie François Xavier Bichat (1771-1802).
31 Jean-Baptiste Bouillaud (1796-1881).
32 See [127a,b].
33 See [347a].
34 Augustin Serres (1786-1868).

35 See [127a,b,c].
36 Nicolas Saucerotte (1741-1814).
37 Philippe Pinel (1745-1826).
38 Pierre Marie: see note 9 above.
39 He had some difficulty accepting the dissociation of the brain into specialized zones, and admitted being completely hostile to phrenology ([285], p. 16).
40 Gabriel Andral (1797-1876). In his *Clinique* of 1834, he had pointed to the coincidence of unintelligibility of speech and babbling with right hemiplegia by lesion localized in the left corpus striatum. See Moutier ([285], p. 15).
41 *Bulletin de l'Académie de Médecine*, IV, pp. 282-328.
42 ibid., 1848, *1er trimestre*, pp. 699-719.
43 Simon-Alexandre Ernest Auburtin (1825-1893).
44 See note 10 above.
45 F. Lallemand (1790-1854).
46 See [163b].
47 See note 40.
48 Louis Léon Rostan (1790-1866).
49 Jean Pierre Frank (1745-1821).
50 Jacques Lordat (1773-1870) of the Montepellier Medical School. On July 17, 1825 a chronic sore throat triggered the attack which for weeks deprived him of speech and reading.
51 See [395].
52 We must mention here, as a source of documentation, the article by Riese [343a].
53 Moutier ([285], p. 16) mentions Lordat's book *L'Analyse de la Parole* (1823). In fact Lordat published, or rather authorized his student Kühnholtz to publish his lectures from the course in physiology from the academic year 1842-43, under the title "Analysis of speech, to serve the theory of various cases of alalia and paralalia (mutism and imperfections of speaking) which nosologists have failed to recognize", in the *Journal de la Société de Médecine Pratique de Montpellier* VII, pp. 333-353 and 417-433; VIII, pp. 1-17 (1843). This is also the view of Quercy and Bayle (see [24]).
54 Benton [29b], like Riese (note 52), emphasizes Lordat's influence on Dax Sr. and Jr. The father, Marc Dax, a doctor in Sommières, has presented a communication to the Medical Conference in Montpellier in July 1836; in this communication he established a relationship between forgetting the signs of thought and lesions of the left hemisphere. Marc Dax even noted that this observation had been made by Schenkius.

55 The patients Broca concerned himself with were practically hopeless cases where speech had almost completely disappeared.

56 "When I wished to glance at the book I was reading when my illness had struck, I found myself unable to read the title" [243].

57 See note 53.

58 "The difficulty increased rapidly, and, in the space of 24 hours, I found myself deprived of the value of almost all words. Though there were a few left to me, they were becoming almost useless, because I could no longer remember the way to coordinate them in my mind so that they could express a thought..." [243].

59 "...For all that, it was necessary to 'corporify' all the ideas in my mind; as a result, to exercise memory, to recall to mind the ideas of sounds; that could only be done with efforts that tired me for a long time, and which have never ceased to be a burden to me" [243].

60 See ([24], p. 300, n. 1): "Language is a pananthropic function."

61 As we know, this preoccupation with thought and language has turned out to be a focus for 20th-century linguistic debate.

62 See p. 109, note 55.

63 See [220b], pp. 114f.

64 See p. 108, note 26. Flourens ([127e], p. 251) himself refers to [127d].

65 See p. 110, note 62. The work cited here was published in Heidelberg in 1821.

66 See p. 110, note 63.

67 See note 28 above.

68 Claude Bernard (1813-1878).

69 See p. 107, note 3.

70 Christian Gottfried Ehrenberg (1795-1876).

71 The achromatic microscope was gradually developed from lenses used for telescopes. Its aim was to eliminate chromatic aberrations from the image by using prisms.

72 Gabriel Gustav Valentin (1810-1883).

73 Jules Gabriel François Baillarger (1806-1891).

74 See p. 58, note 16.

75 See note 55, p. 109.

76 Indeed Malpighi had suggested that the "conduits" of white matter were connected with the "glands of the cortex".

77 Robert Remak (1815-1865) identified myelinated fibre, which Leeuwenhoek and Fontana may have seen.

78 Rudolf A. von Koelliker (1817-1905).

79 See p. 107, note 8.

80 See [276] and [277a,b].

81 See note 77.

82 It is perhaps of interest to point out that there may be correlations between the myelination process and speech and language development. See [225].

83 Rudolf Berlin (1833-1897).

84 Theodor Meynert (1833-1892).

85 Vladimir Alexewitsch Betz (1834-1894).

86 Eduard Hitzig (1838-1907) and Gustav Theodor Fritsch (1838-1927): the names of these two physiologists are linked as a result of their experiment in electrical stimulation of the canine brain.

87 See [337].

88 Jan Evangelista Purkyne (1787-1869).

89 See note 70.

90 Theodor Schwann (1810-1882).

91 Adolf Hannover (1814-1894).

92 See note 78.

93 Koelliker presents his point of view in [210c], but he had already done so in his communication [210a].

94 Otto Friedrich Karl Deiters (1834-1863).

95 Anastomosis is the contact of two blood vessels, arterial or lymphatic, and by extension between two conduits of similar nature, such as two nerves.

96 Rudolf Johann Wagner (1805-1864).

97 Joseph von Gerlach (1820-1896).

98 Camillo Golgi (1843-1926).

99 See pp. 182ff.

100 See [256].

101 See p. 109 note 40.

102 Johannes Müller (1801-1858).

103 See p. 112, note 95.

104 See p. 113, note 98.

105 Du Bois-Reymond: see [108b].

106 Hermann Ludwig Ferdinand von Helmholtz (1821-1894).

107 Ludimar Hermann (1838-1914)

IV
The Birth of Neurolinguistics

1. THE BROCA ERA

THE MYTH OF THE THIRD LEFT FRONTAL CONVOLUTION

> The great experimental principle, then, is doubt, that philosophic
> doubt which leaves to the mind its freedom and initiative, and from
> which the virtues most valuable to investigators in physiology and medi-
> cine are derived.
> Claude Bernard ([35], p. 37)

How does it happen, one may ask, that an investigator allows his mind
to become trapped in a closed system of relations between the fact he has
discovered and the hypothesis he has boldly proposed to account for it? In
such cases we seem to witness the rapid transformation of hypotheses into
truths; and in the case of nineteenth-century brain science, the metamor-
phosis was further hastened by the climate of impassioned debate in which
the key events occurred.

Towards the end of the 1840's, Bouillaud[1] had offered a prize of 500
gold francs to anyone who could produce a patient having lost the faculty
of language without presenting a lesion of the frontal lobes.[2] In 1861, the
challenge had still not been taken up. At this time, as Pierre Marie[3] explains,

> Broca was 37 years old, and he was secretary of the Société d'Anthro-
> pologie... Bouillaud was 65... He was a person of some importance by
> reason of his age, his talent, his university honours... ([253c], p. 75).

In February and March of that year, several controversies broke out in
the Société d'Anthropologie between Gratiolet[4], Auburtin[5] and Broca[6] about
the question of parallels between the development of the brain and the
races of man. Gratiolet held that research to establish such relationships
had no foundation in reality. Auburtin, Bouillaud's son-in-law, vigorously
supported the doctrine of localizations.

Undecided, Broca took neither side, but at the meeting of March 21,
1861, in replying to Gratiolet, he considered this question among others:
do the various parts of the brain serving thought have the same characteristics?

Pierre Marie comments:

> In this connection he expounded his ideas on brain localization; his
> speech deserves much admiration, for in it he reveals his superiority over
> most men of his time. While repudiating Gall's system and the doctrine

155

of bumps on the skull, he recognises that the principle of localization
does not stand or fall with it... ([253c], p. 82)

During the April 4 meeting, Auburtin addressed the society on the seat
of the language faculty. Referring to a patient on his ward who had lost the
use of speech, he had no hesitation in saying that, after this man's death, if
no lesion of the frontal lobes was found, he would abandon the theory.
This communication fell into place at just the right psychological moment
for Broca.[7] A few days later, there arrived on his ward a patient named Leborgne, mentally feeble, an epileptic in his childhood, and paralysed on the
right side for ten years. He could pronounce only the meaningless mono-
syllable "tan".[8] His admission to Broca's ward at Bicêtre, due to a massive
blood-clot, occurred on April 12, 1861. The potential interest of the case
prompted Broca to ask Auburtin to come and examine the patient.

What was Broca's state of thinking at the time of these events? Bouillaud's authority was considerable, and his work commanded Broca's respect;
but he was not in agreement with the highly dogmatic conclusions in which
it was couched. Broca, then, would be quite willing to believe the thesis of
the localization of the language faculty in the frontal lobes if, like Doubt-
ing Thomas, he could see it for himself.[9]

On April 17 Leborgne died and an immediate autopsy revealed that:

the frontal lobe of the left hemisphere was softened in the greatest
part of its area. ([57a], p. 237)

Let us take note of the phrasing of this statement; it is the beginning of
all that was to follow.

The communication to the Société d'Anthropologie from which the above
quotation is taken, and the presentation of the "exhibit", took place on
April 18, the day after Leborgne's death and autopsy.

These few details indicate the rapid succession of events, and the impassioned quality of the proceedings. As Marie stated much later:

There were other lesions as well in the posterior part of the Sylvian
region, but they were scarcely mentioned. [253c], p. 82f.)

In August 1861 Broca presented to the Société Anatomique[10] his "Remarks on the seat of the faculty of articulate language, followed by an
observation of aphemia [loss of speech]". The paper is in two parts.

In the first, Broca constructs a kind of theory of language on the basis of
pathological data. He recalls that the Phrenological school placed the language faculty in the frontal part of the brain, in one of the convolutions
that rest against the orbital vault.

Such an opinion, claimed without sufficient evidence and resting only on a very imperfect analysis of the phenomena of language, would no doubt have disappeared with the rest of the system,

> if M. Bouillaud had not salvaged it by subjecting it to significant modifications and surrounding it with a series of proofs taken particularly from pathology. ([57b], p. 330)

Broca then comments that there are several kinds of language, and that any sign system enabling the expression of ideas in a more or less intelligible, complex or rapid manner is "a language in the widest sense of the word". However, there is only one general faculty of language presiding over all these modes of expression of thought, which can be defined:

> the faculty of establishing a constant relation between an idea and a sign, whether that sign be a sound, a gesture, a figure or some kind of outline... ([57b], p. 331)

The absence or abolition of this faculty makes any kind of language impossible. However, there are cases where the language faculty persists, the auditory apparatus is intact, all the muscles (those of voice and articulation not excepted) obey the will, and yet where:

> a cerebral lesion abolishes articulate language. This abolition of speech in individuals who are neither paralyzed nor idiots constitutes a rather specific symptom, so that it seems to me useful to designate it by a special name. I will accordingly give it the name aphemia (α, privative + $\varphi\eta\mu\iota$, I speak or pronounce); because what these patients lack is only the faculty of articulating words... ([57b], p. 332)

Broca next points out that these patients have retained total motor activity of the tongue and lips, and that what has collapsed in them is neither the faculty of language, nor word memory, nor the action of the nerves and muscles of phonation and articulation:

> It is a faculty considered by Dr Bouillaud as the faculty of coordinating the movements proper to articulate language, or more simply as the faculty of articulate language, since without it no articulation is possible.
> ([57b], p. 333)

He then examines the validity of the theory of localizations as Bouillaud had tried to establish it for the faculty of language, and declares for the extreme likelihood of the principle, while refraining from the claim that each faculty has its seat in a particular convolution:

> It is a question that seems to me quite insoluble at the present state
> of science. ([57b], p. 338)

Clearly, at this stage in his thinking, Broca did not regard the Leborgne case as sufficient evidence to warrant throwing his unconditional support behind Bouillaud's theories, which he accepted only as working hypotheses.

In the second part of his discussion, Broca returns to the study of the Leborgne case, reiterates its circumstances and states the results of his anatomical exploration during the autopsy as follows:

> If one wished to go into further detail, one would note that the third
> frontal convolution is the one which presents the greatest loss of mat-
> ter... and that, as a result, in all possibility it is in the third fontal convo-
> lution that the disease began... ([57b], p. 353)

This is the first time that such specific mention is made of the third frontal convolution. In concluding, Broca specifies the role he believes can be assigned to this site in the cortex:

> In our patient, the primitive seat of the lesion was in the second or
> third frontal convolution, more likely in the latter. It is therefore possible
> that this faculty of articulate language is located in one or other of these
> two convolutions; but one cannot be sure of it as yet, seeing as previous
> observations say nothing about the state of each convolution individu-
> ally, and one cannot even anticipate it since the principle of localization
> by convolutions does not yet rest on any firm basis. ([57b], p. 357)

Broca cautiously eschews further comment. However, he does find in the facts proof enough to conclude emphatically that these facts can hardly be fitted to:

> the notion of the faculty of articulate language being situated in a
> fixed, circumscribed locus situated under any bump of the skull... but
> that, on the other hand they can be reconciled with the system of local-
> ization by convolutions.[11]

On October 27, 1861, six months after the Leborgne case,[12] an old man of 84 years of age named Lelong was brought to the Bicêtre Infirmary to be treated for a fracture of the left femur. Admitted to the hospice eight years before due to senile debility, and the victim of a stroke in April 1861, he was almost incapable of speaking although he retained the use of a few common words. His daughter believed that his tongue was paralyzed. His intelligence seemed intact and he understood what was said to him. On examining him, Broca found absence of paralysis of the tongue, and the pertinence of his gesture responses to questions put to him led Broca to the conclusion that Lelong was suffering from aphemia.

Lelong died on November 8. The autopsy gave Broca a real surprise as far as the site of the lesion was concerned:

> This lesion is incomparably more circumscribed than that which existed on Tan's brain; but comparing the two specimens, we find that the centre of the lesion is identically the same in the two cases. ([57c], pp. 403f.)

He accordingly reminds his colleagues at the Société Anatomique of his reluctance[13] to assign circumscribed points to localizations, and states:

> I will therefore not hide that I experienced surprise akin to stupefaction when I found that on my second patient the lesion occupied exactly the same seat as on the first... and on the very same side (the left). ([57c], pp. 406f.)

Broca is aware of the arguments that partisans of Phrenology might draw from his observations. Calling on the testimony of other anatomists without, however, ascribing too much importance to the insufficiently detailed observations that preceded his own, he declares that the data gathered are perfectly compatible with the hypothesis of localization by convolutions, but difficult to reconcile with the principle of localization into zones.[14]

In the months that followed, several identical cases were reported, particularly in Charcot's[15] ward at the Salpêtrière, where Broca had been appointed surgeon in January 1862. Broca gave an account of the situation in a paper presented to the Société d'Anthropologie at its meeting of April 2, 1863. During this same meeting, however, a theme appeared which would soon take on greater and greater significance in Broca's thinking. He found that in all the patients considered, the lesion was on the left side. Always circumspect, Broca added that he did not venture to draw any conclusion from that, and that he awaited new data. The continuation of the discussion on the same day reveals another theme too, whose future was still more promising: the relationship between loss of speech, memory and intelligence.[16] This April 2 was indeed a red-letter day for brain science.

All during these years Bouillaud's behavior is rather curious. As Marie[17] notes, as long as the site of the lesion in the third frontal convolution could be considered as an argument in favour of localization in the frontal lobes, Bouillaud applauded Broca enthusiastically; but when it was only a matter of considering the third frontal convolution as a special centre with a remarkably fixed and limited localization, Bouillaud just kept a cool silence.

Broca himself, however, developed a tendency to listen only to the voices that were favourable to him. At the 97th meeting of the Société d'Anthropologie on March 3, 1864, he read a communication by Prof. Ange Duval[18]: "Seat of the faculty of articulate language. Two cases of traumatic aphemia produced by lesions of the left third frontal convolution." The first case was that of a 34-year-old man who, after a fall on his head, presented complete loss of speech with retention of intelligence. Duval diagnosed a lesion of the left frontal lobe. The injured man died twelve days after the accident, and the autopsy proved Duval right. The second case was that of a child who, after a fracture of the left part of the frontal bone, lost the use of speech at the age of five. A year later, the child drowned, and the autopsy revealed a cyst that had replaced a blood clot produced by a deep contusion of the corresponding part of the brain. The continuation must be quoted:

> The observation was recorded in Toulon in 1849, and at that time there was no question of giving a name to the lesioned convolutions. But the situation of the cyst was determined with enough precision for it to be impossible to doubt a lesion of the third frontal convolution. ([57g], p. 214)

This tardy recovery of an old finding was somewhat inconclusive; what struck Broca, however, was that on well-nigh twenty autopsies to date it had been constantly found that aphemia lesions were situated on the left side. Again, a large number of aphemics still alive presented a more or less complete right-sided hemiplegia. Finally, lesions had several times been found on the third right frontal without impairment of the language faculty. Broca accordingly proposed the following cautious, provisional conclusion:

> It seems to follow from this that the faculty of articulate language is localized in the left hemisphere of the brain, or at least that it depends mainly on that hemisphere. ([57g], p. 216)

As Moutier[19] notes, Parrot[20] in 1863 had produced a right hemisphere on which was found:

> complete atrophy of the lobule of the insula and of the third convolution of the right frontal lobe, with preservation of intelligence and of the faculty of language.

For Broca, the piece of evidence that would have falsified his thesis would have been that of an aphemia produced by lesions of the right hemisphere. It is thus quite understandable that, in 1864, Broca began to feel confident. He withdrew into an increasingly dogmatic attitude in the face of Dax Jr.'s[21] claims of his father's priority in observing the specialization of the left hemisphere as well as Trousseau's[22] aspersions on the propriety of the term "aphemia". It was at this point that he wrote the long paper entitled "On the seat of the faculty of articulate language" which was published in the *Bulletin de la Société d'Anthropologie* on June 15, 1865.

Broca shows where he stands right from the opening:

> My communication relates to the singular predilection of aphemia lesions for the left hemisphere of the brain. ([57h]; see ([107], p. 109)

He then reiterates point by point his closing argumentation of March 3, 1864[23], emphasizing his last point: the presence of lesions of the right third frontal convolution without aphemic disturbances. These,

> only corroborated my opinion, since it was in the left third frontal convolution and not in the right that I had localized the faculty of articulate language. (ibid.)

Thus what had been only a tentative hypothesis now became a scientifically established fact. He goes on to deal with the theoretical difficulties raised by the special influence of the left hemisphere on articulate language. An initial fact established by Charcot and Vulpian[24] was that diseases of the right hemisphere were as frequent as those of the left, and yet "the vast majority of aphemics... have their lesion in the left hemisphere." That, says Broca, raises the question of functional differences between the two hemispheres. There clearly exists a manual preference for the right hand, which suggests left-hemisphere dominance. At a level of greater complexity, "that amounts to saying that, for language, we are cerebral left-handers."

Moreau de Tours[25] had observed a 47 year old woman, epileptic since childhood, who had never presented the slightest trace of aphemia in spite of extensive destruction of the left third frontal convolution. Broca has a clear explanation:

> ...Just as there are left-handed people... one supposes that there can be a certain number of individuals in whom the native preeminence of the right-hemisphere convolutions will reverse the order of phenomena which I have just indicated... ([57h]; [107], p. 115)

The patient observed by Moreau de Tours would have had to be aphemic

if the left third frontal convolution was the exclusive and constant site of
the faculty of coordinating word articulation, but in this case the deficiency
of the left hemisphere had caused a compensatory switch to the right hemisphere.

Broca then wonders why such a phenomenon of substitution does not
happen in all cases of aphemia if both hemispheres take part in the language function. From the explanations he gives, the conclusion is that
hemispheric specialization is the result of training, and efforts at reeducating aphemics have never gone very far.

Thus was forged the theory of left-brain dominance. As Moutier ironically remarks,

> the dogma had been created. From now on observers or brains would
> be in the wrong when observations did not confirm the reigning doc-
> trine, but the third frontal could no longer be left out. ([285], p. 25)

For quite a long time afterwards, scientists would define themselves in
relation to these positions.

Pierre Marie[26] would be the one to put an end to this long magisterium
- to some extent at least - with his article entitled "The left third frontal
convolution has no special role in the function of language", published in
the *Semaine Médicale* of May 23, 1906. In the meantime, systematic exploration of the phenomena of speech loss generated an extensive body of
practical clinical knowledge. This many-side activity initially took the form
of an effort to specify Broca's picture of aphemia, which, thanks to Trousseau,[27] took on the definitive name "aphasia."

THE SEARCH FOR APHASIA

> The state about which I am to speak to you was called "alalia" by
> Prof. Lordat in 1820; M. Broca, in 1861, thought it necessary to call it by
> the name "aphemia"; but since "aphemia" in Greek means "infamy",
> the term was clearly inappropriate. M. Chrysaphis, a distinguished
> Greek-born scholar of Greek, thought the word "aphasia" far
> preferable.
> Trousseau [395]

What was the reason behind Trousseau's[28] polemic against Broca regarding the appropriateness of a single term? The pedantry of the issue has
been raised by many, the first of them being Broca himself. In his reply to
Trousseau, he gives etymological justification for his rejection of the word
aphonia, meaning loss of voice, the word *alalia*,[29] which signifies muteness,
particularly deaf-muteness, and the word *aphasia*, expressing the state:

of an individual... whom timidity or confusion momentarily prevents
from speaking. [57f]

He goes on to say that he would have preferred the word *aphrasia*, derived from a Greek verb meaning not only to speak but to speak clearly:
"My desire to stray as little as possible from the usage of the Greek language made me give up this word" and choose *aphemia*, as yet untried for
scientific applications. The whole reply is courteous in tone, and ironic,
too, when he dissipates the ambiguity of *aphemia* as a synonym of *infamy*.[30]
But did Broca really believe that there was only a lexical disagreement between
himself and Trousseau?

Whereas language loss was accepted by all as a self-evident fact, the choice
of a label presupposed an interpretation of the nature of that loss, if not of
the underlying etiology. Two theses were available. Some regarded it as no
more than a mechanical disturbance of the organisation of speech movements[31] corresponding to a kind of motor amnesia, as Bouillaud and Broca
thought. Others saw in it a deeper disturbance of a conceptual nature that
impairs not only the speech formation mechanisms but also the mechanisms of thought formation. This dilemma had been latent in discussions
for a long time.[32] It acquired particular acuity in the late nineteenth century.

Laborde,[33] Parchappe[34] and Baillarger[35] would express their doubts as to
the intellectual integrity of aphasics; Trousseau stated his certainty. In his
clinical lectures, the account of each of the cases could be the opening
chapter of a novel in the Naturalist style. From his literary education Trousseau derived the art of observing others, and his sensitivity to each person's
language mannerisms. He possesses a sense of the arresting phrase,
and of the quaint or touching detail.[36]

One essential characteristic strikes him in the picture of the disturbance:
the presence of amnesia. However, the accepted notion of amnesia makes
him wonder what the exact nature of the disturbance is in an aphasic who
shows himself incapable of pronouncing the words of his own language.
Have aphasics forgotten only the words, and not the thoughts of which
they are the expression? With Condillac[37] and Warburton,[38] he leans towards those who regard words as necessary and even indispensable to thought.[39]
Intelligence, he finds, has to "corporify" its ideas;

> thus there is in aphasia not just loss of speech, but there is lesion of
> the understanding. ([395]: see [107], p. 257)

In 1906 - more than 40 years later - Pierre Marie[40] was still pointing the
finger at the dominant aspect of the picture of aphasia. In all aphasics, he
finds,

there is a more or less pronounced disturbance in the comprehension
of spoken language. ([253a], p. 5)

However, this disturbance of comprehension is not limited to language
alone, and Marie reports simple experiments[41] which, according to him, demonstrate this. He arrives at the following viewpoint:

It is that in aphasics there is something much more significant and
much more serious than loss of word-meaning; there is a very marked
diminution in general intellectual capacity... ([253e], p. 7)

At the time of Broca and Trousseau, in 1865, Baillarger[42] read a paper
"on aphasia from a psychological viewpoint" to the Académie de Médecine. He first examines simple aphasia, which presents two categories of
disturbances:
(1) loss of speech and writing,
(2) loss of speech with writing intact.

One could therefore:

become aphasic in two ways, either by losing one's memory of the
signs of language, or by forgetting the movements required for the articulation of words. ([18b], p. 586)

Though it may seem possible to agree in the first case on an explanation
in terms of amnesia, in the second case such agreement is more difficult. Is
there really a memory of the movements necessary for speech? Baillarger
disputes this, basing himself on observation of the behaviour of the child
during acquisition of the native language.
It is not the effort to remember the organisation of articulatory movements that holds the child back in his verbal development, but the obstacles that the instrument places in his way. The conclusion is inescapable:
"in these conditions memory factors are therefore almost non-existent."
([18b], p. 587)
Bouillaud had proposed another explanation for these disturbances. They
are to be attributed to the lesion of a coordinating or legislating organ of
speech.[43] Baillarger does not conceal his skepticism about this; but he appeals
to the authority of Parchappe[44] who believes, "that it is not indispensable
here to bring in a special organ for the coordination of movements."
(p. 590)
Baillarger then studies: "aphasia with perversion of the faculty of language where there is no disorder in the coordinating apparatus." He postulates that there exists: "for speech, besides the voluntary motor incitation,
the involuntary or spontaneous motor incitation." ([18b], p. 593)

We shall soon hear this idea again.

Whereas Broca came to believe that there is only a single focus of the lesion causing loss of speech, his approach met with two kinds of objections in the years 1865-1870.

The first is of a philosophical if not metaphysical nature. Parchappe writes:

> Human speech is a highly complex act which presupposes in the agent various skills, and which requires, for it to be realized, the involvement of perfectly distinct organic actions. ([300b], p. 679)

He seeks a middle way between supporters of localization and those who, like Gratiolet, held as unassailable the principle of organic unity of the brain:

> The structural arrangement of the brain[45] allows us to understand how the brain, as a centre of action, preserves its organic unity while including a multiplicity of organic elements of action relative to various conditions of realization of the unitary function. ([300b], p. 690)

The second group of objections were anatomical in nature. Two reasons were principally advanced:

(1) the multiplicity of lesions routinely encountered in the course of autopsies. Such was the position of Archambault[46] in 1866, and of Proust.[47] Pierre Marie, citing Vulpian's[48] 1864 lectures, criticises Broca for failing to recognise the importance of lesions of the temporo-parietal lobe, later to be demonstrated by Wernicke.[49]

(2) the existence of cases of aphasia without lesion of the left third frontal convolution. Already in 1863, Parrot, with a case of lesion of the right third frontal but without aphemia,[50] and Charcot, with a case of aphemia with lesion of the left hemisphere but an intact frontal lobe, had provided data which should perhaps have made Broca more cautious.[51] Besides those who embraced the dogma of the left third frontal, like Charcot,[52] observers following Bastian[53] and especially Wernicke[54] became open to the idea that aphasia might come from lesions situated in different cortical territories. We thus find a twofold expansion taking place: an expansion of anatomical sites where a lesion is found to cause disturbances of speech; an expansion of the clinical features of aphasia - the clinical picture would diversify continually.[55]

Investigators were accordingly on the way to a pluralistic conception of the disorder, while still striving to integrate each particular aspect into a systematic theoretical perspective. The discoveries of Fritsch and Hitzig[56] and those of Meynert[57] gave a new somatic reality to these undertakings. The era of Associationist theories had begun.

Fleury established a contrast between "aphasia", the disturbance of language through lack of transmission of the cerebral conamen to the motor apparatus, and *aphrasia*, the disturbance of intelligence conceived as an inability to construct a sentence intellectually.[58] William Ogle, in his *Aphasia and Agraphia*, proposed a coherent picture of language deficits, contrasting *amnemonic aphasia* with *ataxic aphasia*, and *amnemonic agraphia* with *ataxic agraphia*.[59]

In London in 1869, Bastian[60] published an article "On the various forms of loss of speech in cerebral disease".[61] For Bastian, words are basically re-vivifications of sound impressions.

Referring to Bain's[62] ideas on the sensation of muscular movements, and holding with Maudsley[63] that words are "motor intuitions" of thought, he identifies the centres known as motor language centres as "kinesthetic centres". The speech centre is a "glosso-kinesthetic centre";[64] the centre for writing is a "cheiro-kinesthetic centre". The language function is supported by the interaction of four specialised centres: the visual-verbal centre, the auditory-verbal centre, the glosso-kinesthetic centre and the cheiro-kines-thetic centre.

Language disorders are derived from this schema. There are four different types of disorder: *amnesia* (inability to remember words, and significant disturbance of thinking), *aphasia* (loss of speech and writing), *aphemia* (loss of speech), and *agraphia* (loss of writing).

When Bastian published his first communications in 1869, the location and even the existence of sensory and motor or kinesthetic centres had not yet received experimental verification. The discoveries of Fritsch and Hitzig, which followed shortly afterwards, provided the concept of "centre" with an indisputable status of scientific truth, while in 1873 Ferrier[65] localised the auditory centre in the first temporal convolution.

From this point on, Associationism enjoyed a period of success. In 1872, Broadbent[66] adopted Bastian's model and added an intellectual centre having the function of higher coordinating centre.

At the same time, Wernicke[67] was attempting to define a systematic picture of aphasia. To understand aphasia, it is necessary to distinguish language and thought, two independent processes. Normal language (oral at the basic level) is made up of arbitrary symbols, verbo-motor and auditory elements which contain no characteristic peculiar to the symbolised object. It is an error on the part of psychologists and linguists[68] to claim that the driving force of language is the conceptual synthesis of sensory impressions provided by the object.[69]

Integrity of hearing is therefore the sine qua non for language. In the case of the individual who has learned to speak, the visual images of objects can trigger the word directly, but auditory verbal images are always activated during this process and exert a monitoring function. Wernicke excludes from the domain of aphasia disorders of a conceptual nature which Finkelnburg[70] had described with the name *asymbolia*. Asymbolia is a disturbance of intelligence, that is, a disturbance of the synthesis of qualities proper to the object. Aphasia is not a disturbance of intelligence.

Wernicke proposes a systematisation in which the frontal, motor region is the seat of the representation of movements, and the temporal, sensory region is the seat of the representation of sounds. The *fibrae propriae* that converge in the insular cortex form the intermediate arc between representations of sounds and representations of movements. Depending on the site of the lesion along this pathway and the centres involved, the disturbance will take a specifiable form. The diversity of clinical pictures of aphasia can be analysed into the simple or combined forms of *sensory, motor* and *conduction* aphasia.[71]

Kussmaul[72] proposed a model with four word-image centres: *acoustic, phonic, optic* and *graphic*, under the control of a centre of conception, the *ideogenic* centre. For Kussmaul, aphasia could not be dissociated from asymbolia since language cannot be dissociated from thought. Kussmaul, however, rejected the term "asymbolia" in favour of "asemia", which he took from Steinthal.[73] Speech does not merely reproduce what has been thought; it also stimulates thought and produces ideas. As a mechanical expression of thought, speech may be impaired at the various stages along the way from conception and judgement to mechanical articulation.[74] We must accordingly distinguish "dyslalias" or disturbances of articulation due to the peripheral organs, "dysarthrias" or disturbances of articulation due to impairment of the centres for mechanical production of language, "dysphasias" or disturbances of diction, that is of the use and grammatical arrangement of words, and "dyslogias" or disturbances of thought formation.

Aphasia therefore does not exist as a nosological entity. Under this name, a large number of symptoms have been amalgamated which are in fact of different nature.[75]

It is illusory to search for a seat of speech understood as a simple, overall function; one can only describe and analyse disturbances of very diverse functions which come into play in the exercise of speech, writing and other means of expression. As for defining precisely the seat of a particular function, it is found that Exner's[76] efforts at assigning a precise seat to the graphic centre, for example, show the absurdity of such an undertaking.

Lichtheim's[77] monograph *Über Aphasie* (1884) offers a perfect systematisation of the point of view of the hybrid Associationists[78] as well as an excellent illustration of the theoretical character of their method. The forms of aphasia which he describes have been established by deduction. Clinical observation only comes afterwards to confirm its correctness. The basis of his model is taken from the development of language in the child. This, Lichtheim says, begins with a phase of pure reflex imitation, the echolalic phase, in which the child acquires the images necessary for language - acoustic images of words, motor images of articulatory movements[79] - formed in areas of the brain constituting "verbal acoustic centre A" and "articulatory centre M". If we add to this schema centres and connection pathways for reading and writing, we get a complete systematisation of the cerebral organisation of language functions, from which Lichtheim then derives seven forms of disturbance with seven corresponding forms of aphasia.[80]

Up till 1881, Associationist theories had a negligible impact in France. Charcot[81] now began to carry the deductive method preached by Lichtheim to a limit where it became apparent that it must part company with anatomical and clinical fact.

His conception of language is a mosaic made up of many different pieces at the theoretical level, and is just as theoretical when it comes to describing or justifying the different forms of aphasia. Charcot assumes a common intellectual centre, to which the centres of object images are subordinated. Thus the idea of a bell results from the association of auditory, visual, tactile and other images which the perception of the bell has deposited in the brain's sensory centres. These different images simultaneously perceived by the different senses are centralized by the intelligence in such a way that one of the images evokes all the others. Such images come into being independently of language. Ideas are not subordinated to words; words may disappear without the ideas of objects being erased; but we associate, with the images of the object, the images of the word that represents the object.

A cerebral lesion will destroy either a sensory or a motor verbal centre, or several at once. It may also destroy not the centres themselves but the pathways that link them. The picture of aphasia will thus include word-deafness, word-blindness, motor aphasia and agraphia. Ombredane remarks:

> Thus aphasia would be dismembered into a multiplicity of partial deficits which would lead to loss or dissociation of sensory or kinesthetic input in which language finds its raw material. ([293], p. 69)

Reaction became necessary, and the reaction that occurred opened the way to a new understanding of the discoveries that had been made in the study of aphasia over the previous quarter-century.[82]

EMERGENCE OF KEY CONCEPTS

> Today the field of aphasia has considerably grown, and subdivisions
> have been established which did not exist ten years ago. Since aphasia
> includes all the disorders of language, there are as many principal forms
> as there are functions of language.
> *Grande Encyclopédie du XIXᵉ Siècle.*

By the end of the nineteenth century, the brain had become familiar, explored territory. Its surface was endowed with a precise toponymy[83] which, in a way, gave anatomists a sense of security. This approach, however, belonged to an earlier stage of knowledge in which science was classification and inventory.

The physiologist's approach was newer. It borrowed its analytical tools from physics and mathematics and relied on the objectivity of measurement as a means of grasping the essence of the phenomena it sought to explain. A new discourse on objects grew up, from which clinicians for a time seemed to be separated.

As clinical study concentrated on the concept of aphasia itself, that concept seemed to become submerged in the multitude of detailed observations, and inquiry seemed to have lost its object along the way. Reaction had to occur, as Ombredane[84] remarks, even among supporters of the notion of verbal imagery.

A unitary vision of aphasia first required an understanding of the structural unity of the brain in its functional diversity. Opponents of localization theory had probably sensed this. Thus Parchappe, who had objected to an excessively limited conception of speech localization.[85] In the same communication, he stressed that it is the integrity of coordination between the different zones of the cortex that guarantees the integrity of its functioning. ([300b] p. 698)

The idea that the central nervous system as a whole contributed to the production of language was destined for considerable development, but that development was anticipated by Sigmund Freud[86] when, at the end of the century, reacting against geometric Associationism, he cast the problem of aphasia in a new light. By replacing the narrow concept of centres with the concept of functional circuits (anticipated by Wernicke in his theory of conduction aphasia), Freud led clinicians to a better understanding of what they observed.[87] The clinical form of aphasia depends on the site of the lesion, its proximity to or distance from a given motor or sensory functional centre, or its situation on the coordination pathways between those centres.

Freud was joined by Déjérine[88] in this effort of simplification and clarification. Déjérine defined aphasia as the loss of one or more of the modalities of language, with preservation of the apparatus for reception and exteriorisation of words. He distinguished "true aphasias" (impairment of "inner speech" and lesion of the language zone as he defines it)[89] and "pure aphasias" (inner speech intact and lesions having their focus outside the language zone).

All the disturbances making up the true aphasias can be reduced to loss of verbal images imprinted on brain cells and the disorders remotely caused by these losses in all modes of language, because of the intimate connections uniting the different verbal centres.[90]

Pure aphasias appear as extrinsic symptoms, not affecting verbal images. They are determined by the isolation of one part of the language zone. According to Miraillé,[91] the lesion is then constituted by the destruction of linking fibres of the language zone with one of the general centres of corticality.

Déjérine described one of these types of pure, sub-cortical aphasias: "pure word blindness".[92] He also claimed the existence of "pure word deafness", but held that it was much rarer. Later, after numerous controversies, Déjérine was compelled to accept the idea that only the motor form should be recognized as a sub-cortical aphasia.[93] Like Wernicke, he constantly refuted the hypothesis of the existence of a graphic centre, which Exner[94] had localized at the foot of the second frontal convolution, because clinical work had never provided a single instance of pure, isolated agraphia which was not the relic of a motor or sensory aphasia.[95] Déjérine's thinking meshes significantly with the ideological context of his time. He rejected the extreme consequences of an excessively systematic Associationist theory because he believed in the basic unity of the central nervous system, but he could not completely give up the simplifying notion of language centre. He pluralized it. He borrowed from the technology of his time, especially the notion of "image" from photography. The model of what occurs in the nerve cell is found in the chemical operation occurring on the photographic plate. For the mechanistic theories of preceding periods, brain science at the turn of the century substituted theories suggested by chemistry and electricity.

A quarter of a century before Déjérine's ascendancy in France, Hughlings Jackson[96] in England was expressing views not in conformity with the teaching of Broca. Jackson's thoughtful opposition to the views of Broca concerned Broca's determination to localize the seat of the language faculty with indisputable anatomical precision. The very notion of language faculty bothered Jackson, who saw in this sort of terminology a throwback to the medieval mentality. For him, the brain was only the instrument of a

THE BIRTH OF NEUROLINGUISTICS

function that could not be reduced to brain alone; the motor aspect of language behaviour was only the most complete form of the mechanisms governed by the cortex, but not thought itself. It thus followed that the site of thinking could not be identified with the site of the movements facilitating its communication.[97]

The man who is now regarded as a founder of the English school of neurology had difficulty in getting a hearing until Arnold Pick,[98] who recognised the value of his theories, dedicated to him *Die agrammatischen Störungen*, published in 1913, two years after Jackson's death. This is why (leaving aside chronological order) we have postponed discussion of Jackson and his work until this point.

Henry Head,[99] who was in a sense Jackson's successor, gives three main reasons why Jacksonian theory remained in limbo for so long:[100] the pedantic cautiousness of Jackson's style, the fact that his thinking and his terminology had been heavily influenced by Herbert Spencer,[101] and finally the very nature of Jackson's ideas, so far removed from those then current in medicine that they isolated him from any support he might have received from normal science.

Jackson himself was not cut off from the scientific world of his time. He knew its predominant ideas, but retained a critical attitude to them. He had met Broca at the Norwich Conference,[102] and was aware of the contributions of Dax and Trousseau. His teachers in neurology had been Thomas Laycock[103] and later Brown-Sequard;[104] however, it was the writings of Herbert Spencer[105] that served as the catalyst to his thinking.

In Spencer's work he found the conception of dissolution, which he applied to the interpretation of pathological phenomena. That lead him to a new conception, a hierarchy of functional levels within systems.

In his theory of brain and consciousness, Spencer, who had studied the work of Hartley,[106] claimed that the reflex act was the borderline between physical and mental life. The more perfected and ingrained a behaviour is, the more automatic and unconscious it is. The instincts are innate reflex sets. Human behaviors are not innate but acquired in the first years of life. To the extent that human behaviour becomes more and more complex and less and less automatic, the role of memory becomes crucial. Interpreting clinical phenomena of aphasic impairment in this context, Jackson put forth the view that there are two hierarchically dependent levels of speech production, which are linked to one another: the automatic and the voluntary.

Such an interpretation, which was close to that of Baillarger[107] but also provided it with a theoretical framework, was obviously not well received. Bastian objected that it seemed improbable that the same phenomenon, language, could be served by two different anatomical substrates. At any rate, Bastian claimed, the preservation of the automatic aspect of language could be explained in terms of the strength of emotional states releasing the inhibitions preventing the voluntary act.

As Riese[108] notes, the dissolution theory derives from a surprisingly simple observation. An aphasic who, in the course of an examination, is unable to repeat simple words such as "yes" and "no", is nevertheless able to produce these very same words when he is brought around by the examiner to giving a spontaneous answer. How could it then be thought that lack of speech can be attributed to the destruction of a hypothetical language centre when, in certain circumstances, the lack of speech disappears?

For Jackson, the voluntary, being the least organized, is therefore the most fragile and disappears first in a pathogenic situation. The automatic, on the other hand, the most organized, is the most ingrained and therefore the last to disappear, by a kind of functional involution. In fact, the voluntary has been built on the automatic, which appears the first in phylogenetic order. What is voluntary and reasoned emerges from what is automatic and impulse-driven. The Jacksonian perspective was already close to Darwin's; it was preparing the way for a coming generation of anatomists who would see the traces of slow evolution in the structure of homo sapiens' brain.

Voluntary language thus appeared to Jackson as the highest stage in its evolution, the most complete production of creative mind, and (as Herder[109] and Wilhelm von Humboldt[110] had also believed), the very expression of human freedom. The basic unit of language thus defined is not the word, with its imprecise contours and its semantic diffuseness, but the proposition.

Supported by the work of Hitzig and Ferrier,[111] Jackson believed that at different levels of automatisation, movements that appear identical are in fact governed by different hierarchised centres. All the zones of the central nervous system with their functional specialisations are thus involved in speech behaviour at some point.

In the left hemisphere is the seat of expressive, propositional, purely voluntary language. Speech perception is localized in the right hemisphere, as is automatic, involuntary language. It is in the right hemisphere that the processes of activating images take place, while voluntary reproduction of images depends on the left hemisphere. One may dispute the contrasts set up by Jackson, but his basic position anticipates the present direction of research.

Jackson's work is wide-ranging and complex. He saw, for example, the problem of outward speech as opposed to inner speech, but he relates it to a difference in degree of intensity. From Monakow[112] to Vygotsky[113] and Goldstein,[114] authors closer to our own time have confronted this problem without being able to provide more satisfactory explanations. To clinician and anatomist alike, Jackson showed the error of localizing a brain function at the site of the lesion that seems to cause impairment or loss of that function. Jackson took some time to come to this conclusion.[115] It opened the way to a fruitful line of thinking that led to the present state of our knowledge in this area where, as Jasper[116] once noted, it is perhaps preferable to speak of centres of destruction rather than centres of function.

To theorists of aphasia Jackson showed that the nature of what would later be called linguistic competence had more to do with the ability to formulate propositions and link them together than with recall or articulatory command of words in isolation. He was therefore the first clinician to attempt a theory of language where the mechanism of the individual act of speech is defined in terms of the functionality of the discourse produced, thus contrasting the automatic with the conscious. Pick[117] and then Monakow[118] and Head[119] would pursue this direction.

However, Jackson had already begun the analysis of intelligence in evolving behaviors which do not merely succeed one another in the course of the child's development but which will be an integral part of the adult's behaviour, anticipating in this approach the later work of Piaget.[120] At the same time, he had shown the futility of separating intelligence from language and of using impairment of intelligence as an explanation of language deficits. Pierre Marie, in undertaking a complete reevaluation of the problem of aphasia, would soon find himself at the same crossroads.

NOTES

1   See p. 138.
2   Ombredane ([293], p. 28) notes the curious attraction of the frontal lobes for observers of the period. Zoologists and anthropologists had come to believe that the exceptional development of these lobes was a specifically human characteristic.
3   See p. 149, n. 9.
4   See p. 149, n. 28.
5   See p. 149, n. 28.
6   See p. 149, n. 10.
7   "...When, a few days after hearing M. Auburtin's arguments, I found in my ward one morning a dying man who had lost the faculty of articulate language 21 years before."
8   "...Whatever question was put to him, he always replied "tan, tan"... That is why throughout the hospice he was known by the name Tan" [57a]. Tan was 51 years old.
9   "Until then, without rejecting that theory and without overlooking in the slightest the data favourable to it, I had felt a great deal of hesitation before the contradictory data that exist in science."

10 See [57b].
11 "...Since each of the three great convolutions of the upper level of the
frontal lobe successively crosses in the frontal-posterior pathway all the
regions in which aphemia lesions have been found up till now" ([57b],
p. 357).
12 MacDonald Critchley [84b] is mistaken about Leborgne's age, for he
refers to him as "an old hemiplegic" (p. 61f.). In fact, Leborgne (Critchley actually writes "Laborgne") was only 51 years old. Then, on p. 62,
he writes of the Lelong case: "One month or two later..." Nearly six
months had actually passed between the two cases: 17/iv - 27/x 1861.
13 "...It is a much more doubtful question if the faculty of articulate language depends on the frontal lobe as a whole or specifically on one of
the convolutions of that lobe..." ([57b], p. 357).
14 "I am therefore inclined to attribute to pure coincidence the absolute
identity of the seat of the lesions in the two patients" ([57c], p. 407).
15 Jean-Martin Charcot (1825-1893). See [62a,b].
16 That same day, Martin explains: "There was at Montpellier a famous
example of partial loss of the language faculty. Broussonnet had lost
his memory or the ability to pronounce nouns; he could not articulate
one" (*Bulletin de la Société d'Anthropologie* 4, 1863). Note that this case
in mentioned by Lordat, who speaks of verbal amnesia.
17 Pierre Marie [253c].
18 He was an honorary member of the Société d'Anthropologie of Brest.
19 Moutier ([285], p. 22).
20 Parrot [301].
21 Marc Dax, author of a paper presented in 1836 at the South of France
Medical Congress at Montpellier, in which he claimed that forgetting
the signs of thought was caused by lesions of the left hemisphere. This
communication, fallen into oblivion, was recalled by Gustave Dax, son
of the foregoing, in 1863 (on March 24 to be exact), in a paper submit-
ted to the Académie de Médecine. The editorial committee did not
publish this paper until almost two years later.
22 See p. 131, n. 34, and p. 162.
23 Only his statement of March 3, 1864 was much more cautious. "These
two facts support an observation I made two years ago, and which is so
strange and so subversive that it could not be presented without a great
deal of qualification. I had been struck by this fact that, in my first
aphemics, the lesion always occupied not only the same point in the
brain but also the same left side" ([57g], p.216).
24 Alfred Vulpian (1826-1887).
25 Jacques Joseph Moreau de Tours (1864-1884).
26 See p. 185.

27 See above.
28 See [395] as well as [57f].
29 A term used by Frank and Lordat. The term "aphasia" was apparently used for the first time by *Sextus Empiricus*. See [302].
30 "A modern Greek told you he was shocked to see a degrading expression being applied to decent patients. Aphemia for him is a synonym of infamy. I do not disagree; it would not be the first time that a word had changed its meaning" ([57b], p. 269).
31 Those movements that Lordat regarded as "synergies".
32 See pp. 112ff.
33 Jean-Baptiste Vincent Laborde (1830-1903).
34 J. Parchappe (1800-1866): [300a].
35 See p. 151, n. 73.
36 He writes: "Marie Keller read for a large part of the day, however, and we were all fooled by this appearance of intelligence; but some time after, when she was cured, she admitted to us that she read with her eyes but not 'with her stomach' - a singular manner of saying that she did not understand what she read" ([395], p. 202).
37 See pp. 68ff.
38 William Warburton (1694-1779).
39 "I therefore find it difficult to subscribe completely to the theory of M. Lordat, who professes the absolute independence of thought and speech" ([395], p. 255).
40 See p. 149, n. 9.
41 He cites the case of a skilled cook who could no longer fry an egg. "He begins by breaking his egg very awkwardly and empties it into the pan without any precaution to avoid bursting the yolk, then he puts butter on top of the egg, adds salt and pepper and puts the whole thing in the oven." ([253a], p. 9). Perhaps the order was what had been misunderstood - the cook had cooked an egg *au miroir* (baked), surely the most difficult type.
42 See [18b].
43 ([50b], p. 17).
44 See [300b].
45 Parchappe states that the matter involves "some figures which I am putting before the Academy, and which show... the reality of the participation of the transverse fibres of the corpus callosum in the formation of the lamellous expansions in the cerebral convolutions" ([300b], p. 690).
46 Théophile Archambault.
47 Adrien Proust (1834-1903) writes: "Trying to make of aphasia 'a means of diagnosis from the point of view of localization'... seemed a risky undertaking" [328].

48 Pierre Marie comments: "Among these cases of disturbances of the left frontal lobe with aphasia of which Vulpian speaks here, almost all presented lesions of Wernicke's area, or the lenticular area; it would have been sufficient for Broca to take these into account in order to avoid his error" ([253c], pp. 88f.).
49 Karl Wernicke (1848-1905): [419b,c].
50 See p. 156.
51 From 1861 to 1869, Moutier [285] believes, 29 cases favourable (to Broca's thesis) and 17 unfavourable cases were added to the dossier.
52 See above, n. 15.
53 Henry Charlton Bastian (1837-1915).
54 See n. 49 above.
55 See the work of Fleury [126], Ogle [291a], and Proust's thesis, n. 47 [298].
56 See p. 152, n. 86.
57 See p. 152, n. 84.
58 Louis-Joseph Fleury (18??-1852): see n. 55 above.
59 Ogle [291]: see n. 55.
60 See n. 53.
61 He also published, in the same year, another article which is the theoretical basis of the article on disturbances of language [21b].
62 Alexander Bain (1818-1903).
63 Henry Maudsley (1835-1918).
64 Ombredane, whom we are following here, points out that these phrases are not found in the 1869 publication but in the 1897 one.
65 David Ferrier (1843-1928).
66 W. H. Broadbent (1835-1907).
67 Here we are speaking of the 1874 paper.
68 See pp. 131ff.
69 ([293], p. 77).
70 F. C. Finkelnburg [124a].
71 Pierre Marie writes: "As far as language is concerned, the cerebral cortex is said to contain a centre for auditory images and a centre for visual images of language. If, by any kind of lesion, these centres happen to be destroyed, the patient, deprived of his auditory images, becomes incapable of understanding what is said to him and to speak in a normal way - he is affected by 'word deafness'. If he is deprived, by another lesion, of his visual images, he becomes incapable of reading or writing - he is affected by 'word blindness'. These two, word blindness and word deafness, are the components of Wernicke's sensory aphasia" ([253c], p. 118).
72 Adolf Kussmaul (1822-1902): [215].

73 Heymann Steinthal (1823-1899).
74 Kussmaul made use of Lordat's analysis.
75 "These disturbances have the common features of being cortical and affecting language" ([293], p. 90).
76 Sigmund Exner (1846-1926). Marie writes: "If there existed - as has been taught - in the human brain innate centres for reading and writing, you can be sure that man would not have taken so many thousand years to be able to translate his oral language into written language" [253c], p. 125).
77 Ludwig Lichtheim (1845-1928).
78 Thus called because they held theories that superimpose on centres for images a higher association centre, an intellectual centre where ideas are said to be formed. See Ombredane ([293], p. 70).
79 ([293], p. 96).
80 ([293], p. 77).
81 See above, n. 15.
82 Marie comments: "One could in all truth give to this period in the history of aphasia the name 'geometric phase'. To sum up, to state the classic doctrine of aphasia, they began with an undemonstrated hypothesis and on this hypothesis erected an entire edifice which then had to be demolished. I have tried my best to do this." ([253e], pp. 119f.)
83 Broca [57i].
84 ([293], p. 107.
85 See p. 164.
86 Sigmund Freud (1856-1939): [343b]; see also [137].
87 Ombredane ([293], p. 107) comments: "The basic aspect of aphasia was said to be not the loss of one or another order of images than difficulty in evoking an image from an order determined by other images".
88 Jules Déjérine (1849-1917) worked with his wife Augusta Déjérine-Klumpke (1859-1937).
89 For Déjérine "the language zone" is that portion of corticality in which are stored the centres of the "language images": the foot of the third frontal, the pli courbe and the back part of the third temporal convolution [96c].
90 "Every brain cell", explains Déjérine, "receives an imprint, an image, and constitutes the basis of the memory of that imprint, that image; memory is only the totality of these partial images. Spontaneous evocation of these images, mnesic evocation, requires the absolute integrity, psychic and material, of these images, that is, of these cells and their connections with neighbouring cells" ([96c], p. 417).
91 Charles Miraillé [269].

92 "Different varieties of word blindness: (1) word blindness with agraphia
or very marked disturbances of writing; (2) pure word blindness with
integrity of spontaneous writing and writing from dictation" [96b].

93 Déjérine [96a].

94 See above, n. 76.

95 ([293], p. 124).

96 John Hughlings Jackson (1834-1911): see [177a,b,c].

97 Riese states ([343b], p. 100): "The target was Broca's assumption of a
faculty of language to which Jackson denied any existence".

98 Arnold Pick (1851-1924), neurologist. See [316a,b,c,d].

99 Henry Head (1861-1940), neurophysiologist. See [177a,b,c].

100 See ([177a], pp. 1f.).

101 Herbert Spencer (1820-1903): [377a,b,c,d,e].

102 According to MacDonald Critchley, Jackson had presented a paper there
[193b].

103 Thomas Laycock (1812-1876): see [223].

104 Charles Edward Brown-Sequard (1817-1894): [60a,b].

105 Riese writes: "It goes without saying that Jackson acknowledged his
great indebtedness to Spencer from whom he borrowed the principle
of evolution and its opposite, i.e. that of dissolution" ([343b], p. 88). In
the same way, MacDonald Critchley, in his article "Jacksonian ideas..."
[84a], points to the influence of Darwin.

106 See pp. 98ff.

107 See p. 151, n. 73.

108 Riese [343b].

109 See p. 84, n. 42.

110 Wilhelm von Humboldt (1767-1835): see [190a].

111 Hitzig: see p. 152, n. 86. Ferrier: see above, n. 65.

112 Constantin von Monakow (1853-1930). [272b] is a classic. The concept
of "diaschisis" is not yet found in the first edition of his book [272a].

113 Lev Semenovitch Vygotsky (1896-1934).

114 Kurt Goldstein (1878-1965): see [155b,c].

115 As Critchley [84a] points out, Jackson, in 1899, admitted that he had
formerly spoken of centres for will, memory or emotion, but added
"To have imagined such centres had been a mere artifice".

116 H. H. Jasper [200a].

117 See n. 98 above.

118 See n. 112 above.

119 See n. 99 above.

120 Jean Piaget (1896-1979).

2. Language as an Object of Science

The emergence of theories of language

> Linguistics will have achieved its finest triumph when it shown that the connections and distinctions which it establishes coincide with the natural divisions based on physical study of the races of man.
> Broca ([57d], p. 239)

The eighteenth century[1] had opened the way to careful investigation, in the nineteenth, of the individual phenomenon of speech in its normal and abnormal aspects.

However, no dialogue took place between grammarians and physiologists. When a grammarian and philosopher of language like Steinthal[2] developed an approach to a linguistic theory of aphasia, his efforts met with little interest.

Clinicians also seemed to believe that nature spoke Latin. This reduction of pathological data to the categories of traditional grammar explains many errors in interpretation of impaired speech. Deficits were characterised in terms of loss of nouns, adjectives or verbs, or of the relations linking these words together in the sentence.[3]

Seventeenth and eighteenth century study of speech articulation with the practical aim of reeducating deaf-mutes laid the foundations of a phonetic analysis from which the comparative grammarians would benefit. Physiologists do not seem to have drawn much profit from it.

At the same time, however, anthropology emerged as a fertile blending of the contributions of various disciplines. Broca, who was one of its most convinced advocates, accordingly found himself interested in contemporary findings of the science of language;[4] but he was looking at the wrong linguistics.

Broca and his contemporaries may perhaps be excused in this. Ferdinand de Saussure, who was only 14 in 1871, would have to take a long detour through historical grammar and comparative method before realising the possibility of a pure linguistics, and laying the foundations of that discipline in his *Cours de Linguistique Générale*, published about fifty years later by his pupils.[5] Nor did the concepts that are presented in that book come easily to Saussure; and they were slow to win recognition.[6]

Saussure's first breakthrough was a clear distinction between two sets of phenomena: one belonging to the sphere of langue (language as linguistic code), the other belonging to the sphere of parole (speech, or the use of the linguistic code by speakers). (This classic distinction was later rounded

179

out by a second one contrasting the individual reality of speech with that of discours, the discourse which it constructs - a contribution of Gustave Guillaume.)

Saussure's second theoretical breakthrough put linguistic analysis on a level where linguists and neurophysiologists would one day be able to understand one another. In it, Saussure subsumed the domain of language and its manifestations under the broader heading of a general semiology.[7] He thus attached language phenomena to the existence of an all-inclusive symbolic function which appears as one of the main constants of cognitive life.

The most decisive contribution of the *Cours* was to regard linguistic units as valeurs (values), that is, as "elements of a system".[8] Saussure thereby made it possible to understand the internal cohesion of these linguistic elements and, eventually, to grasp the processes involved in their dissociation, as found in the pathological manifestations of language. The system concept also implied the concept of oppositions,[9] which would have an equally wide application in the investigation of aphasic impairments.

With Saussure, the term "functioning" synthesises the static concept of "system" and the dynamic concept of "mechanism". He moves from the object, langue conceived of as a catalogue of forms organised into systems, to the subject, the speaker, who invests these forms in a mechanism - which implies movement - resulting in discourse.[10] Of course, Saussure's terms are often outdated: he speaks of "acoustic images",[11] "verbal images",[12] and while he believes the relationship between linguistics and psychology[13] important, he is of the opinion that:

> the study of languages requires explanations from the physiology of sounds, but does not provide it with any in return. ([358b], p. 21)

Thanks to the new ideas in the *Cours*, however, the perception of language phenomena and language itself was being transformed.

Saussure's ideas were introduced in Russia by Karcevskij,[14] who transmitted them to Roman Jakobson[15] and N. S. Trubetzkoy.[16] Baudouin de Courtenay[17] had already put forth the idea that there must be two distinct kinds of phonetics, depending on whether the investigator is studying the concrete sounds as physical phenomena or as phonic signals used for the purpose of communication within a speech community.[18] Under the influence of Saussure's teaching, this statement acquired a fresh new meaning for Jakobson and Trubetzkoy, resulting in the development of phonology. Proposition 22 passed by the First International Congress of Linguistics[19] officially inaugurated the new discipline.

The work of the linguists of the Prague School and the Copenhagen

Linguistic Circle - which benefited along the way from the work of the generalist phoneticians like Rousselot[20] and Grammont[21] - led to the identification of the distinctive features of phonemes and to the definition of the concept of distinctiveness, which emphasises their functional character; also to a more correct representation of what a linguistic system is: a set of minimal elements, all interconnected, each of which has its value only by virtue of the networks of identities and differences which serve to distinguish it from all the other elements. This Structuralist vision of language would be a factor bringing linguists and psychologists closer together.

Most of all, the work of phonological analysis would open up new possibilities for the understanding (from a neurophysiological and neuropsychological point of view) of perceptual and interpretative mechanisms of discourse reception and verbo-motor mechanisms of discourse production.

The convergence of the different scientific disciplines of language and language behavior is due to the consistency with which these phenomena where being grasped in their dynamic aspect. Gustave Guillaume,[22] a linguist whose importance has still not been fully recognised a quarter-century after his death, built his whole theory of language and language behavior on the implications of this dynamic aspect.[23] Guillaume summed those implications up in a striking phrase: "It takes time to think, like it takes time to walk."

He called this time "operational time", the necessary substrate of "any phenomenon and any movement". The study of the processes by which thought is invested in discourse during the language act constitutes a new linguistic discipline which Guillaume called the "psychomechanics of language".

Guillaume's ideas actually answered to the concerns of clinicians, who, following the directions started by Pick,[24] Monakow[25] and Goldstein,[26] would find that the impaired verbal behaviors of aphasics involved a dissociation of the conceptual impetus from the motor impetus of the language act.[27]

From now on, the complementary parameters of time and space could no longer be excluded from linguistic thinking, while the very concept of language found itself redefined under a new perspective.[28]

Beginning in the 1930s, a method of analysis of language data known as "distributional analysis" developed in the United States. It attempted to liberate the linguist's investigation from the Greek and Latin framework that had too often weighed on the thinking of those studying languages historically related to the classical languages. Its development was favoured in America by the fact that New World linguists were dealing with 150 language families which were totally alien in their structure to the Indo-European languages and posed novel problems of analysis. On the basis of a significant but limited number of utterances collected in natural conditions and constituting the "corpus", the distributional linguist proceeded to compare utterances in various ways and attempted to isolate characteristic groupings and configurations. When this task was completed, the elements were isolated and their environments defined.[29] The regrouping of "distributions" of elements then led to the setting up of distributional classes at the different levels of organisation of the utterance.[30]

Constraints that hold between elements by virtue of their environment, as also possibilities of substitution of one element for another at a given point in the utterance, are expressed in a diagrammatic representation in which the horizontal axis, called the "syntagmatic" axis, represents the combinations of elements of a lower rank to make up those of a higher rank, while the vertical, "paradigmatic" axes represent the substitutions possible at any given point:

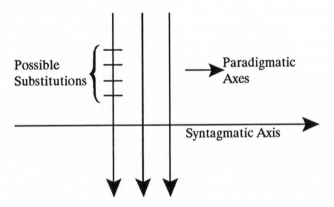

This kind of representation returns by another route to the dynamism of language behavior and the two factors of space and time on which Guillaume built up his theory. However, the progress of these two approaches occurred quite independently, for reasons geographic and historical as well as cultural.[31] It was not till after the Second World War that the two currents of inquiry succeeded in meeting, as exemplified on the European side by the post-war Structuralism of André Martinet.[32]

Born from the strict discipline of distributional analysis, and in the very environment in which it had flourished, a new departure was launched in the 1960s which, under the direction of its chief architect, became *Generative-Transformational Grammar.*

Chomsky's book *Syntactic Structures* marks the beginning of this new period of linguistic thinking. The basic goal of linguistic analysis of a language L is to separate the grammatical sentences from the ungrammatical. The grammar of L will thus be regarded as a device which generates all the grammatically correct sentences of L and none of the ungrammatical sentences.[33] From the outset, it became clear what opposed this viewpoint to that of the Distributional school: rejection of the notion of "corpus" and of the rather narrow way in which grammatical formalisation had been conceived.[34]

"Competence" in the new approach was to be defined as the system of rules internalised by speakers, by means of which they are able to utter and understand an infinite number of sentences they have never heard before. The basic goal of inquiry is thus to construct a theory able to account for the linguistic creativity[35] of the speaker. The notion of competence is contrasted with that of "performance", defined as the manifestation of speaker competence in language behavior.

With his keen analysis of linguistic data, Chomsky soon found that below the visible structure of the utterance, which he called its "surface structure", there was a deeper level where thought meets language. He accordingly added into his theory the concept of "deep structures". The process of deriving the surface level from this deep level required the introduction of transformational rules, to complement the initial "rewrite" rules. As a consequence, the problem of meaning came back into linguistic analysis.

In *Language and Mind*, first published in an abridged version in 1968 and then in an enlarged edition in 1972, Chomsky considers the contribution of generative-transformational theory to knowledge of the functioning of mind. He postulates that:

> as far as we know, possession of human language is associated with a specific type of mental organisation, not simply a higher degree of intelligence. ([72d], p. 70)

This finding has two consequences:

(1) There is no reason to believe that the emergence of language is due to a more complex development of structures found elsewhere in the animal world;
(2) There must be universals of language as there are supposed to be universals of thought.

The first consequence, like the second, reintroduces into contemporary debate a dimension that links it to the great philosophical discussions of the past; Chomsky finds a remote ancestor for his views in Cartesianism.[36] In fact, the development of his thought leads Chomsky to even more remote sources, medieval and ancient. Confronted with a body of theory still under development and revision, it is difficult to reach a conclusive assessment. In the debate on innate ideas, to which we will shortly return, Chomsky's contribution is of major significance. Luria[37] with fairness and balance remarks:

The decisive step made by modern structural linguistics, with its theory of generative transformational grammar, opened up for the first time new paths toward the hitherto inaccessible scientific analysis of the stages of conversion of thought into extended speech. ([246k], p. 11)

We shall leave him the last word.

THE NEUROPHYSIOLOGICAL ASPECT OF LANGUAGE THEORIES

Verbal communication, the process of human communication through the use of natural languages has been the subject of considerable study in various disciplines... However, the data of these sciences cover only a part of the whole real complexity of the process of human communication...
Luria ([246k], p. 3)

Lordat's[38] attempt to establish a theory of language on the basis of pathological data had been premature. Jackson[39] restated the problem in more precise terms, while at the same time theorists of aphasia were losing themselves in the maze of Associationist diagrams. This was a period when the emergence of the first concepts of modern linguistics could win the attention of neurophysiologists if the gulf between the two disciplines was not almost unbridgeable. The first step would be taken, not by a linguist or a neurophysiologist, but by a philosopher.

The first edition of Bergson's *Matter and Memory* appeared in 1896.[40] Bergson noted that the concept of "image" as used by the Associationist theories was an abstract and intellectual concept which did not fit with the physical constraints inherent in the very nature of the nervous system. Neither, however, did this concept agree with a linguistic reality that seemed completely misunderstood by medical men:

To hear some theorists discourse on sensory aphasia, we might imagine that they had never considered with any care the structure of a sentence. They argue as if a sentence were composed of nouns which call up the images of things... Consider then the host of different relations which can be expressed by the same word, according to the place it occupies and the terms which it unites... Essentially discontinuous since it proceeds by juxtaposing words, speech can only indicate by a few guideposts placed here and there the chief stages in the movement of thought... But I shall never be able to understand it if I start from the verbal images themselves... For images can never be anything but things, and thought is a movement. ([32b], pp. 158f.)

The capital error of Associationism has been:

> that it substitutes for this continuity of becoming, which is the living
> reality, a discontinuous multiplicity of elements, inert and juxtaposed.
> ([32b], p. 171)

These images that the philosopher attacks in the name of linguistic realism would in turn be knocked down by the neuro-physiologist. In 1906, Pierre Marie[41] began a series of articles on "Revision of the question of aphasia". In the very first article published in the *Semaine médicale* of May 23, 1906, and entitled "The left third frontal convolution has no special role in the function of language", we find the following statement:

> If we wish to acquire true ideas on aphasia, we must get rid of every-
> thing we have read and learned about word images, about receptive or
> conduction aphasia, about language centres, etc., etc. ([253a], p. 5)

In fact, the Associationists had abandoned the anatomical and clinical method. When sensory aphasia was created,[42] it met with general acceptance. Such an attitude led to an inflation of the concept of verbal images, with each taking its place in some special centre interconnected with all the others.

In the article in the *Semaine médicale* of October 17, 1906, "What is to be thought of subcortical aphasias (pure aphasias),"[43] Marie states:

> Writers have claimed that words, syllables, penetrating by means of
> hearing to the level of that sensory zone [i.e. the zone of auditory per-
> ception of words], left there a special category of images of language
> called by them auditory images, which are supposed to be stored in a
> piece of convolution next to that already supposed to house the com-
> mon auditory centre, i.e. in the posterior region of the left first tempo-
> ral... First we should be told how these wonderful auditory images are
> actually put in place. Does every word get inscribed in this verbal audi-
> tory centre? But then what an enormous development this centre would
> require, especially in polyglots!
> ([253b], p. 36)

The speculative imagination had placed an obstacle in the way of inquiry, the metaphor of the image. The later introduction of the term *engram*,[44] first used in German, and which soon entered universal usage, would enable the concept to establish itself. On the other hand, the real nature of minimal linguistic units was far from being grasped by the scholarly mind of Pierre Marie.

In his effort at specification and classification, Marie forcefully indicates the necessarily intellectual character of aphasic impairment.[45]

Aphasia is thus not merely a loss of word meaning, and it is apparent,

> that there is a considerable deficit, especially in the stock of things
> learned by didactic procedures. ([253a], p. 8)

With the aphasic impairments he has just characterised, Marie contrasts anarthric impairments:

> In contrast with aphasics, anarthrics understand perfectly well what is
> said to them, even if it involves complicated sentences; they can read
> and write....[46]

By means of this distinction between aphasia and anarthria, Marie reintroduced into the debate a dimension of language too often forgotten during the nineteenth century: its twofold character, which for Cordemoy[47] had made it the unique meeting-point of the spiritual and the material. This is the reality Saussurean theory sought to capture with the langue-parole distinction, although this latter pair of terms is both wider in scope and more flexible. In Marie's view, this twofold nature of language is matched by a twofold nature of pathological disturbances.

That interpretation would be opposed by some - Head[48] in particular, who, sharing Déjérine's[49] ideas on this point, denied the existence of anarthria, and saw aphasia basically as a disturbance of statement. It was, however, in relation to Marie's viewpoint that noeticians and antinoeticians[50] would subsequently define their positions, which bears witness to the importance of his role at the time.

Marie's opposition to Associationist theories and schemata culminates in his article "On the function of language" [253d], which presents itself as a "rectification with regard to an article by M. Grasset".[51] Reviewing the constant contradictions he has found in the course of his clinical career between the expectations of theory and the facts he has encountered, Marie states that the clinical picture of aphasia appears to be quite different depending on whether it is studied in books or after nature.

Marie also recalls the classic view of sensory centres of reception, and declares: "In one word, out of the four centres of language claimed by M. Grasset, I claim only one" ([253d], p. 96)

Some years before, Binet,[52] in his *Experimental study of intelligence* (1903), had brought together several pieces of research on the relations between thought and image, and thought and word. He had shown that thought could on no account be reduced to an automatic set of images, and that there could be thought without images. This kind of psychological research would later find its counterpart in the work of linguists.[53] For Binet, what can best define thinking as a feeling, an intention of the mind: "to think is to refrain from acting".

Around the same time, the psychologists of the Würzburg school were following a parallel course.[54] To explain the process of directed recall, Watt speaks of an attitude of consciousness, a general orientation of attention, a set (*Einstellung*) on the part of the subject, all this formation requiring the involvement of a time factor which Gustave Guillaume would later place at the core of language behaviour.[55] In these several approaches, one idea in particular points to the most profound element in Jacksonian thinking: thought like speech is a dynamic process which includes the parameters of time and space. That was also the position held by Bergson, who spoke of the "movement of thought".

Investigating the problem of the understanding of verbal propositions, Bühler[56] covered the same ground. In 1919, Lotmar,[57] studying an aphasic who basic impairment was in word-finding, set up a series of tests the results of which corroborated the hypotheses of the Würzburg school.

These investigations situated the problem of the interpretation of language impairments on a level of much greater complexity than Associationist theories had led to expect. In this context, the work of two researchers was of particular significance: Pick[58] and Monakow.[59]

Presenting language as a dynamic, temporal process, Pick devoted a monograph published in 1913[60] to the study of agrammatical impairments. Wilhelm von Humboldt[61] and, following him, several linguists of the end of the nineteenth and beginning of the twentieth centuries, held the basic principle that the unit of thought is not the word but the sentence, a definition of which Pick borrows from Stern:[62]

> The sentence is the expression of a general attitude embodied or about to be embodied in a content of consciousness. ([385], p. 164)

As Swoboda[63] showed, in order to understand, a human being must be in the very psychological situation where what is to be understood has been said. The relationship between speaker and hearer is a basic determinant of the sentence. Reasoning in accordance with these broad principles, Pick finds that in aphasia - as the Jacksonian principle of dissolution would predict:[64]

> the affective component of the mental attitude expressed by the sentence is what is most resistant. ([293], p. 213)

Grammaticalisation and syntax are the milestones that mark the transformation of unformulated thought into verbal expression. The analysis of the stages of this transformation is very important, because for the aphasiologist the question is to what extent agrammatism results from a disorder of thinking, a disorder of speech or an elective disorder of the grammaticalisation function. Pick distinguishes the conceptual impetus and the linguistic impetus of the sentence, recognising that they are not conterminous. He concludes that agrammatism may be related either to a fault in thought formation,[65] or to a difficulty in word-finding, or to a particular inability to manipulate the grammatical categories within the sentence.[66]

Already in 1900 at the Twelfth International Medical Congress in Paris[67], Pick had developed the idea that the auditory centre could be regarded as a stopping-point for the language mechanism.

This conception was found useful for the explanation of clinical facts. In 1902, Monakow and Bonhoeffer[68] noted the difference in agrammatisms proper to motor aphasia and sensory aphasia,[69] Kleist[70] in 1913 distinguished agrammatism and paragrammatism; and in 1922 Isserlin[71] went on to reformulate the question completely. It was first necessary to identify an agrammatism due to impairment of the thought impetus prior to language - Pick's pseudo-agrammatism which Goldstein[72] had in fact isolated in 1913 - and then an agrammatism caused by an impairment of language activity; the first type revealing itself in a faulty arrangement of grammatical forms, the second by an impoverishment of grammatical forms.

Monakow attempted to go beyond clinical phenomena and account for the neurophysiological processes underlying them.[73] The innovative character of his investigation was due firstly to the importance he ascribed to the time factor in his interpretation of cortical localizations. He therefore spoke of "chronogenic localization of functions" such as movement and language, contrasted with "geometrical localization of symptoms". He believed that the cortex functions because of the interaction of all of its parts.

Cortical activity is an associative activity facilitating the synchronisation of sensorimotor processes, and the integration of successive processes. It ensures, Monakow says, "the development in time of kinetic melodies", with each elementary process having to intervene at the precise moment for a specific action. Thus a brain lesion does not destroy stored images but opposes an action of diaschisis[74] to the activation and ecphoria[75] of time-ordered sensorimotor processes.

Monakow and Mourgue[76] in 1928 undertook a study of language behaviour as a process subtended by a chronological structure. Their description shows how right the intuitions of Lordat had been, in spite of their subjectivity.[77]

In this system of representation of neurophysiological phenomena, the notion of "engram" has replaced that of "image". The engram is a dynamic entity whose localisation should be considered in a chronogenic way, according to a specified order of occurrence in time.

Thus, while linguistics would define the language act according to the parameters of space and time, models of neurophysiological explanation of verbal behaviour were appearing that emphasised the very same factors.

Discussing the "spatial schematics" of thinking, Van Woerkom[78] identified an impairment that he called "impairment of the geometric sense". The patient is able to recognise forms, even complicated ones, but cannot grasp relationships between the elements of these spatial complexes. Three concepts are affected in aphasia: space, time and number.

Mourgue[79] expanded the notion of geometric sense put forward by Van Woerkom. Behind impairment of the geometric sense he saw a more complex impairment of the function of "dividing up" (découpage) and "opposition". Space is basically distinction, dividing up, differentiation and opposition. Note how familiar these terms are to modern linguistics! A neurophysiologist had understood:

> Language is a system of conceptual differences represented by a system of phonic differences. ([293], p. 246)

The aphasic is able to perceive concrete units, forms, durations and simple numeric groups, but he is unable to apply analytical procedures to "divide them up", just as he is unable to relate them one to another.

Subsequently, the work of Lhermitte[80] provided support for these views by presenting aphasia as a basic impairment of constructive thinking in which disorders of spatial schematism occur.

These viewpoints broaden with Goldstein[81] and his Gestaltist explanation of aphasia as disturbance of figure-ground variations and loss of the categorial attitude. The effect of the lesion is to blunt the preeminence of figure processes over ground processes. It allows only global and diffuse reactions, and brings about a "de-differentiation" of figure and ground effects.

In aphasia, Goldstein finds, it is still legitimate to postulate forms in which motor impairment predominates. One should also postulate sensory forms, however, linked to the de-differentiation of sensory functions in general. In what is called verbal knowledge, there is an element of motor learning which is triggered in certain circumstances either by the stimulation of will or in a more involuntary manner. It is beyond doubt that in motor aphasia this motor content of memory is affected.

Goldstein also notes, however, that in numerous cases of motor aphasia the impairment seems to overlap into the representative sphere. The patient understands instructions imperfectly, and no longer grasps information given to him. He has lost the concept of number and the concept of spatial direction. Names of things have become true proper names for him - they no longer represent groups or classes. The patient has lost the "categorial attitude".

A common denominator is discernible in all these theories: language behaviour as a dynamic phenomenon closely involving the factors of space and time. Although some (first Head,[82] then Brain[83]) claimed that the study of aphasia has experienced a development without any contact with linguistic study, the two disciplines have followed pathways that are finally not just parallel but pointing to a single reality. From that point on, dialogue is possible.

NEW PERSPECTIVES ON IMPAIRED DISCOURSE

> When writers seek to conclude the analysis of aphasia with a general conception of language, we find them still more clearly abandoning the intellectualist language they had adopted following Pierre Marie, and in reaction against the conceptions of Broca. One can say of speech neither that it is an operation of the intelligence nor that it is a motor phenomenon; it is completely motor and completely intelligence.
> Merleau-Ponty ([266a], pp. 226f.)

Roman Jakobson was a scholar gifted with an acute sense of synthesis. From the outset of his career he grasped the unity in the teachings of Baudouin de Courtenay and Saussure, and, guided by Kruszewski,[84] he defined his own orientation. To him belongs the credit for having initiated the most fruitful dialogue with neurophysiologists. If neurolinguistics can now aspire to the status of an autonomous discipline, it owes this in the first instance to Jakobson and A. R. Luria, who were able to listen to and understand one another.

For Jakobson, linguistics should be called to play an important role in the study of aphasic phenomena. He was indignant whenever he found this role underestimated or ignored,[85] and he was pleased when it was recognised.[86] The studies of impaired communication opened up new pathways to linguistics for understanding its own central problems.[87] Luria shared this attitude of mind.[88]

It was the development of linguistic thought from Structuralism on that made such interdisciplinary cooperation possible as well as useful.[89] However, when the linguist tackles these kinds of problems, he must adopt a cautious and attentive attitude.[90]

In his effort to bring linguists and neurophysiologists into a common discussion, Jakobson begins by specifying the convergences:

> It is remarkable that already in 1878, two great pioneers, the Polish linguist Baudouin de Courtenay and the neurologist Jackson, had quite independently refuted the idea of an immediate transition between

words (or rather morphemes or minimal grammatical units) and 'an articulatory movement', a physical state. ([198b], p. 134)

He then points out the stages that marked the insertion of linguistic knowledge into the discussions of clinicians:

Some fifty years later, in 1928, the First International Congress of Linguists produced a call for systematic phonological research that would coherently link sound and meaning.[91](pp. 134f.)

In 1929, Wolpert:

was opposing the possibility of dissociating *Wortklangverständnis*, comprehension of the sound of a word, from *Wortsinnverständnis*, comprehension of the meaning of a word. (p. 135)

Phonology was nonetheless the initial meeting-point of the two approaches, as was apparent at the Sixth Congress of the French Phoniatric Society, where Froment and Pichon[92] "showed phonology's importance for the study of language disorders" (p. 135). According to Froment's view, a motor aphasic is not phonetically but phonologically impoverished.[93]

In 1939, Jakobson presented a paper to the Fifth International Congress of Linguists entitled "The phonetic laws of child language and their place in general phonology".[94] There he highlighted the relative regularity of child learning and the principle of interdependence of such learning. During the months that followed, Jakobson made a "comparative study of linguistic - particularly phonological - systems, in development and disintegration".[95] He presented his findings to the Uppsala Linguistic Society in 1941 in the monograph *Kindersprache, Aphasie und allgemeine Lautgesetze* (Child Language, Aphasia and Phonological Universals).[96]

A vision of synthesis was worked out[97] here in which Jakobson perceived:

an identity of the laws of implication in phonetic development of child language and in the synchrony of the languages of the world.[98]

This point of view to some extent reintroduced into the discussion the theme which we have met from antiquity to the eighteenth century according to which ontogeny repeats phylogeny. However, the most significant idea is brought in by means of this statement:

One cannot erect the superstructure without having created the necessary foundations, nor destroy the foundations without having destroyed the super-structures. ([198b], p. 100)

It is possible to speak of a "mirroring between phonological construction and dismantling".

It is worthwhile not to oversimplify this idea, which Jakobson refined and deepened as he went along. Kruszewski, in his *Summary of the Science of Language* (see note 84) showed that the two basic operations underlying verbal behaviour - selection and combination - are linked to two models of relation, explains Jakobson. Selection is based on similarity, combination on contiguity.[99]

In the combination of linguistic units there is an ascending scale of freedom. At the level of combining distinctive features of phonemes, this freedom is zero. It is marginal at the level of word formation. It becomes more significant at the level of sentence construction, and peaks at the level of combining sentences into longer utterances. However, speaking regularly implies selecting certain linguistic entities and combining them into units of a higher degree of complexity.[100] It follows from this that any linguistic sign implies two modes of arrangement: combination and selection.[101]

These two basic operations are affected by aphasic impairments. We can distinguish two kinds of deterioration: impairments affecting the similarity relation, which are accordingly expressed by disorders in selection processes, and those affecting the contiguity relation, which are expressed by disorders in combination processes.

For aphasics of the first type (impairment of the similarity relation, and therefore deficiency in selection), context constitutes an indispensable and decisive factor. The patient is able to complete incomplete words and half-sentences.

The main difficulty is found in initiating a sentence. As Freud noted, key constituents may be jumped, or replaced by vague anaphoric substitutes. A specific noun tends to be replaced by a very general one.[102] Impairment of the similarity relation, which Jakobson calls "internal"[103] causes difficulty in the arrangement of coded units according to this relation. Patients are able to combine two units within one message, but not to substitute one unit for another on the basis of their resemblance or contrast.

For aphasics of the second type (impairment of the contiguity relation, and therefore deficiency in word combination), the context rather "disintegrates".[104]

Discourse is made up of words related to one another in a particular way, and without specific interrelation of its constituents a verbal utterance is only a simple succession of nouns transmitting no proposition.[105] What is in fact impaired here is the ability to construct propositions or to combine simple linguistic entities into more complex units. The patient loses syntactic rules, whence the term "agrammatism" used to characterise the deficit. According to Jackson's observation, the sentence degenerates into a "word-heap".[106]

Disturbance of the contiguity relation, also called "external",[107] leaves the similarity relation intact. The typology of the two impairments is thus opposite. The two contrasting figures of speech, metaphor and metonymy, provide the most condensed expression of the two basic modes of relation: the internal similarity and contrast relation is what underlies metaphor, while the external contiguity and distance relation underlies metonymy.

In a paper presented in London on May 21, 1963 to the CIBA Symposium on Language Disorders, entitled "Toward a linguistic classification of aphasic impairments",[108] Jakobson noted that his views had met with an encouraging response from specialists, but that:

> on the other hand, their discussion of this dichotomy has led me to attribute to this division of aphasia into similarity and contiguity impairments a close connection with the classic sensori-motor dichotomy. ([198b], p. 137)

Following Osgood and Miron,[109] he goes on to say, "a correlation between these two dichotomies in aphasic syndromes" was explored by Wepman (cf. also Fillenbaum, Jones and Wepman, 1961);[110] corroborating experiments led Goodglas[111] to a similar conclusion; and the two dichotomies were expressly unified by Luria.[112]

In the light of these considerations, Jakobson suggests what he calls a "first dichotomy": impairments of encoding (combination, contiguity) and impairments of decoding (selection, similarity). Classic motor aphasia (Broca's) is the basic type of encoding impairment, while sensory aphasia (Wernicke's) is the basic type of decoding impairment.

The two other types of aphasia that Luria proposed in his monographs[113] led Jakobson to introduce a "second dichotomy": limitation and disintegration.

We thus find, in the first place, two attenuated forms: among encoding impairments, the aphasia called by Luria "dynamic", and among decoding impairments, the one he calls "semantic".[114] In the first case, which involves contiguity disorders, there is limitation of the combinatory possibilities along the syntagmatic axis; in the second, which involves similarity disorders, there is semantic disintegration along the paradigmatic axes.[115]

A "third dichotomy" involves the last two types of aphasia enumerated by Luria; it contrasts sequence/successivity with co-presence/simultaneity. At the phonemic level, "efferent aphasia" dislocates sequential concatenations of phonemes; in "afferent aphasia", it is the combination of co-present distinctive features that collapses.

In November of the same year (1963), at the Conference on Speech, Language and Communication organised by the Brain Research Institute, University of California, Jakobson presented a paper entitled "Linguistic types of aphasia", in which he takes up the same problem of classification.

His earliest observations on the principal dichotomy (contiguity vs. similar-ity[116]) were passed over in silence, he says. Towards the end of the 1950s he:

> was fortunate in finding the support and approval of experts in the field.[117]

He then returns to the concepts of efferent aphasia and dynamic aphasia and the second dichotomy.

Following this, Jakobson recalls the two most complex varieties of apha-sia: the one called by Luria "afferent" or "kinesthetic", in which - contrary to the efferent type of combinatory disorders affecting sequences of pho-nemes - it is the amalgams of individual phonemes that are disturbed at the time of encoding; and sensory aphasia, which also manifests loss of phone-mic distinctions. "Thus three dichotomies underlie six cardinal types of apha-sia," he concludes:

(1) combination (which implies contiguity), affecting encoding, as op-posed to selection (implying similarity), affecting primarily decoding;
(2) successivity as opposed to simultaneity;
(3) disintegration as opposed to limitation (the afferent and amnesic types do not belong in this final dichotomy).

Luria's long article "Basic Problems of Neurolinguistics" published in *Current Trends in Linguistics* (Vol. XII, Part 4, 1974) is a rather belated measure of recognition for the new discipline.[118] Luria begins by noting that the decisive role was played by linguists in their first steps to defining the problems of an analysis of phonetic structure. Since Trubetzkoy and Jakobson, it has been known that speech uses a set of elementary units which contrast by features in accordance with systems peculiar to each language. Thus as a kind of echo to Jakobson's ideas, Luria presents the birth of neurolinguistic research as dependent on the emergence of struc-tural linguistics, with its initial breakthrough being the description of the constituent features of the phoneme.

Citing Boskis and Levina's work on the perception of sounds by children affected by congenital aphasia, and that of Chistovich and Koshevnikov on the processes of identification and reproduction of phonemes, Luria finds that this kind of research illustrates the possibility of establishing a bridge between the analytical result of a linguistic theory, phonology, and the neurophysiological realities which are the origin of the activities of produc-tion and reception of speech.

The identity of Luria's views with those of Jakobson is shown in the conceptualisation of the problems posed by aphasia, which he deals with in chapters 2 and 3 of Part I of his book.[119] For the purposes of his own discussion, he takes up Jakobson's dichotomy, contrasting a neurophysiological analysis of encoding impairments (chapter 2) with an analysis of decoding impairments (chapter 3). He thus poses the problem of the linguistic encoding mechanisms:

> ...The encoding of verbal communication is based on two principal types of organisation: the syntagmatic organisation of coherent expression, on the one hand, and the paradigmatic organisation of the phonemic, lexical, morphological, syntactic and semantic units, of which the language is composed, on the other hand... ([246k], p. 52)

The question that arises is to what extent these two forms of language organisation are independent, and which brain mechanisms underlie them:

> The first person to ask this question was the eminent contemporary linguist Roman Jakobson. (In a series of articles published by him between 1956 and 1965). ([246k], p. 52)

These impairments have different somatic dependencies. Those manifesting themselves at the level of syntagmatic organisation are all caused by lesions situated in the frontal parts of the language areas, while those involving paradigmatic organisation are localized in the posterior parts of these same areas.[120] Luria's statements are very specific regarding the strict nature of these localizations, and he shows that they are not incompatible with the point of view he had already argued, according to which the idea of a direct localization in certain zones of the brain of the complex forms of psychological activity is best rejected.

> ...These factors are not localized in circumscribed areas of the cortex, but are distributed in the cortex and subcortical formations; moreover, each area of the cortex or subcortex makes its own specific contribution to the organisation of every complex functional system. ([246k], p. 53)

Luria discusses the question of cerebral mechanisms of language for encoding processes on the basis of these same views. There is no difficulty in postulating that the construction of a syntagmatically organised utterance is founded on psychological processes and brain mechanisms different from those processes and mechanisms underlying the mastery and use of phonemic, lexical and logico-grammatical codes.[121]

Luria thus basically seeks to illustrate, on a neurophysiological level, the interpretation of the linguist Jakobson. Further on, dealing with impairments of communication in patients who use what has come to be known as "telegraphic style", he again stresses the importance of Jakobson's contribution, noting the part played by Jakobson in studying impairments involving disorganisation of paradigmatic systems which are, he says, formed by relations of opposition at the phonetic, lexical and semantic levels.[122]

At this point, between neurologists and linguists, dialogue is henceforth well established; it remains to consider now the convergences of neurolinguistic discourse that have resulted.

NOTES

1   See p. 65.
2   See p. 177, n. 73.
3   Pierre Marie writes: "It would be particularly erroneous to think, as formerly, that this or that cell or cell group constitutes a centre for one of the parts of speech - nouns, adjectives, verbs, etc. - or even for syntax, which regulates the use of the different parts" ([253e], p. 138). See also Déjérine's remark, p. 177, n.90.
4   See Broca's text [57d].
5   The Cours de Linguistique Générale was first published in 1916. It was edited by Charles Bally and Albert Sechehaye with the collaboration of Albert Reidlinger.
6   "Nothing across the Atlantic matched Saussure's feeling for Whitney", as is noted by De Mauro [358b] and Hagège [170].
7   "One may thus imagine a science that studies the life of signs in social life... We shall call it semiology" (from the Greek semeîon, sign) ([358b], p. 33).
8   The concept of system recurs frequently in the Cours; p. 106 [358b].
9   "Up till now units have appeared to us as values, i.e. as elements of a system, and we have considered them mainly in their oppositions" ([358b], p. 182).
10 See chapter V of the Cours:"Syntagmatic relations and associative relations" (pp. 170-175); and chapter VI: "Mechanisms of language", pp. 176-184 [358b].
11 p. 26 of the Cours: "Man could also have chosen gesture and used visual images instead of acoustic images" [358b].
12 p. 30 of the Cours: "If we could embrace the sum total of verbal images stored in all people, we would find the social bond that constitutes language" [358b].
13 "What relations exist between linguistics and social psychology? Basically everything in language is psychological..." ([358b], p. 21).
14 Karcevskij had attended Saussure's lectures in Geneva from 1905 on. He returned to his homeland in 1917.

15 Roman Jakobson (1896-1982).
16 Nicholas Sergeievitch Trubetzkoy (1890-1938). He is, with Jakobson, the creator of *phonology.*
17 Jan Baudouin de Courtenay (1845-1929).
18 This presentation is found in Trubetzkoy's [396].
19 This Congress was held in The Hague, April 10-15, 1928. The text of this proposition is contained in ([198c], pp. 3-6).
20 Jean-Pierre Rousselot (1846-1924). He was the founder of experimental phonetics. See [351a,b].
21 Maurice Grammont (1866-1946), pupil of the Abbé Rousselot. See [160].
22 Gustave Guillaume (1883-1960).
23 See Roch Valin [398].
24 See p. 178, n. 98.
25 See p. 178, n. 112.
26 See p. 178, n. 114.
27 The collection of unpublished writings by Guillaume, with an introduction by Roch Valin [168c] may be consulted.
28 Particularly the Würzburg school. See p. 187.
29 "The environment of an element A being the effective arrangement of its co-occurrents (what remains when A is removed from the utterance), we speak of left, right environment", says the *Dictionnaire de Linguistique,* (G).
30 According to Jean Dubois' phrase, "Linguistic analysis is... distributional to the extent that, at each rank, the constituent units are analysed on the basis of the segments they belong to..." [106b].
31 These reasons are well analysed by Hagège ([170], p. 30).
32 André Martinet (1908-).
33 "The fundamental aim in the linguistic analysis of a language L is to separate the 'grammatical' sequences which are the sentences of L from the 'ungrammatical' sequences which are not sentences of L and to study the structures of the grammatical sequences. The grammar of L will thus be a device that generates all of the grammatical sequences of L and none of the ungrammatical ones" (Chomsky [72a]).
34 Bloomfield is the originator of the method of distributional analysis.
35 Creativity is defined as the speaker's ability to produce spontaneously and to understand an infinite number of sentences which he has never spoken or heard before, (G).
36 *Cartesian Linguistics,* 1966 [72b]. See Bouton ([51b], pp.28ff.).
37 Aleksandr Romanovitch Luria (1902-1982).
38 See p. 150, n. 50.
39 See p. 178, n. 96.
40 Henri Bergson (1859-1941). See [32a,b,c,d].

41 Pierre Marie was then 53 years old. He was beginning to enjoy the stature of a major figure.
42 See p. 176, n. 71.
43 See p. 163, and p. 178 nn. 92 and 93.
44 The concept of "engram" is still very much alive today. See for example an article by Richard F. Thompson ([392], pp. 209-226).
45 See p. 175, n. 41.
46 He adds: "...From these different characteristics, one can easily recognise the clinical picture whose description is to be found in the classic treatises under the name subcortical motor aphasia" ([253a], p. 16).
47 See p. 82, n. 3.
48 See p. 178, n. 99.
49 See p. 177, n. 90.
50 "We have got into the habit of grouping under the name 'noeticians' those writers who regard aphasia as a general modification of behavior... the 'antinoeticians' are those who have created a reaction against the foregoing tendency" ([293], p. 255).
51 Joseph Grasset (1849-1918).
52 Alfred Binet (1857-1911).
53 See p. 151, n. 61.
54 The main figures are: Marbe, Ach, Messer, Bühler, Selz.
55 See p. 179.
56 Karl Bühler (1879-1963): [62].
57 F. Lotmar [244].
58 See p. 178, n. 98.
59 See p. 178, n. 112.
60 [316c].
61 See p. 178, n. 110; ([190b], p. 42) and Gesammelte Schriften v, p. 445.
62 W. & C. Stern: ([385], p. 164).
63 Swoboda: Viertelj.schr. f. Wiss. Philos. 1903, p. 169.
64 See p. 172.
65 "As is found in certain imbeciles, just as in certain aphasics" ([293], p. 216).
66 "...because of uncontrollable verbigeneration that is freed up by impairment of the inhibiting centres whose existence Pick assumes at the level of the temporal region" ([293], p. 216).
67 See [316a].
68 See [44].
69 In motor aphasia, nouns are correctly used whereas the structure of the sentence is very deficient; in sensory aphasia, the general form of discourse is often preserved while within the sentence mistakes in wording occur ([293], p. 217).

70 See [209].
71 See [192].
72 See p. 178, n. 114.
73 See [272b].
74 This notion came to replace Goltz's (1834-1902) irritation by inhibition in Monakow's mind. He presented his views on diaschisis in 1911 in "Lokalisation der Hirnfunktionen", Neurol. Psychiatr. 17, 185-200.
75 Literally, "production outside".
76 C. v. Monakow and R. Mourgue [273].
77 Monakow and Mourgue wrote: "It seems indeed that it is the weakening of this [the first stage of the chronological language process - the setting in motion, originally instinctive] that conditions the enormous elevation of the threshold of ecphoria."
78 W. van Woerkom: see [46a,b].
79 By Mourgue should be mentioned [283a,b]. For the theory presented, see ([293], p. 247).
80 J. Lhermitte: see [237a,b,c].
81 We should mention in particular here [155a].
82 See p. 178, n. 99 [177c].
83 W. R. Brain: [54].
84 Roman Jakobson discusses him in his article "The Kazan' school of Polish linguistics and its place in the international development of phonology" ([198d], pp. 394-428).
85 Thus, in "Two aspects of language and two types of aphasia" ([198c], vol. II, pp. 239-259).
86 "Linguistic types of aphasia", which is contained in [198d], vol. II, pp. 307-331, begins as follows: "At present only a few workers in the field of language disorders still believe that the role of linguistics in the study of aphasia is unimportant."
87 "Aphasia as a linguistic topic" ([198d], p. 229).
88 Luria [246g]: "It is very important to mention that these studies have great significance for the further development of linguistics as well" (p. 10).
89 Jakobson often returns to this idea: for example ([198d], p. 290). We find the same idea slightly modified in Luria, e.g. in ([246k], p. 11).
90 ([198d], p. 240).
91 "This request was discussed at length at the First International Congress of Slavists", Prague 1929 ([198b], pp. 133-142).
92 J. Froment and E. Pichon: [139].
93 In the report cited in n. 92.
94 A paper prepared at Charlottenlund, Denmark, in the summer of 1939.
95 See the preface to ([198b], p. 7).

96 "When I was in Sweden, Collinder, who detests phonology, told me that he would like me to write a book for the Linguistic Society of Uppsala" ([198b], p. 11).

97 See "Phonology and phonetics" in [198a].

98 p. 55 of [198b].

99 Jakobson cites Alice in Wonderland: " 'Did you say pig or fig?' said the cat. I said 'pig', replied Alice." Which, by the way, in French becomes: "*Avez-vous dit 'cochon' ou 'cocon'? dit le chat. J'ai dit 'cochon', répondit Alice.*" What better illustration could there be of the universal character of the system?

100 The part played by these two operations had been noticed by Saussure. See chapter V of the *Cours*, p. 170: "Syntagmatic relations and associative relations" ([198a], p. 48).

101 ([198a], p. 49).

102 "Thus, in French, *machin, chose*, or in German, *Ding* or *Stückle*" ([198a], p. 51).

103 ([198b, p. 112).

104 "...which gives rise to the so-called 'telegraphic style' "([198b], p. 114).

105 ([193a], p. 65).

106 "a mere word heap."

107 "The components of any message are necessarily connected to the code by an 'internal' relation of equivalence and to the context by an 'external' relation of contiguity" ([198b], p. 110).

108 ([198b], pp. 134-154.

109 C. E. Osgood and M. S. Miron [270].

110 S. Fillenbaum, L. V. Jones and J. M. Wepman, in *Language and Speech* (1961), 4-9.

111 H. Goodglass and J. Mayer [158]. H. Goodglass and J. Berko [159].

112 A. R. Luria, 1947 [246a,b,d].

113 ([246d], p. 132 and p. 182); ([246b], p. 30); ([246a], p. 51).

114 Jakobson points out that the meaning of "Semantic" with Luria "deviates a little from the meaning given to this term with Head" ([198b], p. 144).

115 ([198d], p. 298).

116 There are two articles: "Aphasia as a linguistic problem", "Two aspects of language and two types of aphasic disturbances" ([199], pp. 53-82).

117 See nn. 109-110-111-112 above.

118 ([246i], p. 2561).

119 [246k].

120 In [246g] Luria is quite explicit: "As mentioned by R. Jakobson (1955, 1956, 1964, 1966, jointly published in 1971), lesions of the anterior parts

of the major hemisphere result in a marked deterioration of 'syntag-matic' organisation of verbal communication while the 'paradigmatic' of linguistic codes remains relatively preserved. In contradiction, lesions of the posterior cortical areas of the major hemisphere result in a breakdown of the paradigmatic organisation of linguistic structures in different levels (phonemic levels in lesions of the posterior parts of the left temporal lobe, articulatory systems in lesions of the lower part of the left post-cortical zone, semantic or logicogrammatical level in lesions of the posterior tertiary zone) while the syntagmatic organisation of the fluent speech remains preserved."

121 ([246k], p. 53).
122 on p. 95 [246k].

3. NEUROLINGUISTIC DISCOURSE

THE BRAIN AND LANGUAGE TODAY

> Injuries of the skull by weapons of war, causing superficial wounds of the cerebral cortex underneath, allow us to appreciate - often with remarkable closeness - the localization of the various brain centres.
> Marie [254] (1917)

Thirty years after Marie's statement, Luria comes back to the same theme in his *Travmaticheskaya Afaziya*:[1]

> As a rule brain lesions inflicted by firearms... provide one the opportunity to observe the effects of quite limited lesions. ([264a], p. 26)

Certainly, between 1917 and 1947 methods had evolved, concepts were specified, and the power of tools of observation and analysis increased, but the intention behind the approach and its teleological scope remained unchanged: to discover the sites deep within the enigma of the brain where language is articulated with the human body.

In carrying out this exploration, the neurologist now had available a body of knowledge that had widened considerably since the end of the last century. Note for example the establishment of a precise toponymy for the central nervous system.[2] This was a modest but necessary task in order to define the locations that were to be differentiated specifically because of their high degree of functional specialisation. That specialisation was now based on precise data, both histological and physiological. We have today a very detailed knowledge of the nervous tissues that is constantly being refined by improvements in preparation techniques and the use of the electron microscope. Following Meynert,[3] investigators precisely established the fact of a constant relationship between the cytoarchitectonic nature of these tissues and their function.

Forel[4] showed the error of the classic reticular conception. He stated that whereas each cell body is in contact with its neighbour, this contact is established by contiguity, not by continuity. Ramón y Cajal's[5] work corroborated the well-foundedness of this interpretation. With the identity of the nerve cell now established, all it needed was a name. In 1891, in an exposition of the findings of Ramón y Cajal, Waldeyer brought in the term *neuron*.[6]

There remained the problem of the nature of this contiguity of cell bodies. Out of the discussion that developed, the concept of *synapse*[7] was born. However, the very concept of synapse raised a fresh question concerning the mechanisms by which activity in the presynaptic element determines effects in the postsynaptic element. To the concept (going back to Galen) of excitation, i.e. production of activity in the postsynaptic element by the presynaptic element, had been added the concept of "inhibition"[8] following the work of the brothers Weber in 1845.[9] In an attempt as early as 1874 to resolve this problem of synaptic transmission, Du Bois-Reymond[10] had considered two hypotheses: the transmitting agent could be either the electrical current accompanying the activity of the nerve fibre, or a chemical stimulant secreted by the ending of the nerve fibre. Explanatory models were gradually developed. With Eccles,[11] these led to a kind of synthesis of the two theories.[12]

This was the background[13] against which the study of the mechanisms of neurosensory and neuromotor behaviors (language in particular) developed, as well as the interpretation of their pathological disturbances.[14]

In 1929, Hans Berger[15] demonstrated the possibility of gathering and recording variations in the electrical potentials of the human brain. His discovery gave birth to electroencephalography. Around the same time, the work of L. Lapicque became known; it showed the existence of a basal centre regulating nervous impulses by reflex self-regulation of neuronal polarisation. In 1941, P. Chauchard showed that this explained the physiology of sleep.[16] This regulatory centre was rediscovered in 1950 by neurologists of the English-speaking world.[17]

Also during this period, Western scientists became receptive to the work of Pavlov.[18] This provided both a method for exploring higher nervous activity and a coherent theory of learning processes. Syntheses appeared possible between these various paths of inquiry. P. Chauchard declares:

> ...One does not localize functions, but one finds elective zones where certain neuronal circuits involved in these functions are collected. This neurodynamics of the cerebral cortex... we owe our knowledge of it to the fifty years of efforts that led us, with Pavlov, to dynamic stereotypes, with Sherrington to spatio-temporal patterns, and with Lapicque to differentiations and fluctuations of chronaxies of subordination.
> ([70], pp. 10f.)

Luria arrives at a similar statement. It would be inappropriate, he says, to represent to ourselves this complex functional system by assigning faculties to limited groups of cells, and to localize these functions in definite, independent zones of the brain. This interpretation, he adds, can be readily adapted to representation of the cerebral organisation of speech processes.[19] Wilder Penfield,[20] an attentive and brilliant student of Sir Charles Sherrington, demonstrated this throughout the years 1946-1950.

At that time, Penfield was beginning to establish his cartography of the speech area with the help of Dr Preston Robb. His method, in cases where surgical intervention was deemed indispensable, consisted of various preliminary explorations ranging from X-ray to EEG and the Wada test[21] followed by exploration of the exposed area by electrical stimulation prior to actual cortic exaeresis:

> The invariable effect of simple electrical stimulation in any area of cortex is to produce interference with the normal employment of that area. ([307], p. 108)

These explorations, carried out with the patient continuing to speak, and used as a treatment for focal epileptic crises,[22] resulted in the accumulation of valuable data. We remain relatively uninformed as to the precise character of the language disturbances that could be provoked. The salient fact is the language arrest, termed aphasic arrest. On a more solid linguistic basis, the same procedure aided by new technologies would be taken up again during the 1970s by a number of neurologists in association with linguists.[23]

The mapping of the speech-area which Penfield succeeded in establishing by this method remains nonetheless highly instructive. Penfield distinguishes between the motor mechanisms of language - in which he identifies "vocalisation", elicited initially in the right hemisphere and later several times in both hemispheres, in a place in the precentral rolandic gyrus between those providing motor responses of the hand and throat,[24] and "control of voice" and "articulation", which are situated between the two main areas for ideational language, in the two rolandic areas[25] - and the mechanisms of "ideational language". Three areas are circumscribed:

(1) an extended area in the temporal posterior and parietal postero-inferior regions;
(2) a small area in the posterior part of the third frontal convolution, in front of the motor area for control of voice; and
(3) part of the supplementary motor area in the interhemispheric fissure, just in front of the rolandic motor area of the foot.

Having noted that the ideational mechanism of language is organised so as to function in one single hemisphere, Penfield observes that the transcortical association fibres are of certainly less importance that subcortical integration. He then states that the major posterior language area probably has projective connections with the pulvinar and the lateral kernel of the thalamus.[26]

In the 1970s, the implications of these findings and hypotheses were influential in the reorientation of perception to the search for locations in the brain where language is constructed.

During his explorations of the cortex, Penfield found himself several times in the presence of a curious phenomenon which he first reported in *The Sherrington Lectures*[27] of 1958. When electrical stimulation touches certain points in the temporal lobe, he explains, psychological responses are elicited from the patient which can be divided into two groups: "experiential responses" and "interpretative responses". If the electrical stimulation recalls the past, the patient experiences a "flashback".

These observations led Penfield to posit the existence of an 'interpretative cortex', besides the sensory cortex and the motor cortex,[28] by means of which:

> Every individual forms a neuronal record of his own stream of consciousness ...The thread of time remains with us in the form of a succession of 'abiding' facilitations. This thread travels through ganglion cells and synaptic junctions.[29] ([307])

Faced with the infinite complexity of a reality he was discovering for the first time, perhaps, by a quasi-experimental route, Penfield was acutely aware that this reality escaped his grasp every time he seemed to be getting close to it. He therefore came to believe that it must be situated at a completely different level.[30]

> We must claim, [he declares,] the existence of a brain mechanism of coordination and integration. If this machine (note the persistence of the metaphor) has any resemblance to other machines, there must be a place on which sensory influx currents converge; there must be a place whence emerge the motor influx currents to move the two hands in concerted simultaneous action.[31] We should therefore postulate neuronal circuits in which the activity of both hemispheres is in a way synthesized and blended - circuits whose activation facilitates the conscious organisation of activity.[32]

Already in 1936,[33] Penfield had arrived at the following conclusion:

> All regions of the brain may well be involved in normal conscious processes, but the indispensable substratum of consciousness lies outside the cerebral cortex... not in the new brain, but in the old... probably in the diencephalon. ([307], p. 21)

This statement raised many objections.[34] However, Penfield was able to point to the work of Morison, Magoun, Jasper[35] and many others on the reticular system with its non-specific connections, which he believed constituted an important initial anatomical confirmation.

In *The Mystery of the Mind*, published in 1975 with the subtitle *A Critical*

Study of Consciousness and the Human Brain, Penfield returned to these major themes that had marked his career as a scientist.

By virtue of the very dichotomy which he stresses between brain and mind, Penfield takes his place in a lineage of thought opposed to a completely materialistic view of man.

That position does not, however, bar him from some humour found at the end of the book. He has just pointed out that to suppose that consciousness or mind have a localization is to forbid oneself the understanding of physiology, and he finds that "the great Descartes"[36] was in error when he placed them in the pineal gland. He adds, bitingly:

> The amusing aspect is that he came so close to that part of the brain in which the essential circuits of the highest brain-mechanisms must be active to make consciousness possible. ([305c], p. 109)

A parallel reorientation of perception is expressed in Luria's work. Regarding disorders of verbal communication in patients affected by profound brain lesions, he notes that lesions involving the diencephalon and hypothalamus impair what he has described as "the regulator of the general tonus of the brain".[37] In such cases, of course, cortical tone drops significantly. The patient's whole behaviour bears the mark of a kind of basic inactivity, and his verbal communication is seriously disturbed, to the point of organic mutism.[38]

Penfield and Luria both seem to have realised here that they were touching on a deep level of conscious integration of the organisation of speech. However, on this point of agreement their interpretations diverge. For Penfield, investigation only touches mechanisms that leave beyond reach the very mystery of the mind, which science nonetheless aspires to reach some day. For Luria, investigation touches on the very wellsprings of conscious thought conceived as a phenomenon that is clearer and closer to the nature of linguistic phenomena.

Luria's view is as follows. The processes of analysis and synthesis of external stimuli, when they are mediated by speech, acquire a new structure. The formation of verbal behaviours is linked in a phylogenetic perspective to significant changes in the very structure of the functional system of the brain. With the emergence of what Pavlov called the "second signalling system", derived from abstraction and generalisation, a large number of direct signals,[39] the most complex forms of reflex activity, formerly the basis of animal behaviour, acquired specific new characteristics in man.[40]

The highest level of organisation of mental activity, which appears when the relation of the organism to the outside world is mediated by language, is of such a complex systematic character[41] that it cannot be regarded as resulting from the activity of any isolated cortical area. In the final analysis the nervous system as a whole is involved in this activity, if one thinks of its highest functions - in particular, the semantic function, and that very remarkable function of regulating and organising behaviour which language assumes in man.[42] At the present time, Luria writes, considering the state of our knowledge, we can only make conjectures as regards the cortical organisations underlying such systems.[43] That does not mean that we should throw in our lot with the noeticians[44] and, "limit ourselves to speaking of the activity of the brain as a whole." ([246a], p. 23)

Still less, he adds, should we speak: "in terms of spiritual processes which themselves have nothing in common with the brain".

Following such a path leads to the kind of "dead end" in which the great Sherrington found himself at the end of his career: "To separate mental activity from the brain would be to commit a grave mistake against the progressive development of science."

Despite the convergence of their approaches, both of which move towards the hidden inner structures of the central nervous system, the ideological gulf separating Luria and Penfield is quite apparent.

In 1976, the first volume of *Studies in Neurolinguistics*[45] appeared. We will focus on an article by George A. Ojeman entitled "Subcortical Language Mechanisms"; its approach is exemplary. Following a brief review of the history of the search for language localizations, Ojeman shows that, contrary to the classic approach which consisted of looking only at the surface of the cortex, an interiorisation of the investigation facilitates grasping of the deepest sites in the brain where language emerges, notably the thalamus and pulvinar regions.[46] He puts forward the hypothesis that from the pathological and experimental data gathered hitherto it would appear that the language functions of the thalamus go beyond those assigned to it by Penfield.

In the space of a few years techniques for exploring the central nervous system have become more and more sophisticated. There is no longer any need to open up, to explore directly, or to stimulate with points that, no matter how fine they may be, are like sledgehammers compared to the micromillimetre size of the structures under investigation. Scanning, axial tomography, radio-immunocalibration[47] - these are some of the procedures that now enable us to grasp the external and internal reality all at once. The models used to conceptualise nervous activity have also evolved. Electronics, cybernetics, and the use of computers provide the image of self-regulating systems (should one still say machines?). The mirror effect has become complicated by now, but it is still a mirror effect in which the creation of the human brain provides an image for the brain itself. In this perspective, what advances, practically speaking, have occurred? Taking up again the main themes of this long debate conducted down through the centuries, we shall attempt to provide an answer.

CONSTANT THEMES

> If there is one field where both a clear continuity and a formidable
> change between the biological world and the anthropo-social world are
> apparent, it is that of communication. Indeed, to consider the anthropo-
> social field, we are struck by these innovative features: (1) a cerebral
> apparatus of unprecedented complexity... (2) a language with double
> articulation, the only such system established in history and the develop-
> ment of life outside the genetic code.
> Morin, E. (1977): *La Méthode*: Paris: Seuil: I, pp. 336f.

Since antiquity, man's reflexion on his language has found itself faced
with the same questions at every new stage of knowledge; and in every age,
the formation of a learned discourse in keeping with contemporary mythologies and ideologies has given him the illusion of having satisfactory
answers.

At the beginning of this century, Pierre Marie believed that he was at
last putting an end to the thorny problem of innateness and learning in
human language: "I am convinced today that in the human brain there are
no more innate centres for spoken language than there are for written language" ([253e], p. 127).

Marie always opposed the concept of language centres, or even any centres
at all.[48] Up till the present time, he declares, we have never found the existence of a speech fibre which, originating from a cortical centre, would
travel into the pons and the medulla to innervate groups of nerve cells
controlling the executive organs of speech - the tongue, the lips, the palate,
and so on.[49] If there was an innate language centre, how could it be held
that centre lacks an anatomical executive pathway? The motor convolutions, which are innate centres, have their executive pathway, the pyramidal
tract.

The specialisation of language on the left side in the views of the time
affords Marie another argument, anatomical as much as physiological. The
innate centres, he finds, are always bilateral and even symmetrical: "How
can one claim the existence of an innate speech centre which is neither
bilateral nor symmetrical?"[50] ([253e], p. 135). Finally, pathology provides
him with an argument of a different kind. Deaf-mutes do not speak because they are deaf.

If there was an innate speech centre, Marie decides, deaf-mutes should
be capable of spoken language without any reeducation - it would be incomprehensible, to be sure, since it would fall outside the bounds of conventional language, but it would still be language, containing true words
with a "human form".[51] If this is not so and if the reality is in fact very
different, it is simply because "there is no innate speech centre" ([253e], p.
136).

Marie then goes on to pathological data and cites the case of children affected by right hemiplegia who never present aphasia provided that the hemiplegia occurred in the first years of life. The most natural explanation of such a fact would be to recognise that:

> since there is no innate centre for language, [language] could not have been destroyed by the brain lesion, the cause of the hemiplegia. ([253e], p. 137)

While there is no preformed centre for language in the brain, Marie continues, one must, on the other hand, recognise the presence in the left hemisphere of a zone in which lesioning gives rise to an aphasia all the more severe as the lesion is deeper and more extensive.[52] It is ironic to find that, in a footnote, Marie states that he is only using the word "centre" for ease of exposition, as it would be "impossible to suppose that these cases involved true centres according to the old conception of that word".[53]

There is really nothing surprising in this neurologist's position at a time when language was seen first and foremost as a social fact by linguists themselves.[54] Saussure mentions Broca's discoveries only to present (rather unconvincingly) the idea that[55] the localization of language in the left third frontal convolution "has been used to attribute a natural character to language" ([358b], p. 26).

Such an attitude was maintained all through the first half of this century. Vendryès, in his book Le Langage published in 1914 and still authoritative in the 1950s,[56] wrote: "Language could only have emerged as a social fact when the human brain was developed enough to use it" (p. 23) - a rather ambiguous statement, really, which leaves everything to the imagination when it comes to phylogeny.

Experiment showed Wilder Penfield that:

> there are four cortical areas in which a gentle electrical current causes a patient, who is lying fully conscious on the operating table, to utter a long-drawn vowel sound which he is quite helpless to stop until he runs out of breath. ([307], p. 199)

He goes on to say:[57]

> Curious as it may seem, this is the most striking difference between the cortical motor responses of man and other mammals, and it seems likely that it bears some relationship to man's ability to talk.

Penfield adds that there is another striking peculiarity of the human cortex which may also have a relationship to speaking and writing, and that is the relatively large areas devoted to mouth and hand. These remarks of Penfield's date from 1959. In 1967, Eric Lenneberg published his *Biological Foundations of Language*. In this book he cautiously tackles the problem of innate mechanisms of perception and response, and remarks that we must know if this hypothesis is compatible with a biological theory in general, and with neurological considerations in particular.

In a final chapter, Lenneberg is more explicit:

> There was a time, [he declares,] when 'innateness' was on the index of forbidden concepts... At present, biology does not more than to discover how various forms are innately constituted. ([230], p. 393)

The relevance of this viewpoint to language is clear, he goes on, if we omit from the discussion the problem of speech and motor production "and focus on understanding of language as a special form of pattern recognition". He appeals to the authority of Chomsky, who, in an appendix of his own, deals with the question under the title "The Formal Nature of Language".

This is not the first time Chomsky had expressed his views on innateness,[58] but Lenneberg's book gave his ideas an audience beyond linguistic circles. Here the domain of strict facts where neurophysiology would wish to confine itself is left behind, and we enter a speculative discourse which is both recursive and evolving, subject as it is to constant reformulation in the face of a reality grasped from various angles. Here the centre of interest moves from language[59] to the speaker, and the notion of competence develops from the object (language) to the subject (the speaker).[60] This shift also entails a modification of the concept of performance.[61]

Language associates sounds and meanings.[62] The concept of an "acquisition model" based on a "perceptual model" can only be understood if one accepts the notion of innateness making this acquisition possible.[63] When interest shifts from languages - particular facts - to Language - a general fact - it must be claimed that the systems underlying competence which develop it on an innate basis are founded on universals existing at all levels of organisation of language.[64] In reviving this concept, Chomsky cites the classic works.[65]

In this generalising perspective, the concepts of deep and surface structure are reformulated as follows:

> The deep structure contains all information relevant to semantic interpretation; the surface structure, all information relevant to phonetic interpretation. ([72c], p. 406)

As for Universal Grammar, a concept which is now revived, it can be defined as "the study of the conditions that must be met by the grammars of all human languages".[66] It is therefore a "theory of language structure"[67] which enables recognition of what is linguistically innate, and in which principles are identified, which, by virtue of the fact that they are not acquired, are to be considered as belonging to the conceptual equipment used by the learner in the process of language acquisition.

The pair of concepts "competence/grammar" thus represents a kind of middle term between two infinite sets of possibles in relation to the contrasting pair of realities "language/performance".

From this complex presentation emerges what some have termed a neo-Kantianism. Some years later, this latent thinking would be more clearly expressed, and Chomsky would be in a position to present a less ambiguous and more cohesive argumentation in debate with Piaget.

Again under the direction of Eric Lenneberg, there appeared in 1975 a volume by several authors entitled *Foundations of Language Development*. The paper by Marcus Jacobson, "Brain Development in Relation to Language", is a valuable contribution. The neurologist begins with a statement that it is still quite difficult to establish a causal relationship between neurobiology and language.[68] Brain localizations of language functions, which nonetheless constitute a preliminary stage for any study of this kind, do not succeed in giving us a clue to a neurophysiological explanation of language itself.[69]

Mentioning the approaches of Generative Grammar, Jacobson bluntly says:

> ...It is very doubtful whether they have any meaning in relationship to brain mechanisms subserving language. It is hardly an exaggeration to say that, in so far as the propositions of linguistic analysis refer to the nervous system, they are uncertain, and in so far as they are certain, they do not refer to the nervous system. ([196b], p. 106)

He does not reject the idea that it might theoretically be possible to establish links between linguistic and neurobiological analyses, seeking to define causal relationships between neuronal activities and regularities found in any natural language. However, such an inquiry into relationships between the brain and languages, with its formal and logico-mathematical character, is open to the criticism that it remains purely phenomenological[70] and therefore non-explanatory. The work of Piaget, he notes, affords an excellent illustration of this viewpoint.

In fact, biology has available concepts that remain valid either at the level of neuronal reality or at a level of maximal generality. Such is for example the case with the progression from neurogenotype to neurophenotype.[71]

Chomsky's hypothesis that natural languages share certain universal features or structures leads to the assumption that such structures derive from innately determined brain functions. Whatever the interest of such a hypothesis, it must be said that at the present time there is no way of verifying it experimentally.[72]

Ontogeny shows that both cerebral hemispheres are functionally undifferentiated with regard to language. Brain lateralization occurs after the thirty-sixth month.[73] Again, pathology indicates that the possibilities of recuperation decline with the maturation of the cortex, from the onset of language (at about 18 months) to age 15 at the latest. These phenomena of progressive narrowing of the functional potentialities of the zones of the cortex and progressive decline of recuperative capacity are not limited to the neurobiological bases of language. They are also attested in the development of other functional systems.

Though the cortex does not seem to present at the outset systems specialized for any kind of cognitive activity, such activities are constructed and can, under certain conditions, be reconstructed.

Whether inquiry seeks to penetrate the mysteries of neuronal organisation and to decipher the code of the genetic program, the lateralization processes and hemispheric functional specialization, or whether it draws the pathology's lesson of disorders observed and behaviors enabling them to be overcome, it still discovers the same self-evident fact: the prodigious arrangement in the space of the body and in the time of its development of a formidable, powerful system, the nervous system, whose purpose seems to be learning. However, in the complexity of nervous structures, how much is innate and how much acquired? The boundaries between the two areas are perhaps not as clear-cut as has sometimes been thought.

A meeting took place at Royaumont in France from October 10 to October 13, 1975, in which a group of investigators from various disciplines, all equally interested in the relationship between innateness and acquisition, joined Jean Piaget and Noam Chomsky to discuss the theme *Theories of Language and Theories of Learning*. Could there be a middle ground between Piagetian constructivism and Chomskyan nativism? In the course of the colloquium, Piaget declared that there are no a priori or innate cognitive structures in man, and that: "only the functioning of intelligence is hereditary" ([311], p. 53). In debate, however, he stated that: "there is no clear and total opposition, with a delimitable boundary, between what is innate and what is acquired" (p. 99).

Chomsky, in his remarks, revealed how much ground he had travelled in a few years. In response to Piaget, he stated at the very beginning of the discussion:

...The study of human language has led me to believe that a genetically determined language capacity which is a component of the human mind specifies a certain class of 'accessible human grammars'. (p. 65)

For Chomsky, the study of cognitive structures like human language must be undertaken in a manner similar to that in which one would study an organ like the eye or the heart.[74] When Bateson asked him "Do you believe that language is an organ?", he answered:

I think that, to the extent that we speak in metaphors, this one is better than the ones used previously... I believe that the growth of this capacity has the general characteristics of that of organs. (p. 125)

One must, of course, read the full text of the debates to grasp the scope of the arguments and to appreciate the viewpoints of the participants, particularly those who were seeking middle ground. One of these was Stephen Toulmin, who concluded the debate, provisionally, in these terms:

We should certainly suppose, against what is claimed by Piaget, that the ability to learn language depends on the fact that the very young child possesses very specific abilities which are innate, that is, 'wired in' to the central nervous system; there are, of course, independent neurological proofs of the existence of such 'innate' abilities. But the particular abilities which Chomsky attributes to the child are apparently much too specific to be probable, let alone that it seems difficult to conceive what their neurological counterparts might be. (p. 405)

Close as we are to the end of our inquiry, we must remark on the constant themes. Innateness and acquisition, competence and performance, sound and meaning, language and thought, genotype and phenotype, to mention only some of the lexical pairs expressing constant dichotomies, express under a different ideological guise the same quest that has continued down through the ages.

The debate on innateness and acquisition is in a sense the geometrical locus of all these themes; it sums them all up. However, in these confrontations where theory and fact are at times irreconcilably opposed, it would seem that the problem of the fundamental relationship between brain and language has often been badly stated. Just as the shape and the weight of a tool depend not only on its use and purpose, but even more on the hand that holds it and the mind that creates it, language is explained not only by its symbolic and communicative use and purpose, but even more by the brain that generates it. There has been a tendency, especially in recent decades, to adopt the opposite attitude, trying to explain the brain by language.[75]

Under what conditions could there now be a neurolinguistic approach that would give our redirected perceptions a new power of resolution? That is the question to be dealt with in the final section of the present study.

EPISTEMOLOGICAL CONSIDERATIONS

> Epistemology: part of philosophy that deals with the critical study of postulates, conclusions and methods of a given science, considered from the view-point of its evolution, so as to determine the logical origin, the value and the scientific and philosophical applicability thereof.
> *Trésor de la langue française (H).*

A new branch of the sciences of man has developed in recent decades on the border of the social and natural sciences, that may be called neurolinguistics, writes A.R. Luria.[76] Under the cover of words we find the same constant duality that we considered in the last section. Could neurolinguistics be a science of the impossible?

Here as in many other cases, the orientation of inquiry that informs neurolinguistics existed long before the term itself was invented.[77]

As it attempted to define the postulates on which its approach is based, neurolinguistics began to recognise its own limits. In 1963, a neuropsychological and neurolinguistic research group was formed at the St. Anne Hospital in Paris. The journal *Langages*[78] has devoted a special issue to the work of this team. In an article for that issue, Jean Dubois wrote:

> Pathological utterances are distinguished from the totality of standard utterances by systematic rules defining these divergences... ([106a], p. 3)

There is a basic question of the relationship between the disorganised utterance and that which is considered normal. The author considers three possible levels of disorder:

(1) disorders of speech[79]
(2) disorders of language[80]
(3) disorders of the utterance[81]

He then attempts to define the object of neurolinguistics. It is:

> The study of the correlations existing between anatomical/clinical typology and linguistic typology of aphasias. The basic postulate is that this correlation is meaningful for the analysis of the functioning of language and of its disorganisation. ([106a], p. 6)

Neurolinguistics involves two kinds of models, anatomical/clinical and linguistic.

> The number and definition of the deficits will depend on the number
> and definition of levels that we have been able to identify in language.
> ([106b], p. 9)

The distinction between synchronic functioning and the diachronic stages of development has led to aphasia being seen as a regression of language; this was a mistake.[82]

One may question the validity of this restrictive view of the field of neurolinguistics. It is far from being accepted by all. The neurologist Grewel (1966) defines neurolinguistics as the study of language and speech disorders due to neurological impairment; and he rejects the identification of neurolinguistics with aphasiology.[83] According to Luria, the task of neurolinguistics is to make use of available clinical data to discover the physiological and neurophysiological mechanisms determining disorders of verbal behaviour and thus to arrive at an integrated view of verbal pathologies of central origin.[84] In fact, neurolinguistic research has extended to the widest possible scope, and now covers the whole area of language pathology.[85] There is more involved here than a mere argument about words, for the definition that is given to a specialty will determine its scope and its aims, its assumptions and its methods.

This brings us back to the problem of the semiological interpretation of deficits. Roman Jakobson, who was very much aware of this problem, recalled Hughlings Jackson's view:

> An aphasic mutation may be regarded as presenting, by its nature, a
> twofold aspect: when a patient says 'chair' for 'table', he is revealing first
> of all a deficit, in that he does not say 'table', and then a compensation,
> in that he says 'chair'. (Jackson 1879).[86] ([198b], p. 105)

Jakobson comments: "...aphasia can lead to a redistribution of linguistic functions." ([198b], p. 105)

Consequently, to establish a one-to-one relationship between the deficit and the site of the lesion, and to attempt, on this basis, to determine "aphasic grammars" - leading inevitably to a static evaluation of competence, whereas performance indicates an evolving impairment - may seem to be somewhat presumptuous and to go beyond the constraining reality of the facts.

As Kinsbourne[87] notes, the non-dominant hemisphere is far from remaining neutral in the formation of language behaviour.[88] Aphasic discourse does not necessarily express the limited functioning of a language area impaired by a lesion, as has generally been assumed. That discourse, with all its imperfections, may very well be the product of unsophisticated attempts at compensation by the intact non-dominant hemisphere.[89] However, this finding, which has emerged from particular clinical cases, cannot be generalised.[90] It is not yet possible to know exactly what kinds of impairment allow or do not allow this recourse to the right (non-dominant) hemisphere. The non-dominant hemisphere in the adult reveals a skill in decoding verbal communication in an immediate manner when the left (dominant) hemisphere is inactivated or excluded from "transcallosal communication" with the right. However, the situation is completely different when the speech act - encoding - is involved. Some time must pass after the beginning of the lesion before the right hemisphere can assume relative control of verbal production even to a limited extent. This finding suggests that the right hemisphere plays no part in the normal speech act and, furthermore, that it is excluded by some neuronal arrangement that needs time to reverse itself under certain conditions.

The conclusion to which these findings lead, Kinsbourne believes, is that the left hemisphere is not totally dominant at the outset of language development but that this dominance is gradually established. The right hemisphere seems always to retain some language potential, particularly in the matter of receiving verbal messages. While both hemispheres are equipped for language functions, cerebral dominance presupposes an active competition between them that the left hemisphere is genetically destined to win.

It is premature to study problems from the top down and to attempt right away to formalize a theory of methods and principles of neurolinguistics, as some not long ago were led to do. The most fruitful approach is probably to accumulate findings established with the maximum rigour in observation and interpretation.

The series *Studies in Neurolinguistics* published by Haiganoosh and Harry A. Whitaker regularly since 1976[91] is the best exemplar of the fruitfulness of this approach. Within the framework of a strict method in which discipline of inquiry (for anatomical and clinical observation) and discipline of thinking (for physiological and linguistic interpretation) complement one another in a felicitous manner, a large number of facts have been observed, analysed and (where possible) ranked in relation to one another.

This and other information efforts[92] nevertheless bring difficulties if not dangers of their own. Immediate communication of provisional research results concerning a wide range of pathological manifestations of verbal behaviour[93] and touching both on surface linguistic phenomena and the somatic phenomena that underlie them can sometimes give an impression of diffuseness and lack of clarity.

At the present time, inquiry - whether it be linguistic, clinical, neurophysiological, psychological or re-educative, depending on the background of the investigator - is solicited in many different directions at once, and it seems obvious that the moment of great syntheses that marks the achievement of maturity by a discipline has not yet occurred. We must therefore get used to this open and insecure attitude that makes us constantly question the knowledge acquired the day before.

As a model of its kind we may cite the research of Lecours and Lhermitte reported in *Cortex*[94] under the title "Phonemic Paraphasias: Linguistic Structures and Tentative Hypothesis". The theme[95] is a very attractive one for phoneticians and phonologists.

Already in 1939, the phonetician Marguerite Durand had carried out a study in conjunction with Drs Théophile Alajouanine and A. Ombredane on *The Phonetic Disintegration Syndrome in Aphasia*.[96] The work of Lecours and Lhermitte shows the gains that have been made in rigour and precision of observation due to careful use of a coherent linguistic theory, in this case an extrapolation of the concepts of distributional analysis under the influence of Martinet[97] and Buyssens.[98] Every language being considered as a specific, ranked system of units, impairments can be situated at the different ranks of the hierarchy: syntagms, monemes, phonemes and distinctive features. Beginning with the lowest-level units, the distinctive features, it is possible to identify the kinds of transformations appearing in "aphasic jargon". There is a tendency towards replacement of some phonemic units with morphologically similar units.

The authors thus reveal regular modalities of more and more complex transformations which characterise discours produced by these patients. They can then attempt, as a hypothesis, to establish correlations between linguistic facts and physiological facts.[99] Dysfunction of the same physiological mechanism may very well lie at the origin of different phenomena at the level of verbal behaviour, because these mechanisms may act simultaneously at the different assembly-points of the linguistic system of ranked units. If one wishes to speculate further about the postulated types of physiological organisation, they conclude, it is not inconceivable that (for example) each linguistic unit might correspond to one neuronal circuit and one only, of undetermined complexity and localization, which has learned this program of realization and whose function is to govern all realizations of that particular unit.[100] The problem of activation, selection and integration of linguistic units reveals the twofold action of processes which develop in the syntagm or in paradigms, and which rest on these basic functional units as posited by the authors, assumed to be present at all levels of organisation of language. So as not to wander off into the imaginary, the authors suggest experimental computer simulations based on mathematical parameters aimed at integrating all possible behaviors.

One must note how closely and faithfully this argumentation takes up and renews the fundamental themes of a debate that has gone on over the centuries, and that forms the basis of present-day neurolinguistic discourse: to know the brain and penetrate what Penfield calls "The Mystery of the Mind";[101] to probe, consequently, beneath the surface of appearances so as to grasp the underlying reality, in an approach that we find from Plato to Gustave Guillaume; in this way, to reduce the complex to the simple; and finally, to find an explanation for the normal in the manifestations of the abnormal.

The present stage of development of neurolinguistic studies allows us to make a (very provisional) evaluation. In a volume published under the title *The Neurosciences: Paths of Discovery* in 1975,[102] we find the names of A.R. Luria, R.W. Sperry and Wilder Penfield. By following the path they have set out by their research efforts, we shall attempt such an evaluation.

The view that complex psychological processes could be localizable in specific areas of the cortex has not established itself without debate. As Luria states, a century of history of what we might nowadays call the theoretical propositions of neuropsychology (the theory of cerebral organisation and of human psychological activity), torn between supporters of narrow localization and champions of broad localization, in fact led to a deadlock.[103]

In the recent past, however, the principle of localization of complex psychological functions in circumscribed aggregates of cells was receiving apparent confirmation.[104] To get beyond oppositions between theories it was first necessary to review the concepts of localization and function.

The term 'function', says Luria, can be understood in two completely different ways. It can refer to the 'function' of a particular tissue. In this sense the function of the pancreas is to secrete insulin... However, the term has another meaning, as has been made clear in particular by the work of the Soviet psychologist P. K. Anokhin:[105]

> A 'function' can be understood as a complex adaptive activity aimed at the performance of some vitally important task... Perhaps the best and the simplest examples are the 'functions' of respiration and locomotion. ([246j], p. 340)

This also applies to higher psychological processes. Vygotsky stated that psychological processes are not elementary and inborn "faculties".

The two characteristic features of higher psychological functions are:

(1) their mediated character - tools for movements and actions, language for perception, memory and thought;
(2) basic transformations of the structure of these complex processes during ontogeny: a young child thinks by remembering, while an adult can remember by thinking.[106]

Leontiev[107] and Gal'perin[108] have shown the decisive role of the active manipulation of objects in the development of complex human psychological processes, and the complexity of both the pathways of formation and the structures of these processes. We thus reach the indisputable conclusion, Luria says, that complex forms of psychological processes... are functional systems,[109] using different methods and having a complex structure.

Revision of the concept of function leads to revision of the concept of localization. Pavlov[110] had stated that whereas at the beginning of the century it had been thought that the respiratory centre was:

> something the size of a pinhead in the medulla, now, however, it has proved extremely elusive, climbing up into the brain and sinking down into the spinal cord, so that nobody knows its precise boundaries.

As for the centres involving the higher psychological processes, all that can be said about them is that: "any attempt to localize them in circumscribed groups of cells is meaningless." ([246j], p. 341)

Revision of the concepts of function and localization also entail revision of the concept of symptom. If a localized brain lesion led to a clearly defined loss of function, or, in other words, if it caused a definite symptom, earlier observers concluded that the particular area of the brain was the "centre" in which the corresponding "function" was localized.

> The idea that the concepts of function and symptom coincide, even though they are opposite in sign, gave basic support to the idea of the direct localization of functions. However, despite the apparent simplicity and attractiveness of this idea, [says Luria,] it began long ago to arouse fundamental misgivings, and the idea that the concept of 'symptom' is by no means equivalent to the concept of 'function' gradually began to penetrate deeper and deeper into classical neurology. (p. 342)

Kurt Goldstein[111] played an important role in this regard.

If a local brain lesion produces a certain disturbance of a complex form of psychological activity - perception, thinking, speech, writing, reading - this does not necessarily imply that the complex function is localized in a particular area of the brain. Goldstein, with Gelb[112] introduced the concept of basic or primary disturbances and associated disorders,[113] which helped symptomatology to break the deadlock.

Luria concludes that:

> The higher forms of human psychological activity... take place with the participation of all parts and levels of the brain,[114] each of which makes its own specific contribution to the work of the functional system as a whole.

In the same volume,[115] Sperry[116] writes:

> Conscious mental experience in our present interpretation is con-
> ceived to be a holistic emergent of brain activity, different from and
> more than the neural events of which it is composed. ([378], p. 430)

Penfield, too, studying memory mechanisms, shows the extent to which
that function involves the activity of the sum total of structures of the central
nervous system.[117] It is interesting to note the community of viewpoints
here.

After so many efforts to discover specialized structures in the organisation of the nervous system, inquiry comes back to an overall vision of the
central nervous system as the locus of formation of conscious, verbalised
thought, even as it immerses itself in the innermost parts of the brain's
internal structure - the limbic system and the brain stem.[118]

*

*   *

At this arbitrary end of a long journey, we must declare that language
continues to be perceived, in a new scientific discourse, as the locus where
the material and the spiritual, the visible and the invisible, form and meaning are articulated in man - with all the dichotomies only serving to repeat
the same "eternal questioning" in different words.

The entire debate that is unfolding in present-day neurolinguistic discourse comes down to the age-old search for a definition of the locations
in the human body by which language becomes possible. Some have always
tried to identify language with these locations, while others have striven to
distinguish it from them.

However, it is not unthinkable that in seizing on the ever-increasing complexity of the organisation of matter, inquiry will only see the limits of
what is accessible and possible recede further into the distance. Neurolinguistics has to recognise that it only grasps evanescent forms while the key
to those mechanisms remains hidden. Is it, as we wondered earlier, a science of the impossible? At the present time, it is clear that neurolinguistics
addresses itself to that question by a discourse whose object constantly escapes
investigation. The frontiers may be pushed back, but the problem remains.

NOTES

1   Published in the USSR in 1947.
2   See p. 177, n. 83.
3   See p. 152, n. 84.
4   Auguste-Henri Forel (1848-1933). His contribution can be summed up in three points:
    (1) the nervous network does not exist as such, and each nerve cell is in contact but not in continuity with its neighbours. This is what is called Forel's contact theory.
    (2) Nerve fibres originate from the cell.
    (3) As a result, fibre degenerates if the cell is damaged, and pace Waller, the converse may also occur.
5   Santiago Ramón y Cajal (1852-1934).
6   H. Wilhelm Gottfried von Waldeyer (1836-1921). He in fact gave a new meaning to the Greek term long used for "nerve".
7   Charles Scott Sherrington (1857-1952). The term "synapse" was also used in 1897 by M. Forster.
8   E. H. Weber (1795-1878) and E.F.W. Weber (1806-1871). Their experiment is described in the *Handwörterbuch der Physiologie mit Rücksicht auf physiologische Pathologie* (Braunschweig, 1846, Vol. III, pp. 1-222: *'Muskelbewegung'*). They showed that stimulation of the pneumogastric nerve halted the heartbeat; in other words, the activity of a nerve caused the interruption of the activity of the organ innervated by it.
9   To express the phenomenon demonstrated by the Brothers Weber, Brown-Sequard pressed into service the term "inhibition" in allusion to a legal sense: "put in opposition".
10 See p.152, n. 105.
11 J.C. Eccles (1903-): [256].
12 See [1a,b] and [188].
13 [256], p. 37.
14 "...The neuron appears to us as a cell endowed with various functions; but all these functions are organised to ensure the transmission of information from one point of the organism to another..." ([256], p. 37).
15 Hans Berger (1873-1941). See [65].
16 Pierre Chauchard [70], pp. 4 and 64.
17 [250a], pp. 480-492.
18 Ivan Petrovitch Pavlov (1849-1936).
19 [246d], p. 20.
20 Wilder Graves Penfield (1891-1976).
21 "An injection of sodium amytal made into the inner carotid artery causes

a contralateral hemiplegia" ([307], pp. 89-90). See [51a], pp. 52 and 164.

22   "Cortical exaeresis... did not abolish the ability to speak in the patient, although aphasia frequently appeared as a postoperative reaction, to disappear again when convalescence was complete" ([307], p. 110).

23   See [420b].

24   Penfield [305a].

25   In [306], p. 215.

26   "The optic layer or thalamus is an ovoid nucleus of grey matter whose internal and superior surfaces protrude into visibility from the third ventricle and the lateral ventricle, and whose external and inferior surfaces are attached to neighbouring regions. The posterior extremity presents a voluminous inflation: the pulvinar, reaching out over two eminences, the external and internal geniculate bodies, where the conjunctival arms end." ([98], p. 102). This complex set of different structures is referred to as the limbic system. See [19], p. 10.

27   This is a short but crucial text among Penfield's writings. See [305b].

28   We are here following the text of [307].

29   The word "abiding" is borrowed from the oft-quoted description by Sherrington (Adrian, 1947, p. 17) ([307], p. 55, n. 1).

30   [307], p. 18.

31   [307], p. 18.

32   [307], p. 18.

33   *The Harvey Lectures*, New York Academy of Medicine, 1938. Title: "The Cerebral Cortex and Consciousness".

34   [307], pp. 19f.

35   See in particular Jasper (1960) ([200b], pp. 1552-1593). We might add that research up till 1975 in this area is well summed up in a special issue of *Brain and Language* 2, 1 (1975).

36   See p. 49.

37   A. R. Luria ([246k], p. 55). On the concept of regulative centre, see Luria [246f], part 3, "Synthetic mental activities and their cerebral organisation", pp. 245ff.

38   See [246k], pp. 55f.

39   [246a], p. 21.

40   [246a], p. 21.

41   On this aspect of the problem, see Luria [246c]. See also Luria and Yudovich [247].

42   [246a], p. 21.

43   "On the basis of all this there is no reason to consider the semantic aspect of speech to result from the functioning of some cortical 'center' which acts as a 'depot' for those images which language dominates.

We have every reason to believe that the speech activity associated with abstraction and generalisation is a product of highly complex systems of temporary connections which arise in the process of communication with other people" ([246a], p. 22).

44   See p. 198, n. 50.

45   Four volumes have appeared to date: I and II (1976), III (1977), IV (1979). Space does not allow us to summarize these volumes, but they are rich in content [420A].

46   See n. 26.

47   Yalow, Guillemin and Schally, who devised this method, received the Nobel Prize for their work in 1977.

48   See p. 186.

49   [253e], p. 135. See [125].

50   "All that is said here is aimed at a psychic centre of speech, but as regards the mechanism of articulation, we must state that it may be impaired by a lesion sited in either hemisphere at the level of the 'quadrilateral' region" ([253e], p. 135).

51   [253e], p. 136.

52   A zone that Pierre Marie situated at the level of the gyrus, the gyrus angularis and the first temporals.

53   [253e], p. 138.

54   [358b], p. 33.

55   He says, a few lines previously: "...One might say that it is not spoken language that is natural to man, but the faculty of constituting a language, i.e. a system of distinctive signs corresponding to distinct ideas..." ([358b], p. 26).

56   It was published in a new edition in 1968.

57   He adds the following details to this claim in a footnote: "Leyton and Sherrington (1917) observed that they could not produce vocalization in anthropoids by faradic stimulation" ([307], p. 199).

58   See [72a,b]; the first version of [72d] goes back to early 1967. Chomsky returns to this question in [72e].

59   "...In studying the behavior of a complex organism, it will be necessary to isolate such essentially independent underlying systems as the system of linguistic competence..." ([72c], p. 399).

60   "...A person with command of a language... has developed what we will refer to as linguistic competence" ([72c], p. 397).

61   [72c], pp. 397f.

62   [72c], p. 398.

63   "The existence of innate mental structure is, obviously, not a matter of controversy. What we may question is just what it is and to what extent it is specific to language" ([72c], p. 401).

64 [72c], p. 402.
65 For example, Bishop Wilkins ([72c], p. 402).
66 [72c], p. 407.
67 [72c], p. 407.
68 [196b], p. 105.
69 [196b], p. 105.
70 [196b], p. 106.
71 "We may expect to find genetic preconditions for the development of language and mechanisms that regulate language ontogeny, just as there are these genetic and regulatory mechanisms in the development of the structural components of the developing organism" ([196b], p. 107).
72 See [51a], "Phylogénie et ontogénie", pp. 138ff., and [196b], pp. 107ff.
73 "As the cerebral cortex matures postnatally, certain linguistic functions become increasingly restricted to the left cerebral hemisphere" ([196b], p. 111).
74 [311], p. 67.
75 "I would say, therefore, that a rational approach would consist of supposing that, in the domain where we have certain non-trivial results concerning language structure, the organizational principles determining the specific structures of language are simply part of the initial state of the organism" ([311], p. 257).
76 See [246i,e]
77 Yvan Lebrun [224], p. 1).
78 Issue 5 of the journal Langages, Paris, March 1967.
79 "Lesion of the peripheral organs of the bulb or the cerebellum" ([106b], p. 3).
80 "Lesions localized in the left hemisphere of right-handers and varying with this localization" ([106b], p. 3f.).
81 "General modifications of behavior of the subject in relation to the world" ([106b], p. 4).
82 [106b], p. 10.
83 F. Grewel [165]: "To limit neurolinguistics to aphasiology is inaccurate."
84 [246e].
85 See [420a].
86 [193d].
87 [208b].
88 "Mere disconnection of right from left hemisphere suffices to reveal at once that the right hemisphere can decode speech to a fairly complex level..."
89 "It appears that aphasic speech does not necessarily, as has been generally assumed, represent the limited functioning of a damaged domi-

nant language area. Rather it may result from the unsophisticated compensatory efforts of the intact minor hemisphere" ([208b], p. 110).

90 [208a].
91 We may also mention the *Applied Psycholinguistics Series* edited for Plenum by R. W. Rieber.
92 *Brain and Language, Neuropsychologia.*
93 This can be demonstrated by a look at the tables of contents of some publications.
94 See [226a].
95 "The first step in linguistic analysis of any string of aphasic language is to achieve reliable identification of the transformed unit..." ([226e], p. 193).
96 See [246k], p. 95.
97 [255].
98 [65].
99 [226a], pp. 212ff.
100 [226a], p. 219.
101 "The mind remains a mystery" ([305c], p. 83).
102 *The Neurosciences: Paths of Discovery*, Frederick J. Worden, Judith P. Swazey and George Adelman, editors, MIT Press, Cambridge, Mass. & London, 1975.
103 [246j], pp. 335-361.
104 See D. H. Hubel & T. N. Wiesel (1962): "Receptive fields: binocular interaction and functional architecture in the cat's visual cortex": *J. Physiol.* 160: 106-154.
105 [9].
106 [415], p. 341.
107 [233].
108 [144].
109 It may be useful to point out that the word "system", in Russian sistema, is to be taken in its strong sense. "It indicates that there is a multitude of complex interconnexions between the elements (signs and verbal relations) which make of it a very complicated network of liaisons and reciprocal actions; it is indeed a structure" ([231], p. 138).
110 See above, n. 18.
111 See p. 178, n. 114.
112 [148].
113 [246j], p. 342.
114 [246j], p. 346.
115 See n. 102.
116 See [378]. He was particularly interested in the consequences of hemispherectomies and deconnexions of the two hemispheres (the "split brain" phenomenon).

117 See [305d]. This text was actually incorporated into his book *The Mystery of the Mind*; see n. 26 (pp. 437-454 of the book).

118 See [246j], p. 353; [379] and [59], of which we will quote the conclusion: "Finally, it might be said that the proposed model, however briefly depicted, does represent a radical departure from the classical approach. According to the latter, local function was interpreted either as a result of disruption of a mechanism, 'representations', 'strategies', etc., or as a pathway-mediated influence upon some other area. The 'centers' of traditional neuropsychology are rather to be considered as levels by means of which cognition is carried one stage further. Similarly pathways do not serve to associate ideas, perceptions to movements, written words to sounds, etc., but rather link up temporally transformations occurring at different points in the microgenetic sequence. Cognition is a lawful unfolding of evolutionary forms, not a pastiche of more or less fragmentary elements."

BIBLIOGRAPHY

1. Adrian, E.D.
   a) *The Mechanism of Nervous Action. Electrical Studies of the Neurone*: Philadelphia: 1932.
   b) The Physical Background of Perception: Oxford: 1947.

2. Aetius: in: Voilquin, J. (ed.): *Les penseurs grecs avant Socrate*: Paris: Garnier: 1941.

3. Alajouanine, T., A. Ombredane & M. Durand: *Le syndrome de la désintégration phonétique dans l'aphasie*: Paris: Masson: 1939.

4. Albertus Magnus:
   a) *Summa*
   b) *De Anima*
   c) *De Spiritu*
   d) *De Animalibus*
   A. Borgnet, ed.: Paris: Vives: 1896. Meerssemann, *Introductio in Opera Omnia Alberti Magni*: Bruges: Beyaert: 1931.

4'. Alberti, S.: *Oratio de surdite et mutitate*: Nuremberg: 1591.

5. Aldini, G.: *An Account of the Late Improvements in Galvanism*: London: 1803.

6. Altman, J.: "Postnatal Growth and Differentiation of the Mammalian Brain with Implications for a Morphological Theory of Memory": in: *The Neurosciences: A Study Program*: G. Quarton, T. Melnechuck and F.O. Schmitt, eds.: New York: Rockefeller University Press: 1969.

7. Altschule, M.D.: *Origin of Concepts in Human Behavior*: chap. 9: "The Calcified Pineal Gland": Washington/London: John Wiley & Son: 1977.

8. Amman, J.C.
   a) *Surdus Loquens*: Harlemii: 1692.
   b) *Dissertatio de Loquela*: Amstelodami: 1700.
   c) *The Talking Deaf Man* [Eng. trans. of **a**]: London: 1694.

8'. Angelergues, R., & H. Hecaen: *Pathologie du Langage*: Paris: Larousse: 1965.

9. Anokhin, P. K.: *Biology and Neurophysiology of the Conditioned Reflex and its Role in the Adaptative Behavior* [Eng. trans.]: Oxford: Pergamon Press: 1974.

10. Arceo, F.:
    a) *De Recta Curandorum Vulnerum Ratione*: Antwerp: 1574.
    b) *A Most Excellent and Compendious Method of Curing Wounds in the Head*: London: Thomas East for Thomas Cadman: 1588.

11. Aristotle:
    a) *De Partibus Animalium*: (Parts of Animals): with an Eng. trans. by A.L. Peck: Loeb Classical Library: London: Heinemann.
    b) *De Animalibus*
    c) *Rhetoric*
    d) *De Anima*
    e) *Parva Naturalia: De Memoria et Reminiscentia.*

12. Arnauld, A. & C. Lancelot: *Grammaire générale et raisonnée*: re-publication Paulet, Paris, 1969.

13. Auburtin, S.A.E.: Considérations sur les localisations cérébrales, et en particulier sur le siège du langage articulé: in: *Gazette Hebdomadaire de Médecine et de Chirurgie*: 1863.

14. Augustine, St.:
    a) *Confessions*
    b) *De Libero Arbitrio.*

15. Aulus Gellius: *Noctes Atticae*: with Fr. trans. by M.V. Verger: Paris: 1820.

16. Avicenna: *Canon*: 1030 (?)

17. Bacon, Sir Francis:
    a) *Novum Organum*: 1620.
    b) *Sylva Sylvarum*: 1627.

18. Baillarger, J.G.F.:
    a) Recherches sur la structure de la couche corticale des circon-volutions du cerveau: in: *Mem. Acad. Roy. Med.*: Paris: 1840: 8: 149-183.
    b) *Recherches sur les maladies mentales*: Paris: Masson: 1890.

19. Barbizet, J., & P. Duizabo: *Neuropsychologie*: Paris: Masson: 1977.

20. Bartholin, G., & T. Bartholin: *Anatomicae Institutiones Corporis Humani*: 1611.

21. Bastian, Henry Charlton:
    a) "On the various forms of loss of speech in cerebral disease": *Brit. & Foreign Med. Chir. Rev.* 43: London: 1869.
    b) "The Physiology of Thinking": *Fortnightly Review* (new series) 5: 1869.
    c) *The Brain as an Organ of Mind*: 3rd ed.: London: Kegan, Trench & Co.: 1882.
    d) "On some problems in connection with aphasia and other speech defects": The Lumleian Lectures: *Lancet* I: 1897.

22. Bauhin, G.: *Institutiones Anatomicae*: 7 eds.: 1590-1629.

23. Baverius de Baveriis: *Concilia Medicinalia Sive de Morborum Curationibus Liber*: Bologna: 1489.

24. Bayle, & Quercy: "Les fondateurs de la doctrine française de l'aphasie": *Ann. Med. Psych.* 15ᵉ série, 98ᵉ année, Tome I: 1940 pp. 297-310.

25. Beauzee, N: *Grammaire générale* (1767): with an introduction by Barrie Bartlett: Stuttgart-Bad Cannstadt: F. Frommann Verlag (Gunther Holzboog).

26. Bede, The Venerable: *Historia Ecclesiastica Gentis Anglorum*: 731

27. Benson, D.F.: "Neurological Correlates of Anomia": in: *Studies in Neurolinguistics*, H. & H.A. Whitaker, eds.: New York/San Francisco/London: Academic Press: Vol. 4: 1979 pp. 293-326.

28. Bentley, D. R.: "Genetic Control of an Insect Neuronal Network": *Science* 174 (1971): pp. 1139-1141.

29. Benton, A.L., & R.J. Joynt:
    a) "Early descriptions of aphasia": *Arch. Neurol.* 1960-3.
    b) "Contributions to aphasia before Broca": *Cortex* 3 (1964).

30. Berengario da Carpi:
    a) *Commentaria cum amplissimis additionibus super anatomia*

Mundini una cum textu ejusdem in pristinum et venum nitorem redacto: Bologna: Benedictis: 1521.
b) *Isagoge breves*: 1522.

31. Berger, H.: "Über das Elektrenkephalogramm des Menschen": *Arch. f. Psychiatr.* 87 (1929): 527-570.

32. Bergson, H.:
a) *Essai sur les données ímmédiates de la conscience*: 1889.
b) *Matière et mémoire*: Paris: 1896
c) *L'Evolution créatrice*: 1907.
d) *La Pensée et le mouvant*: 1934.

33. Berko, J. & H. Goodglass: "Agrammatism and inflexional morphology in English": *J. Speech & Hearing Res.* 3 (1960): 257-267.

34. Berlin, R.: *Beitrag zur Strukturlehre der Grosshirnwindungen*: Erlangen: 1858.

35. Bernard, C.: *An Introduction to the Study of Experimental Medicine*: trans. H.C. Greene: Henry Schuman: 1949.

36. Bernier, F.: *Abrégé de la philosophie de Gassendi*: Lyon: Anisson et Posuel: 1678.

37. Betz, V.A.: "Anatomischer Nachweis Zweier Gehirncentra": *Zbl. Med. Wiss.* 12 (1874): 578-580; 595-599.

38. Bichat, M.F.X.: *Traité d'anatomie générale*.

39. Binet, A.:
a) *Introduction à la psychologie expérimentale*: 1894.
b) *Etude expérimentale de l'intelligence*: 1903.

40. Bloomfield, L.: *Language*: 1933.

41. Bodin, J.:
a) *Universae Naturae Theatrum*: Lyon: 1596.
b) *Le Théâtre de la Nature de Jean Bodin*: Fr. trans. by F. de Fougerolles: Lyon: 1597.

42. Boissier de la Croix de Sauvages, F.: *Nosologia Methodica Sistens*

Morborum Classes, Genera et Species, Juxta Sydenhami Senten et Botanicorum Ordinem: Amsterdam & Geneva: 1763.

43. Bonet, J. P.: *Reducción de las letras y arte por enseñar a hablar los mudos*: 1620.

44. Bonhoeffer, K.: "Zur Klinik und Lokalisation des Agrammatismus und der Rechts-Links-Desorientierung": *Monatsschr. f. Psychiatr. u. Neurol.* 54 (1923).

45. Bonnet, C.: *Essai analytique des facultés de l'âme*: Copenhagen: 1760.

46. Borelli, J.A.: *De Motu Animalium*: Rome: 1680-1681.

47. Borel-Maisonny & Launay, C.: *Les Troubles du langage, de la parole et de la voix chez l'enfant*: Paris: Masson: 1972.

48. Borst, A.: *Der Turmbau von Babel*: Stuttgart: Hiersemann: 1947.

49. Boskis, R.M., & R.E. Levina: "On the form of acoustic agnosia": *USSR Neuropathology and Psychiatry* 5: 1938.

50. Bouillaud, J.B.:
    a) *Traité clinique et physiologique de l'encéphalite*: Paris: Baillière: 1825.
    b) "Recherches cliniques propres à démontrer que la perte de la parole correspond à la lésion des lobules antérieurs du cerveau, et à confirmer l'opinion de Monsieur Gall sur le siège de l'organe du langage articulé" [paper read to the Académie Royale de Médecine, Feb. 21, 1825]: Arch. gen. de Med. IIIe année (1825), T, 8: pp. 25-45.
    c) "Recherches expérimentales tendant à prouver que le cervelet préside aux actes de la station et de la progression, et non à l'instinct de la propagation" [paper to the Académie Royale de Médecine, 1827].
    d) "Recherches cliniques tendant à réfuter l'opinion de Monsieur Gall sur les fonctions du cervelet, et à prouver que cet organe préside aux actes de l'équilibration, de la station et de la progression" [paper to the Académie Royale de Médecine, 1827].
    e) "Recherches cliniques propres à démontrer que le sens du langage articulé et le principe coordinateur des mouvements de la parole réside dans les lobes antérieurs du cerveau" [paper to the

Académie Royale de Médecine, 1848: pp. 699-719. See [107], pp. 34-53]

51. Bouton, C.P.:
    a) *Le développement du langage: aspects normaux et pathologiques*: Paris: UNESCO/Masson: 1976.
    b) *La Signification*: Paris: Klincksieck: 1979.
    c) *La Linguistique appliquée*: Paris: P.U.F.: 1979 (*Que sais-je* series, no. 1755).

52. Boyle, R.: *Experimenta et observationes physicae* [trans. from Eng. original]: Geneva: 1680.

53. Bradbury, S.: *The Evolution of the Microscope*: Oxford: Pergamon Press: 1967.

54. Brain, W.R.: *Speech Disorders*: London: Butterworths: 1961.

55. Brazier, M. A. B.: *A History of the Electrical Activity of the Brain: the first half century*: London: Pitman Medical Publishing: 1961.

56. Broadbent, W.H.: "On the Cerebral mechanisms of speech and thought": *Med. Chir. Trans.* 15 (1872): 145-194.

57. Broca, P.P.:
    a) "Perte de la parole, ramollissement chronique et destruction partielle du lobe antérieur gauche du cerveau" [April 18, 1861]: *Bull. Soc. Anthropol. de Paris* 2 (1861): 235-238.
    b) "Remarques sur le siège de la faculté du langage articulé, suivies d'une observation d'aphémie (perte de la parole)" [August 1861]: *Bull. mens. Soc. Anat. de Paris* Vol. 36 (1861): pp. 330-357.
    c) "Nouvelle observation d'aphémie produite par une lésion de la moitié postérieure des deuxième et troisième circonvolutions frontales" [Nov. 1861]: *Bull. mens. Soc. Anat. de Paris*, Vol. 36 (1861): pp. 398-407.
    d) "Linguistique et anthropologie": *Bull. Soc. Anthropol. de Paris*, t. III (Ie série) (1862): pp. 261-319 [reprinted in *Mémoires d'Anthropologie*: Paris: C. Reinwald: 1871: pp. 232-275].
    e) "Localisation des fonctions cérébrales. Siège du langage articulé" [April 2, 1863]: *Bull. Soc. Anthropol. de Paris*, 4 (1863): pp. 200-204.
    f) "Sur les mots aphémie, aphasie et aphrasie, lettre à Monsieur le

Professeur Trousseau" [January 18, 1864]: *Gaz. Hôp. Civ. et Mil.* (1864): pp. 35-36.

g) "Siège de la faculté du langage articulé. Deux cas d'aphémie traumatique produite par des lésions de la troisième circonvolution frontale gauche" [communication by Ange Duval, presented by Broca, March 3, 1864]: *Bull. Soc. Anthropol. de Paris* 5: 213-217.

h) "Communication sur le siège de la faculté du langage articulé" [June 15, 1865]: *Bull. Soc. Anthropol. de Paris,* t. VI: pp. 337-363.

i) "Nomenclature cérébrale: dénomination des divisions et subdivisions des hémisphères et des anfractuosités de leur surface": *Revue d'Anthropologie* (1878): pp. 193-236.

58. Brosses, C. de: Traité de la formation mécanique des langues et des principes physiques de l'étymologie: Paris: 1765.

59. Brown, J.: "The Neural Organization of Language: Thalamic and Cortical Relationships": *Brain and Language* 2 (1975): 18-30.

60. Brown-Sequard, C.E.:
a) "Mémoire sur la transmission des impressions sensitives dans la moelle épinière": *C.R. Hebd. Séance Acad. Sci. Paris* 31 (1850): 700-701.

b) "Recherches cliniques et expérimentales sur les entrecroisements des conducteurs servant aux mouvements volontaires": *Arch. Physiol. norm. et path.,* 21 (1889) 219-245.

61. Brunot, F.: *La Pensée et la Langue*: Paris: Masson: 1926.

62. Buehler, K.: "Tatsachen und Probleme zu einer Psychologie der Denkvorgaenge: I: Über Gedanken": *Arch. f. d. Ges. Psychol.* IX (1907); "II: Über Gedankenzusammenhaenge": *ibid.* XII (1908); "III: Über Gedankenerrinerungen": *ibid.* XII (1908).

63. Bulwer, J.: *Philocophus, or the deaf and dumb man's friend, exhibiting the philosophical verities of that subtil art which may enable one with an observant eye to hear what any man speaks by the moving of his lips*: London: 1648.

64. Burloud, A.: *La pensée d'après les recherches expérimentales de Watt, Messer et Buehler*: Paris: Alcan: 1927.

65. Buyssens, E.: *La communication et l'articulation linguistique*: Paris: P.U.F.: 1967.

66. Cabanis, P.J.G.: *Traité du physique et du moral de l'homme*: Paris: 1802 [in: Corpus général des philosophes français XLIV, I: Paris: P.U.F.: 1966].

67. Chanet, P.:
    a) *Considérations sur la sagesse de Pierre Charon*: 1643.
    b) *De l'instinct et de la connaissance des animaux*: 1646.
    c) *Traité de l'esprit de l'homme et de ses fonctions*: 1649.

68. Charcot, J. M.:
    a) *Leçons sur les localisations dans les maladies du cerveau*: Paris: 1876-1880.
    b) *Cliniques nerveuses de la Salpétrière*: in: Le Progrès médical: 1883.

69. Charpentier, F.: *De l'excellence de la langue française*: 2 vols.: 1683.

70. Chauchard, P.: *Les mécanismes cérébraux de la prise de conscience*: Paris: Masson: 1956.

71. Chistovich, L.A., & V.A. Kozhevnikov: *Speech Articulation and Perception*: Washington, D.C.: Joint Publications Research Service, U.S. Dept. of Commerce: no. 30: 1965.

72. Chomsky, N.:
    a) *Syntactic Structures*: The Hague: Mouton: 1957 (1971).
    b) *Cartesian Linguistics*: New York/London: Harper & Row: 1966.
    c) "The Formal Nature of Language": Appendix A to Lenneberg [230].
    d) *Language and Mind*: New York: Harcourt, Brace, Jovanovich: enlarged edition: 1972.
    e) "Biological Basis of Language Capacities": in: Rieber, R.W. (ed.): *The Neurophysiology of Language*: New York: Plenum: 1976.

73. Cicero: *De Natura Deorum; Academica*: with an Eng. trans. by H. Rackham: Loeb Classical Library: London: Heinemann: 1933.

74. Clarke, E.:
    a) "Aristotelian concepts of the form and function of the brain": *Bull. Hist. Med.* 37 (1963): 1-14.
    b) "Brain anatomy before Steno": in: Scherz, G. (ed.): Steno and Brain Research in the Seventeenth Century: *Analecta Medico-Historica*: 1968: pp. 27-34.

75. Clarke, E., & J. Stannard: "Aristotle on the Anatomy of the Brain":
     J. Hist. Med. 18 (1963): 130-148.

76. Clarke, E., & C.D. O'Malley: *The Human Brain and Spinal Cord*:
     Berkeley & Los Angeles: University of California Press: 1968.

77. Clarke, E., & K. Dewhurst: *An Illustrated History of Brain Function*:
     Oxford: Sandford Publications: 1972.

78. Condillac, E. B. de:
     a) *Essai sur l'origine des connaissances humaines*: 1746.
     b) *Traité des systèmes*: 1749.
     c) *Cours d'études* [1755]: in: Corpus général des philosophes français
         t. XXXIII, I: Paris: P.U.F.: 1947.
     d) *Principes généraux de grammaire pour toutes les langues, avec leur
         application particulière à la langue française*: Paris: Dugour: An VI
         (1798) de la République.

79. Cordemoy, G. de:
     a) *Discours sur la distinction et l'union du corps et de l'âme*.
     b) *A Philosophical Discourse Concerning Speech*: Delmar, N.Y.:
         Scholar's Facsimiles and Reprints: 1972.

80. Corneille, T.: *Dictionnaire des arts et des sciences*: 1665, 1694.

81. Court de Gébelin, A.: *Histoire naturelle de la parole ou précis de l'ori-
     gine du langage et de l'écriture*: 1776.

82. Creutz, W.: *Die Neurologie des 1.-7. Jahrhunderts nach Chr.*: Leipzig:
     Georg Thieme: 1934.

83. Crichton, A.: *An Enquiry on the Nature and Origin of Mental De-
     rangement Comprehending a Concise System of the Philosophy and
     Pathology of the Human Mind and an History of the Passions and their
     Effects*: London: T. Caddell, jr., & W. Davies: 1798.

84   Critchley, M.:
     a) "Jacksonian Ideas and the Future, with Special Reference to
         Aphasia": *Brit. Med. Journal* 6, July 2 (1960).
     b) *Aphasiology and Other Aspects of Language*: London: Edward
         Arnold: 1970.
     c) "The Study of Language Disorder: Past, Present and Future": in:
         The Centennial Lectures: New York: Putnam: 1959: pp. 269-292.

85. Cruveilher, J.:
     a) *Anatomie pathologique du corps humain*: 1828.
     b) *Anatomie du système nerveux de l'homme*: 1838.

86. Cucurron Sicard, R.A.:
     a) *Cours d'instruction d'un sourd-muet de naissance*: 1809.
     b) *Théories des signes*: 1810.

87. Cureau de la Chambre, M.:
     a) De la connaissance des bêtes: in: *Caractères des Passions*: T. II:
        1645.
     b) *Traité de la connaissance des animaux*: Paris: 1648.
     c) *Le système de l'âme*: Paris: 1664.

88. Czopf, J.: "Über die Rolle der nicht dominanten Hemisphere in der
     Restitution der Sprache des Aphasischen": *Arch. Psychiatr. Nervenkr.*
     216 (1972): 162-171.

89. Dalin, O.: "Berättelse om en dumbe, som kan siunga": *K. Swenska
     Wetensk. Acad. Handlingar* 6 (1745).

90. Damascene, John: La source de la connaissance: in: *Histoire de la
     philosophie*: Paris: Pléiade: 1969.

91. Damourette, J., & E. Pichon: *Des mots à la pensée: essai de
     grammaire de la langue française*: 7 vols.: Paris: d'Artrey: 1911-1930.

92. Daremberg, C.:
     a) *Fragment du commentaire de Galien sur le Timée de Platon*: Paris:
        Masson: 1848.
     b) *Galien, oeuvres anatomiques, physiologiques et médicales, traduites
        sur les textes imprimés et manuscrits*: 2 vols.: Paris: Baillière: 1854-
        1856.
     c) *Histoire des sciences médicales*: 2 vols.: Paris: Baillière: 1870.

93. Darwin, E.: *Zoonomia, or the Laws of Organic Life*: London: Johnson:
     1796.

94. Dax, M., & G. Dax: "Observations tendant à prouver la coïncidence
     du dérangement de la parole avec une lésion de l'hémisphère gauche
     du cerveau": *Gaz. hebd. méd. et chir.* (1865) [includes the paper by M.
     Dax].

95. Deiters, O.F.K.: *Untersuchungen über Gehirn und Rückenmark des Meschen und der Säugetiere*: Braunschweig: 1865.

96. Déjérine, J.:
   a) "Contribution à l'étude de l'aphasie motrice sous-corticale et de la localisation cérébrale des centres laryngés": *Bull. Soc. de Biol.* (1891).
   b) "Différentes variétés de cécité verbale": *Mém. à la Soc. de Biol. de Paris* 44 [February 27, 1892].
   c) "Sémiologie du système nerveux": in: *Traité de Pathologie*: 1901.
   d) "L'aphasie sensorielle et l'aphasie motrice": *Presse médicale* 14: 1906.
   e) "Aphasie et anarthrie": *Trans. of the 17th. International Congress of Medicine: London*: 1913.
   f) *Sémiologie des affections du système nerveux*: Paris: 1914.

97. Delius, H.F.: *De alalia et aphonia*: 1757.

98. Delmas, J., & A. Delmas: *Voies et centres nerveux*: Paris: Masson: 1949.

99. Descartes, R.: *Oeuvres et lettres*: Bridoux, A. (ed.): Paris: Pléiade: 1953.
   a,b)*Discourse on Method, Optics, Geometry and Meteorology*: trans. by Paul J. Olscamp: Indianapolis: Bobbs-Merrill.
   c) *Passions de l'âme*: 1649.
   d) *Treatise on Man*: 1662 [Latin], 1664 [French].
   e) *De Mundo*: 1664.
   f) *Correspondence*.

100. Dilly: *De l'âme des bêtes, où après avoir démontré la spiritualité de l'âme de l'homme, l'on explique par la seule machine, les actions les plus surprenantes des animaux*: Lyon: Anisson et Poysuel: 1676.

101. Diogenes Laertius: Vie et opinions des philosophes: in: *Les Stoïciens*: Paris: Pléiade: 1962.

102. Dodart, D.:
   a) "Mémoire sur les causes de la voix de l'homme et de ses différents tons": *Hist. Acad. roy. des Sciences* (1700).
   b) "Supplément au mémoire sur la voix et les tons": *Hist. Acad. roy. des Sciences* [part 1] 1706, [part 2] 1707.

103. Drabkin, I.E.: Caelius Aurelianus: *On Acute Diseases and on Chronic Diseases*: Chicago: University of Chicago Press: 1950.

104. Drouin, V.D.: *Description du cerveau*: Paris: 1710[?].

105. Dubois, C.G.: *Mythe et langage au XVIe siècle*: Bruxelles: Ducros: 1970.

106. Dubois, J.:
    a) "Présentation": *Langages* 5, March (1967).
    b) "La neurolinguistique": *ibid.*

107. Dubois, J., & H. Hécaen: *La naissance de la neuropsychologie du langage*: Paris: Flammarion: 1969.

108. Du Bois-Reymond, E.:
    a) *Untersuchungen über tierische Elektrizität*: Berlin: 1849.
    b) *On Signor Carlo Matteucci's letter to H. Bence Jones*: London: Churchill: 1853.
    c) *Motatsberichte der Akademie der Wissenschaften zu Berlin* (1874): pp. 519-560.

109. Du Hamel, J.B.: *De Corpore Animato*: 1673.

110. Duizabo, P.: see [19].

111. Du Laurens, A.: *Historia Anatomica Humani Corporis*: 11 eds.: 1595-1650).

112. Du Marsais, C.: *Logique et principes de grammaire*: 1769.

113. Durand, M.: see [3].

114. Du Vernet, J.G.: *Oeuvres anatomiques*: 2 vols.: 1761.

115. Ebstein, E.: "Das Valsalva-Morgagnische Gesetz: ein Beitrag zur Vorgeschichte der Aphasie": *Deutsche Zeitschr. Nervenh.* 53 (1915): 130-136.

116. Eccles, J.C.: *Reflex Activity of the Spinal Cord*: London: O.U.P.: 1932.

117. Echeverria, J.: *Edition critique du mémoire de Maine de Biran*: de *l'aperception immédiate*: Paris: Vrin: 1963.

118. Ehrenberg, C.G.: "Mémoire sur la structure microscopique de la cellule nerveuse": *Annln. Phys.* 28 (1833): 449-473.

119. Fabre d'Olivet, N.:
   a) *Notions sur le sens de l'ouïe en général et en particulier sur le développement de ce sens opéré chez Rodolphe Grivel et chez plusieurs autres enfants sourds-muets de naissance*: Paris: 1811.
   b) *La langue hébraïque restituée et le vrai sens des mots hébreux rétabli et prouvé par leur analyse radicale*: Paris: 1816.

120. Falconer, W.: *De l'influence des passions sur les altérations du physique*: trans. from Eng. by La Montagne: Paris: 1791.

121. Falret, J.: "Des troubles du langage et de la mémoire des mots dans les affections cérébrales": *Arch. gén. méd.* (1874).

122. Ferrein, A.: "De la formation de la voix de l'homme": *Hist. Acad. roy. des Sciences* (1741).

123. Ferrier, D.:
   a) "Experimental researches in cerebral physiology and pathology": *West Riding Asylum Reports* 3 (1873).
   b) "Experiments on the brain of monkeys": *Phil. Trans. Roy. Soc.* 165 (1875).
   c) *The Functions of the Brain:* London: Smith, Elder & Co.: 1886.

124. Finkelnburg, F.C.:
   a) *Niederrheinische Gesellschaft*, Sitzung vom 21. Marz 1870 in Bonn: Berlin. klin. Wochenschr. 7 (1870).
   b) "Über Aphasie und Asymbolie nebst Versuch einer Theorie der Sprachbildung": *Arch. Psychiat.* 6 (1876).

125. Flechsig, P.E.: "Les centres de projection et d'association du cerveau humain": in: *Actes du XIIe Congrès International de Médecine Section neurologie*: Paris: 1900: pp. 115-121.

126. Fleury, L.J.: "Aphasie": *Gaz. des Hop.* 6 (1866).

127. Flourens, P.:
   a) "Détermination des propriétés du système nerveux ou recherches physiques sur l'irritabilité et la sensibilité": *J. de Phys. exp. et pathol.* 2 (1822): 372-384.

b) "Recherches physiques sur les propriétés et les fonctions du système nerveux dans les animaux vertébrés": *Arch. gén. de la Méd.* 2 (1823): 321-370.

c) *Recherches expérimentales sur les propriétés et les fonctions du système nerveux dans les animaux vertébrés*: Paris: Crévot: 1824.

d) *Examen de la phrénologie*: Paris: Paulin: 1842.

e) *De la vie et de l'intelligence*: Paris: Garnier: 1859.

f) *De la phrénologie et des études vraies sur le cerveau*: Paris: Garnier: 1863.

128. Fontana, F.G.F.: *Traité sur le venin de la vipère*: Florence: 1781.

129. Forel, A.H.: "Einige hirnanatomische Betrachtungen und Ergebnisse": *Arch. Psychiat. Nervenkrankh.* 18 (1887): 162-198.

130. Forge, L. de la: [De l'esprit humain, Lat. trans. by J. Flayder]: *Tractatus de mente humana ejus facultatibus et functionibus necnon de ejusdem unione cum corpore secundum principia Renati Descartes*: Paris: 1666.

131. Forster, M.: *A Textbook of Physiology*: Part III: London: MacMillan: 1897.

132. Foucault, M.:
a) *The Birth of the Clinic: an Archaeology of Medical Perception*: trans. by A.M. Sheridan Smith: New York: Pantheon: 1973.

b) *Les mots et les choses*: Paris: Gallimard: 1967.

c) *Archéologie du savoir*: Paris: Gallimard: 1969.

133. Foville, A.L.: *Traité complet de l'anatomie, de la physiologie et de la pathologie du système nerveux cérébro-spinal*: Paris: Fortin, Masson: 1844.

134. Frain du Tremblai, J.: *Traité des langues*: Paris: 1703.

135. Frank, J.P.: *De Curandis Hominum Morbis Epitome*: Mannheim: 1792-1802.

136. Freeman, K.: *The Presocratic Philosophers*: 2nd ed.: Oxford: Blackwell: 1959.

137. Freud, S.: *Zur Auffassung der Aphasien*: Vienna: 1891.

138. Fritsch, G.T., & E. Hitzig: "Über die elektrische Erregbarkeit des Grosshirns": *Arch. Anat. Physiol.* (1870): pp. 300-332.

139. Froment, J., & E. Pichon: "Rapport au sixième congrès de la Société française de Phoniatrie": *Rev. fr. de Phoniatrie* 7 (1939).

140. Furetière, A.: *Dictionnaire universel*: Paris: 1690.

141. Galen:
   a) *Diagnosis of Disease by Means of Dreams.*
   b) *The Dissection of Nerves.*
   c) *On the Opinions of Hippocrates and Plato*: Opera omnia editionem curavit C.G. Kühn: 1831-1833.
   d) *On the Seat of Diseases* (see Daremberg [92b]).
   e) *On the Usefulness of Parts of the Body*: translated from the Greek with an introduction and commentary by Margaret Tallmade-May: Ithaca, N.Y.: Cornell Univ. Press: 1968.

142. Gall, F.J.:
   a) *Discours d'ouverture lu par Monsieur le Dr Gall à la première séance de son cours public sur la physiologie du cerveau* [January 15, 1808]: Paris: F. Didot, Lefort & F. Schoell: 1808.
   b) Article "Cerveau" in *Dic. des Sciences méd.* t. IV: Paris: 1813.
   c) Article "Crâne" in *Dic. des Sciences méd.* t. VII: Paris: 1813.
   d) *Sur les fonctions du cerveau et sur celles de chacune de ses parties*: 6 vols.: Paris: J.B. Baillière: 1825.

143. Gall, F.J., & G. Spurzheim: *Anatomie et physiologie du système nerveux en général et du cerveau en particulier, avec des observations sur la possibilité de reconnaître plusieurs dispositions intellectuelles et morales de l'homme et des animaux par la configuration de leurs têtes*: 4 vols.: Paris: 1810-1818.

144. Gal'perin, P.Y.: "Stages in the development of mental acts": in: Cole, M., & I. Maltzman (eds.): *Handbook of Contemporary Soviet Psychology*: New York: Basic Books: 1969.

145. Galvani, L: *De viribus electricitatis in motu muscularis commentarius*: 1791.

146. Gassendi, P.: *Opera*: Lyon: 1658.

147. Gelb, A.: "Remarques sur l'utilisation des données pathologiques pour la psychologie et la philosophie du langage": *Journ. de Psychol. norm. et pathol.* 30 (1933).

148. Gelb, A. & K. Goldstein (eds.): *Psychologische Analysen Hirnpathologischer Fälle*: Leipzig: Springer Verlag: 1920.

149. Gennari, F.: *De Peculiari Structura Cerebri Nonnullisque Ejus Morbis*: Parma: 1782.

150. Gesner, J.: *Sammlung von Beobachtungen aus der Arzneygelahrtheit und Naturkunde*: Nordlingen: C.G. Beck: 1769-1776.

151. Ghirardelli, C.: *Cefalogia fisionomica, con cento teste intagliate sotto ogni una delle quali e un sonnetto e un distico*: Bologna: E. Dozza: 1650.

152. Gibson, W.C.: "Pioneers in Localization of Function in the Brain": *JAMA* (June 16, 1962).

153. Glisson, F.:
   a) *Anatomia Hepatis*: 1654.
   b) *Tractatus de Natura Substancia Energetica Seu de Vita Naturae e Jusque Tribus Primis Facultatibus*: 1672.
   c) *De Ventriculo et Intestinis*: 1677.

154. Globus, A., & A.B. Scheibel: "Pattern and field in cortical structure: the rabbit": *Journal of Comparative Neurology* 131 (1967): 155-172.

155. Goldstein, K.:
   a) "L'analyse de l'aphasie et l'étude de l'essence du langage": *Journal de Psychol. norm. et pathol.* 30 (1933).
   b) *Der Aufbau des Organismus*: The Hague: Nijhoff: 1934.
   c) *Language and Language Disturbances*: New York: Grune & Stratton: 1948.

156. Goldstein & Gelb: see [148].

157. Golgi, C.: "Recherches sur l'histologie des centres nerveux": *Arch. ital. de Biol.* 3 (1883): 285-317.

158. Goodglass, H., & J. Mayer: "Agrammatism in aphasia": *J. Speech Dis.* (1958): 23-99.

159. Goodglass & Berko: see [33].

160. Grammont, M.: *Traité de phonétique*: Paris: Delagrave: 1933.

161. Grandjean de Fouchy, J.P.: "Observation anatomique": *Hist. Acad. Roy. des Sciences, Mém. de l'Acad.* (1784): pp. 399-401.

162. Grasset, J.: "La fonction du langage et la localisation des centres psychiques dans le cerveau": *Revue de Phil.*, Jan. (1907).

163. Gratiolet, L.P.:
    a) *Mémoire sur les plis cérébraux de l'homme*: 1854.
    b) *Anatomie comparée du système nerveux considéré dans ses rapports avec l'intelligence* [vol. 2 of a work begun by F. Leuret]: 1854.

164. Gregory of Nyssa (St.): *De Hominis Officio*.

165. Grewel, F.: "Neurolinguistiek": *Tijdschrift voor Logopedie en Foniatrie* 38 (1966): 1159-1162.

166. Gruner, O.C.: *A Treatise on the Canon of Medicine of Avicenna, incorporating a translation of the first Book*: London: 1930.

167. Guainerio, A.: *Opera Medica*: Pavia: Antonius de Carcano: 1481.

168. Guillaume, G.:
    a) *Langage et science du langage*: Paris: Nizet; Québec: Presses de l'Université Laval: 1964.
    b) *Leçons de linguistique de G. Guillaume*: ed. by R. Valin: Paris: Klincksieck; Québec: Presses de l'Université Laval: 1971- .
    c) *Principes de linguistique théorique de G. Guillaume*: ed. by R. Valin: Paris: Klincksieck; Québec: Presses de l'Univ. Laval: 1973.

169. Guthrie, W.K.C.: *A History of Greek Philosophy*: C.U.P.: 1962.

170. Hagège, C.: *La grammaire générative, réflexions critiques*: Paris: P.U.F.: 1976.

171. Hales, S.: *Statical Essays, Containing Haemastaticks, II*: London: Innys, Manby & Woodward: 1733.

172. Haller, A. v.: "De partibus corporis humani sensibilibus et irritabilibus": *Comment. Soc. Reg. Sci. Goettingen* 2 (1753): 114-158.

173. Hannover, A.: "Lettre au professeur Jacobson (de Copenhague) sur une nouvelle technique de préparation du tissu nerveux pour observer au microscope": *Arch. Anat. Physiol.* (1840).

174. Harris, J.: *Hermes, or a Philosophical Enquiry Concerning Language and Universal Grammar*: London: 1751.

175. Hartley, D.: *Observations on Man, his Frame, his Duty and his Expectations*: London: S. Richardson: 1749.

176. Harvey, W.: *Exercitatio Anatomica de Motu Cordis et Sanguinis in Animalibus*: Francoforti: 1629.

176'. Hécaen, H.: "Neurolinguistique et neuropsychologie": *Langages* 25 (1972) [introduction].

176". Hécaen, H.: see [8'].

177. Head, H.:
   a) "H. Jackson on aphasia and kindred affections of speech": *Brain I & II*, vol. 38 (1915).
   b) "Aphasia: an historical review": in: *Proceedings of the Section of Neurology of the Royal Society of Medicine*, October (1920).
   c) *Aphasia and Kindred Disorders of Speech*: 2 vols.: C.U.P.: 1926.

178. Hegel, F.: *Phenomenology of Spirit*: 1708.

179. Helmholtz, H.L.F. v.: "Vorläufiger Bericht über die Fortpflanzungsgeschwindigkeit der Nervenreizung": *Arch. Anat. Physiol.* (Anat. Abt. Supplement - Bd.) (1850): pp. 71-73.

180. Heraclitus: in: Voilquin, J. (ed.): *Les penseurs grecs avant Socrate*: Paris: Garnier: 1941.

181. Herder: *Über den Ursprung der Sprache*: 1772.

182. Hérissant, F.D.: "Eclaircissement sur l'osséification": *Mém. Acad. Roy. des Sci. de Paris* (1758).

183. Hermann, L: *Grundriss der Physiologie des Menschen*: Berlin: Hirsch: 1863.

184. *Herodotus*: with an Eng. trans. by A.D. Godley: Loeb Classical Library: London: Heinemann: 1946.

185. Herz, M.: "Wirkung des Denkvermögens auf die Sprachwerkzeuge": *Magazin für Erfahrungsseelenkunde* 8, 2 (1791): 1-6.

186. Hippocrates:
   a) *The Sacred Disease*
   b) *Epidemics*
   c) *Treatise on Wounds of the Head*: in [240].

187. Hitzig, E.: see [138].

188. Hodgkin, A.L.: *The Conduction of the Nervous Impulse*: Liverpool University Press: 1964.

189. Holder, W.: *Elements of Speech, an Essay of inquiry into the natural production of letters with an Appendix concerning persons deaf and dumb*: 1669.

190. Humboldt, W. v.: *Über die Verschiedenheit des menschlichen Sprachbaues und ihren Einfluss auf die geistige Entwicklung des Menschengeschlechts*: 1836.

191. Hunt, R.K., & M. Jacobson: "Development and stability of positional information in xenopus retinal ganglion cells": *Proceedings of the National Academy of Sciences* 69 (1972): 780-783.

192. Isserlin, M.: "Über Agrammatismus": *Zeitschr. f. d. ges. Neur. u. Psychiatr.* 75 (1922).

193. Jackson, J.H.:
   a) *Notes on the Physiology and Pathology of the Nervous System*: 1868.
   b) "On the physiology of language": *Brit. Med. Journal* ii (1868).
   c) "Words and other symbols of mentation": *Med. Press & Circular* ii: p. 205.
   d) "Reprints of H. Jackson's papers on affections of speech": *Brain* 38 (1915).
   e) *Selected Writings of H. Jackson*, J. Taylor (ed.): London: Hodder & Stoughton: 1932.

194. Jacob, A.: *Les exigences théoriques de la linguistique selon G. Guillaume*: Paris: Klincksieck: 1970.

195. Jacobson, C.O.: "The localization of the presumptive cerebral region in the neural plate of the Axolotl 1 larva": *Journal of Embryology & Experimental Morphology* 7 (1959): 1-22.

196. Jacobson, M.:
    a) *Developmental Neurobiology*: New York: Holt: 1970.
    b) "Brain development in relation to language": in: Lenneberg, E.H. & E. (eds.): *Foundations of Language Development* I: Paris/New York: UNESCO/Academic Press: 1975.

197. Jacobson, M., & R.K. Hunt: see [191].

198. Jakobson, R.:
    a) *Essai de linguistique générale*: trad. F. Ruwet: Paris: Minuit: 1963.
    b) *Langage enfantin et aphasie*: Trad. J.P. Boons et R. Zygouris: Paris: Minuit: 1969.
    c) *Selected Writings (I: Phonological Studies)*: The Hague: Mouton: 1971.
    d) *Selected Writings (II: Word and Language)*: The Hague: Mouton: 1971.
    e) *Six Leçons sur le son et le sens*: Paris ": Minuit: 1976.

199. Jakobson, R., & M. Halle: *Fundamentals of Language*: The Hague: Mouton: 1956.

200. Jasper, H.H.:
    a) "Functional properties of the thalamic reticular system": in: The Council for International Organization of Medical Sciences: *Brain Mechanisms and Consciousness*: Oxford: Blackwell: 1954.
    b) "Unspecific thalamo-cortical relations": in: Field, J., Magoun, H.W., & W. Hall (eds.): *Handbook of Physiology*: Section I: Neurophysiology: Vol. II: Washington: American Physiological Society: 1960: pp. 1553-1593.
    c) "The centrencephalic system": *CMA Journal* 116 (June 18, 1977): 1371-1372.

201. Joly, A.:
    a) [Introduction and notes]: *Tableau des progrès de la science grammaticale de F. Thurot*: Bordeaux: Ducros: 1970.

b) [Introduction and notes]: *L'Hermès* traduit par F. Thurot: Genève: Droz: 1972 [see 174].

202. Joubert, L.:
a) *Erreurs populaires aux faits de la médecine et régimes de santé*: Bordeaux: 1570.
b) *Traité du ris, contenant son essence, ses causes et ses merveilleux effets*: Paris: 1579.

203. Joynt, R.G., & A.L. Benton: see [29].

204. Kayser, C.: *Physiologie*: 3 vols.: Paris: Flammarion: 1969.

205. Kayserling, A.: "Die Medizin Alcmeons von Kroton": *Z. klin. Med.* 43 (1901): 171-179.

206. Kempf, K.: *Valerii Maximi factorum et dictorum memorabilium libri novem*: Leipzig: B.G. Toubner: 1888.

207. Kimura, D.: "The neural basis of language *Qua* gesture": in: Whitaker, H. & H.A. (eds.) *Studies in Neurolinguistics II*: New York: Academic Press: pp. 146-154.

208. Kinsbourne, M.:
a) "The minor cerebral hemisphere as a source of aphasic speech": *Arch. of Neurol.*: Chicago 25 (1971): 302-306.
b) "Minor hemisphere language and cerebral maturation": in: Lenneberg, E.H. & E. (eds.): *Foundations of Language Development II*: Paris/New York: UNESCO/Academic Press: 1975.

209. Kleist, K.: "Gehirnpathologische und lokalisatorische ergebnisse über hörstörungen, geräuschtaubheiten und amusien": *Monatsschr. f. Psychiatr. u. Neur.* 68 (1928).

210. Koelliker, R.A. v.:
a) "Neurologische bemerkungen": *Z. wiss. Zool. I* (1849): 135-163.
b) *Mikroskopische Anatomie*: Leipzig: 1850-1854.
c) *Handbuch der Gewebelehre des Menschen*: Leipzig: 1952.

211. Korzybski, A.: "Neuro-semantic and neuro-linguistic mechanisms of extensionalization": *Communication to the American Association for the Advancement of Science*: 1935.

212. Kozhevnikov, A., & Chistovich, L.A.: see [71].

213. Kruszewksi, N.: *Aperçu de la science du langage*: Kazan: 1883.

214. Kühn, C.G.: see [141c]

215. Kussmaul, A.: *Les troubles de la parole* [Fr. trans.]: Paris: 1884.

216. Laborde, J.B.V.: *Traité élémentaire de physiologie*: Paris: 1893.

217. Lallemand, F.: *Recherches anatomiques et pathologiques sur l'encéphale et sur ses dépendances*: Paris: Béchet jeune: 1820-1823.

217'. Lamendella, J.T.: "The limbic system in human communication": in [420']: 3.

218. Lamy, B.: *La rhétorique ou l'art de parler*: Paris: 1675.

219. Lancelot, C., & A. Arnauld: see [12].

220. Lantéri-Laura, G.:
    a) *Les apports de la linguistique à la psychiatrie contemporaine*: Paris: Masson: 1966.
    b) *Histoire de la phrénologie: l'homme et son cerveau selon F.J. Gall*: Paris: P.U.F.: 1970.

221. Launay, C., & S. Borel-Maisonny: see [47].

222. Lavater, J.G.: *Essais physiognomoniques*: 4 vols.: The Hague: 1781-1787.

223. Laycock, T.: "On the reflex function of the brain": *Brit. Foreign Med. Rev.* 19 (1845): 298-311.

224. Lebrun, Y.: "Neurolinguistic models of language and speech": in: [420]: vol. 1: pp. 1-28.

225. Lecours, A.R.: "Myelogenetic correlates of the development of speech and language": in: [230']: I, 7: pp. 121-135.

226. Lecours, A.R., & F. Lhermitte:
    a) "Phonemic paraphasias: linguistic structures and tentative hypothesis": *Cortex* 5 (1969): 193-228.

b) "The 'pure form' of the phonetic disintegration syndrome 'pure anarthria': anatomo-clinical report of a historical case": *Brain and Language* 3 (1976): 88-113.

227. Leeuwenhoek, A.:
a) "Microscopal observations of Mr. Leeuwenhoek concerning the optic nerve": Phil. Trans. *Roy. Soc.* 10 (1675): 378-380.
b) *Epistolae Physiologicae Super Compluribus Naturae Arcanis*: Delft: Beman: 1719.
c) *Arcana Naturae Detecta*: Leiden: 1719-1722.

228. Lefebvre, G.: *Essai sur la médecine égyptienne de l'époque pharaonique*: Paris: P.U.F.: 1956.

229. Leibniz, G.W.:
a) *Nouveaux essais sur l'entendement humain*: 1704.
b) *Brefs essais sur l'origine des peuples déduite principalement des indications fournies par les langues*: 1710.

230. Lenneberg, E.: *Biological Foundations of Language*: New York: Wiley: 1967.

230'. Lenneberg, E.H. & E. (eds.): *Foundations of Language Development*: 2 vols.: Paris/New York: UNESCO/Academic Press.

231. Le Ny, J.F.: *Le conditionnement*: Paris: P.U.F.: 1961.

232. Leonhardt, R.:
a) "Innervatorische und ideokinetische Form der motorischen Aphasie": *Nervenarzt* 25 (1954).
b) "Apraktische Formen von Aphasie": *Neurol. u. med. Psych.* (Leipzig) 9 (1957).

233. Leontiev, A.N.: *Problems of Mental Development* [in Russian]: Moscow: Izd. Akad. Pedag. Nauk.: 1959.

234. Leuret, F.: *Anatomie comparée du système nerveux considéré dans ses rapports avec l'intelligence*: Paris: 1839. [Vol I. For Vol. II, see 163b].

235. Levina, R.E.: see [49].

236. Lhermitte, F.: see [226a,b].

237. Lhermitte, J.:
   a) *Les fondements biologiques de la pathologie*: Paris: 1925.
   b) "Le lobe frontal": *Encéphale* 24 (1929).
   c) "Langage et mouvement": *Encéphale* 33 (1938).

238. Lichtheim, L.: "Über Aphasie" [1884]: *Dtsch. Arch. f. klin. Med.* 36 (1885).

239. Linnaeus, C.: *Gloemska of all substantiva och isynnerhet namn*: K. Swenska. Wetensk. Acad. Handlingar 6 (1745): 116-117.

240. Littré. E.: *Oeuvres complètes d'Hippocrate*: 10 vols.: Paris: Baillière: 1839-1861 [Amsterdam: A.M. Hakkert: 1961].

241. Locke, J.: *Essay concerning human understanding*: 1691.

242. Longet, F.A.: *Anatomie et physiologie du système nerveux de l'homme et des animaux vertébrés*: 2 vols.: Paris: Fortin, Masson: 1842.

243. Lordat, J.: "Leçons tirées du cours de physiologie de l'année scolaire 1842-1843: analyse de la parole pour servir à la théorie de divers cas d'alalie et de paralalie que les nosologistes ont mal connus" [published with Lordat's permission by his pupil Kühnholtz in:]
   a) *Journal de la Société de Médecine pratique de Montpellier* VII: pp. 333-353; VIII: pp. 1-17 (1843).
   b) *Montpellier/Paris*: Castel, Baillière, Fortin, Masson, Béchet & Labé: 1843-1844. [See [107], pp. 129-170].

244. Lotmar, F.: "Zur Kenntnis der erschwerten Wortfindung und ihrer Bedeutung für das Denken des Aphasischen": *Arch. f. Neur. und Psychiatr.* 5 (1919), 6 (1920).

245. Lucretius: *De Rerum Natura*: with an Eng. trans. by W.H.D. Rouse: new ed., revised by M.F. Smith: Loeb Classical Library: London: Heinemann: 1975.

246. Luria, A.R.:
   a) *Travmaticheskaya Afaziya*: Moscow: Izd. Akad. Med. Nauk SSSR: 1947 [Eng. trans.; *Traumatic Aphasia*: The Hague: Mouton:1970].
   b) "Brain disorders and language analysis": *Language and Speech I*, 14 (1958).
   c) *The Role of Speech in the Regulation of Normal and Abnormal Behavior*: London: Pergamon Press: 1961.

d) *Higher Cortical Functions in Man* [1962]: New York: Basic Books: 1966.
e) "Problèmes et faits de la neurolinguistique": *Rev. int. des Sciences soc.* 19 (1967): 39-55.
f) *The Working Brain*: London: Penguin: 1973.
g) "Language and Brain: towards the basic problems of neurolinguistics": *Brain and Language* 1 (1974): 1-14.
h) "Basic problems of language in the light of psychology and neurolinguistics": in [230'] II.
i) "Basic problems of neurolinguistics": in: Sebeok, T.A. (ed.): *Current Trends in Linguistics* 12: The Hague: Mouton: 1974: pp. 2561-2594.
j) "Neuropsychology: its sources, principles and prospects": in: Warden, F.G., Swazey, J.P., & J. Adelman (eds.): *The Neurosciences*: Paths of Discovery: Cambridge, Mass./London: MIT Press: 1975.
k) "Basic Problems of Neurolinguistics": The Hague: Mouton: 1976.

247. Luria, A.R., & F.Y. Judovich: *Speech and the Development of Mental Processes in the Child*: London: 1956.

248. Luria, A.R., & Simernitskaya, G.: "Interhemispheric relations and the functions of the minor hemisphere (note)": *Neuropsychologia* 15 (1977): pp. 175-178.

249. Magnan, V.J.J.: "On simple aphasia: aphasia with incoherence": *Brain* 2 (1879-1880): pp. 112-123.

250. Magoun, H.:
a) "The ascending reticular activating system": *A. Res. Nervous & Mental Disease, Proceedings* 30 (1950): 480-492.
b) "Development of ideas relating the mind and brain": in: Brooks, C., & P.F. Cranefield (eds.): *The Historical Development of Physiological Thought*: New York: Hafner: (1959: 81-107.

251. Maine de Biran, P.F.G.:
a) *Mémoire sur l'habitude*: 1802.
b) *Mémoire sur la décomposition de la pensée*: 1805.
c) *De l'aperception immédiate* [Berlin]: 1807 [see 117].
d) *Observations sur les divisions organiques du cerveau*: 1808.
e) *Nouvelles considérations sur les rapports du physique et du moral de l'homme*: Tisserand, P. (ed.): Paris: Alcan: 1924, 1925, 1949.

252. Malpighi, M.: *De Viscerum Structura Exercitatio Anatomica*: Bologna: 1666.

253. Marie, P.:
   a) "La troisième circonvolution frontale gauche ne joue aucun rôle spécial dans la fonction du langage": *La Semaine médicale* (May 23, 1906).
   b) "Que faut-il penser des aphasies sous-corticales?": *La Semaine médicale* (October 17, 1906).
   c) "L'aphasie de 1861 à 1866. Essai de critique historique sur la genèse de la doctrine de Broca": *La Semaine médicale* (November 28, 1906).
   d) "Sur la fonction du langage: rectification à propos de l'article de M. Grasset": *Revue de philosophie* (1907).
   e) "Existe-t-il chez l'homme des centres préformés ou innés du langage?": in: *Questions neurologiques d'actualité*: Paris: Masson: 1922. [see under heading "Révision de la question de l'aphasie" in Marie, P.: Travaux et Mémoires I: Paris: Masson: 1926.]

254. Marie, P., Foix, C., & I. Bertrand: "Topographie crânio-cérébrale": *Annales de Médecine* IV, 3 (1917).

255. Martinet, A.: *Eléments de linguistique générale*: Paris: Colin: 1960.

256. Marx, C.: "Le Neurone": in: [204].

257. Marx, O.:
   a) "Freud and Aphasia: an historical analysis": *Amer. J. of Psychiat.* 124 (December 6, 1967).
   b) "The history of the biological basis of language": in [230].

258. Massa, N.: *Epistolarum medicinalium: Tomus primus*: Venetiis: ex Officina Stellae Iordani Zilletti: 1558.

259. Matteucci, C.: "Deuxième mémoire sur le courant électrique propre à la grenouille et sur celui des animaux à sang chaud": *Annales de chimie et de physique* (1842).

260. Maudsley, H.:
   a) *Crime and Madness*: 1875.
   b) *Physiology and Pathology of Mind*: 1879.

261. Mayer, J., & H. Goodglass: see [158].

262. Mead, R.:
   a) *Mechanical Account of Poisons*: 1702.
   b) *Mechanica Expositio Venerorum* [Lat. trans.]: Leiden: 1737.

263. Mendelssohn, M.: "Psychologische betrachtungen auf veranlassung einer erfahrung von Spalding": *Mag. Erfahrungsseelenkunde* I, 3 (1783).

264. Mettrie, J. Offray de la:
   a) *Histoire naturelle de l'âme*: The Hague: 1745.
   b) *L'homme machine*: Leyde: 1748
   c) L'art de jouir: in: *Oeuvres philosophiques de la Mettrie*: Amsterdam: 1753.

265. Mercurialis, H.: *De Morbis Puerorum*: Venice: 1583.

266. Merleau-Ponty, M.:
   a) *Phénoménologie de la perception*: Paris: Gallimard: 1945.
   b) *La structure du comportement*: 4th ed.: Paris: P.U.F.: 1960.

267. Mexia, P.:
   a) *Silva de varia lecion*: Seville: 1542.
   b) *Seven Dialogues*: Seville: 1547.

268. Meynert, T.: "Der Bau der Grosshirnrinde und seiner oertlichen Verschiedenheiten": *Vjschr. Psychiat.* I (1867): 77-93, 198-217; (1868): 88-113.

269. Miraillé, C.: *L'Aphasie sensorielle*: thesis: Paris: 1896.

270. Miron, M.S., & C.E. Osgood: *Approaches to the Study of Aphasia: a report on an interdisciplinary conference on aphasia*: Urbana: Univ. of Illinois Press: 1963.

271. Mistichelli, D.: *Trattato dell'apoplexia*: Rome: 1709.

272. Monakow, C. v.:
   a) "Gehirnpathologie": in: *Nothagel, H.: Spezielle Pathologie und Therapie* IX, 1: Vienna: Alfred Hoelder: 1897: pp. 482-579.
   b) *Die Lokalisation im Grosshirn und der Abbau der Funktionen durch kortikale Herde*: Wiesbaden: Bergmann: 1914.

273. Monakow, C. v., & R. Mourgue: *Introduction biologique à l'étude de la neurologie et de la psychopathologie*: Paris: Alcan: 1928.

274. Monboddo, J. Burnett, Lord: *On the Origin and Progress of Language*: 6 vols.: 1773-1792.

275. Mondino de Luzzi: *Anatomia*: Sighinolfi, L. ed.: Bologna: Cappelli: 1930.

276. Monro, A. primus: *Anatomy of the Human Bones and Nerves*: Edinburgh: 1746.

277. Monro, A. secundus:
     a) *The Words of Alexander Monro, M.D.*: Edinburgh: 1781.
     b) *Observations on the Structure and Function of the Nervous System*: 1783.

278. Montesquieu, C.: *Oeuvres complètes*: Paris: Pléiade: 1964.

279. Morgagni, G.B.: *De Sedibus et Causis Morborum par Anatomen Indigatis*: Libri V: Venice: 1761.

280. Morgan, T.: *Experimental Embryology*: New York: Columbia Univ. Press: 1927.

281. Morin, G.: *Physiologie du système nerveux central*: Paris: Masson: 1974.

282. Mounin, G.: *Histoire de la linguistique*: 2 vols.: Paris: P.U.F.: 1967.

283. Mourgue, R.:
     a) "Aphasie et psychologie de la pensée": *Encéphale* (1921).
     b) "Disorders of symbolic thinking due to local lesions of the brain": *Brit. J. Psy. Med. Soc.* I (1921).

284. Mourgue, R., & C. v. Monakow: see [273].

285. Moutier, F.: *L'Aphasie de Broca*: Paris: 1908.

286. Mueller, J.: *Handbuch der Physiologie des Menschen für Vorlesungen*: Koblenz: 1835.

287. Myklebust, H.: *Auditory Disorders in Children*: New York: 1954.

288. McBride, K., & T. Weisenburg: *Aphasia*: New York: Hafner: 1964.

289. Nemesius: *De Natura Hominis*.

290. Nollet, J.A.: *Leçons de physique*: 1743.

291. Ogle, J.W.:
   a) "Aphasia and agraphia": *Saint George Hosp. Rep.* 2 (1867): 83-122.
   b) "Part of clinical lecture on aphasia": *Brit. Med. J.* I (1874): 163-165.

291'. Ojeman, G.A.: "Subcortical language mechanisms": in [420'], 4.

292. O'Malley, C.D.: see [76].

293. Ombredane, A.: *L'aphasie et l'élaboration de la pensée explicite*: Paris: P.U.F.: 1950.

294. Ombredane, A., T. Alajouanine, & T. Durand: see [3].

295. O'Neill, Y.V.: *Speech and Speech Disorders in Western Thought before 1600*: Westport, Conn./London: Greenwood Press: 1980.

296. Orton, S.: *Reading, writing and speech problems in children*: New York: Norton: 1939.

297. Osgood, C.E.: see [270].

298. Paracelsus, P.A.T.: *Opera omnia medico-chymico-chirurgica*: Frankfurt: 1603.

299. Paradis, M.: "Bilingualism and aphasia": in [420'] 3: 65-117.

300. Parchappe, J.:
   a) *Recherches sur l'encéphale, sa structure, ses fonctions, ses maladies*: Paris: Rouvier et Le Bouvier: 1836.
   b) "Sur la faculté du langage articulé": *Bull. Acad. nat. de Méd.* 30 (1865).

301. Parrot: "Atrophie complète du lobule de l'insula et de la troisième circonvolution du lobe frontal avec conservation de l'intelligence et de la faculté du langage articulé": *Gaz. hebd. méd. et chir.* (July 31, 1863).

302. Patrick, M. M.: *Sextus Empiricus and Greek Scepticism*: Cambridge: Deighton Bell: 1899.

303. Pavlov, I.P.: *Typologie et pathologie de l'activité nerveuse supérieure*: Fr. trans. by N. Baumstein: Paris: P.U.F.: 1955.

304. Peirce, C.S.: *Collected Papers*: Cambridge, Mass.: 1932-1934.

305. Penfield, W.G.:
    a) "The cerebral cortex in man: I. The cerebral cortex and consciousness": *Arch. Neurol. Psychiat.* 40 (1938): 417-442.
    b) *The Excitable Cortex in Conscious Man*: Springfield, Ill.: C. Thomas: 1958.
    c) *The Mystery of Mind*: Princeton, N.J.: Princeton Univ. Press: 1975.
    d) "The mind and the brain": in: *The Neurosciences: Paths of Discovery*: Cambridge, Mass.: MIT Press: 1975 [excerpts from 305c].

306. Penfield, W.G., & T. Rasmussen: *The Cerebral Cortex of Man*: New York: McMillan: 1950.

307. Penfield, W.G., & L. Roberts: *Speech and Brain Mechanisms*: Princeton, N.J.: Princeton Univ. Press: 1959.

308. Perrault, C.: *La mécanique des animaux*: 1688.

309. Peyronie, F. Gigot de la: "Mémoire contenant plusieurs observations sur les maladies du cerveau par lesquelles on tâche de découvrir le véritable lien du cerveau dans lequel l'âme exerce ses fonctions": Journal de Trévoux (1709); enlarged in: *Mémoires de l'Académie des Sciences de Paris* (1741).

310. Piaget, J.: *Biologie et Connaissance*: Paris: Gallimard: 1967.

311. Piattelli-Palmarini, M: *Théories du langage et théories de l'apprentissage*: [the debate between Chomsky and Piaget at Royaumont, October 1975]: Paris: Seuil: 1979.

312. Pico della Mirandola, G.: *De ente et uno.*

313. Piccolomini, A.: *Anatomicae praelectiones explicantes mirificam corporis humani fabricam*: Rome: 1586.

314. Pichon, E.: see [91].

315. Pichon, E.: see [139].

316. Pick, A.:
    a) "L'importance du centre auditif du langage comme organe d'arrêt du mécanisme du langage": *XIIe Congrès International de Médecine de Paris*: 1900.
    b) "Studien ueber motorische Apraxie": in *Deuticke* (1905).
    c) *Die Agrammatischen Sprachstoerungen*: Berlin: 1913.
    d) "Des formulations verbales accompagnant les mouvements et les actions": *Journal de psych. norm. et pathol.* 20 (1923).

317. Pinel, P.: *Traité médico-philosophique sur l'aliénation mentale et la manie*: 1801.

318. Plato: with an Eng. trans. by H. N. Fowler et al.: Loeb Classical Library: London: Heinemann.
    a) *Phaedo*
    b) *Phaedrus*
    c) *Timaeus*
    d) *Cratylus*
    e) *The Sophist.*

319. Platter, F., II: *Praxis Medicae*: Basel: Konis: 1656.

320. Pliny the Elder: *Natural History.*

321. Pluche, N.A.:
    a) *Le spectacle de la nature ou entretiens sur l'histoire naturelle et les sciences*: Paris: 1732.
    b) *Le mécanique des langues et l'art de les enseigner*; Paris: 1751.

322. Poliakov, G.I.: "Some results of research into the development of the neuronal structure of the cortical ends of the analysers in man": *Journal of Comparative Neurology* 117 (1961): 197-212.

323. Porta, G.B.: *De Humana Physiognomia*: 1586.

324. Portal, A.: *Histoire de l'anatomie*: 1770-1773.

325. Pourfour du Petit, F.: *Lettres d'un médecin des hôpitaux du Roy à un autre médecin de ses amis*: Namur: C.G. Albert: 1710.

326. Priestley, J.:
   a) *Recherches sur la matière et l'esprit*: 1767.
   b) *Examen de la doctrine du sens commun telle que la concevaient les docteurs Reid, Beattie et Oswald*: 1775.

327. Prochaska, J.: *Adnotationum Academicarum, Fasciculus Tertius*: Prague: Gerle: 1784.

328. Proust, A.: *Thèse sur les différentes formes de ramollissement du cerveau*: 1866.

329. Purkyne, J.E.: "Bericht ueber die Versammlung deutscher Naturforscher und Aertzte in Prag im September 1837": *Opera Selecta*: Prague: 1838: pp. 111-114.

330. Quercy: see [24].

331. Rabelais, F.:
   a) *Aphorismes*: Lyon: Librairie Greiff, S. Gryphe: 1532 [?].
   b) *Lettres latines d'un médecin de Ferrare Giovanni Manardi*: Lyon: 1532[?].
   c) *Pantagruel*: 1542.

332. Ramirez de Carrion, E.: *Maravillas de naturaleza en que se contienen dos mil secretos de cosas naturales*: Madrid: 1622.

333. Ramon y Cajal, S.:
   a) "Estructura de los centros nerviosos de los aves": *Rev. trim. histol. norm. pathol.* I (1888): 305-315.
   b) "Estructura del cerebro": *Gac. med. Catalana* II (1888): 449-457.
   c) "Sur la nature de l'écorce cérébrale de quelques mammifères": *Cellule* 7 (1891): 123-176.
   d) "La fine structure des centres nerveux": *Pro. R. Soc.* 55 (1894): 444-468.
   e) "Structure et connexion des neurones": *Les Prix Nobel en 1906*: Stockholm: Nordstedt & Soener: 1908: pp. 1-25.

334. Rasmussen, T.: see [306].

335. Rasmussen, T., & J. Wada: "Intracarotid injection of sodium amytal for the lateralization of cerebral speech dominance: experimental and clinical observations": *Journal of Neurosurgery* 17 (1960): 226-282.

336. Reisch, G.: *Margarita Philosophica*: Freiburg: 1503.

337. Remak, R.: "Anatomische Beobachtungen über das Gehirn, das Rückenmark und die Nervenwurzel": *Arch. Anat. Physiol.* (1841): pp. 506-522.

338. Rey, A.: *Théories du signe et du sens*: 2 vols.: Paris: Klincksieck: 1973-1976.

339. Richelet, P.: *Dictionnaire français*: Geneva: J.H. Widerhold: 1679.

340. Rieber, R.W., Smith, N., & B. Harris: "Neuropsychological aspects of stuttering and cluttering": in: Rieber, R.W. (ed.): *The Neuropsychology of Language*: New York: Plenum: 1976: pp. 25-45.

341. Rieber, R.W., & J. Wollock: "The historical roots of the theory and therapy of stuttering": *Journal of Communication Disorders* 10 (1977): 3-24.

342. Rieber, R.W., & H. Vetter: "Theoretical and historical roots of psycholinguistic research": in: Rieber, R.W. (ed.): *Psychology of Language and Thought*: New York: Plenum: 1980: pp. 3-49.

343. Riese, W.:
    a) "The Lordat case: auto-observation of aphasia": *Bull. Hist. Med.* 28 (1954): 237-242.
    b) "H. Jackson's doctrine of aphasia and its significance today": *Journal of Nerv. and Ment. Disease* I, 22 (1955): 1-13.

344. Riolan, J.: *Encheiridium anatomicum et pathologicum*: 1649-1658.

345. Roberts, L.: see [307].

346. Rodis-Lewis, G.:
    a) "Le domaine propre de l'homme chez les cartésiens": *Journal of Hist. of Philosophy* 2 (1964): 157-188.

b) "Un théoricien du langage au XVIe siècle: Bernard Lamy": *Le français moderne* 1 (1968): pp. 19-50.

347. Rolando, L.:
a) *Essai sur la vraie structure du cerveau de l'homme et des animaux et sur les fonctions du système nerveux*: Turin: 1809.
b) *Saggio sopra la vera struttura del cervello*: Turin: Marietti: 1828.

348. Rommel, P.: "De aphonia rara": in: *Miscellanea Curiosa Medico-Physica, Academiae Naturae Curiosorum* 2 (ser. 2): 1683: 222-227.

349. Rostan, L.L.: *Cours de Médecine clinique*.

350. Rousseau, J.J.: *Essai sur l'origine des langues*: facsimile ed.: Paris: Copédith: 1970.

351. Rousselot, P.J.:
a) *Les modifications phonétiques du langage étudiées dans le patois d'une famille de Cellefrouin*: Paris: 1892.
b) *Principes de phonétique expérimentale*: Paris: 1897-1908.

352. Rufus of Ephesus: *Du nom des parties du corps humain*: in: Daremberg, C., & C.E. Ruelle (eds.): *Oeuvres de Rufus d'Ephèse*: Paris: Imp. nat.: 1879.

353. Ruysch, F.: *Opera Omnia Anatomico-Medico-Chirurgica*: Amsterdam: Jansson-Waesberg: 1737.

354. Sacy, S. de: *Principes de grammaire générale*: An VII [1799].

355. Santorini, G.: *Septemdecem Tabulae Quae Nunc Primum Edit Atque Explicat*: Parma: 1775.

356. Santro, S.: *Ars Statica Medicina*: 1614.

357. Saucerotte, N.: *Théories des lésions de la tête*: 1777.

358. Saussure, F. de:
a) *Cours de linguistique générale*: Bally, C., Séchehaye, A., & A. Riedlinger (eds.): 4th ed.: Paris: Payot: 1949.
b) *id.*, critical ed. by Tullio de Mauro: Paris: Payot: 1972.

359. Scaliger, J.J.: *Diatriba de Europearum Linguis*: 1599.

360. Scheibel, A.B.: see [154].

361. Schenck von Graffenberg (Schenkius)
   a) *Observationes Medicae de Capite Humano*: Basel: 1584; Lyon: 1585.
   b) *Observationum Medicarum Rararum Novarum ac Mirabilium et Monstrosarum,* Volumen tomis septem de *Toto Homine Institutum*: Frankfurt: 1600.

362. Schiller, J., & J. Theodorides: "Sténon et les milieux scientifiques parisiens": in: Florkin, M. (ed.): *Analecta Medico-Historica* I: Materia medica in the 16th century: Oxford: Pergamon Press: 1964.

363. Schumacher, J.: *Antike Medizin*: 2nd ed.: Berlin: De Gruyter: 1963.

364. Schmidt, J.: "De oblivione lectionis ex apoplexia salva scriptione": in: *Miscellanea Curiosa Medico-Physica Academiae Naturae Curiosorum* 4 (1676): 195-197.

365. Schwann, T.: *Mikroskopische Untersuchungen über die Übereinstimmung in der Struktur und dem Wachstum der Tiere und Pflanzen*: Berlin: Reimer: 1839.

366. Serres, A.: *Anatomie du cerveau*: 1824.

367. Sheehan, J.J.: "Theory and treatment of stuttering as an approach-avoidance conflict": *Journ. Psychol.* 56 (1953): 27-49.

368. Sherrington, C.S.:
   a) *The Integrative Action of the Nervous System*: New Haven: 1906.
   b) *Reflex Activity of the Spinal Cord*: London: O.U.P.: 1932.

369. Siegel, R.E.: *Galen's System of Physiology and Medicine*: Basel: S. Karger: 1968.

370. Skwortzoff, N.: *De la cécité et de la surdité des mots dans l'aphasie*: Thesis: Paris: 1881.

371. Smith, A.:
   a) *Theory of Moral Sentiments*: 1759.

b) *Essay on the Origin of Languages*: 1760.

372. Smith, E.: *The Edwin Smith Surgical Papyrus, in Hieroglyphic Trans-literation with translation and commentary*: vol. I: 1930.

373. Soemmering, S.T.:
   a) *Vom Hirn und Rückenmark*: Mainz: Winkopp: 1788.
   b) *De Corporis Humani Fabrica*: 1794-1801.
   c) *De l'organe de l'âme*: Koenigsberg: 1796.

374. Souques, A.:
   a) *Etapes de la neurologie dans l'antiquité grecque (d'Homère à Galien)*: Paris: Masson: 1936.
   b) "Descartes et l'anatomo-physiologie du système nerveux": *Rev. Neurol.* 70, 3 (1938): 221-245.

375. Soury, J.:
   a) *Les fonctions du cerveau*: Paris: Babé: 1892.
   b) "Le cerveau": in: *Dictionnaire de physiologie de C. Richet II*: Paris: Alcan: 1897: pp. 546-670.
   c) *Le système nerveux central, structure et fonctions, histoire critique des théories et des doctrines*: Paris: G. Carré & C. Naud: 1899.

376. Spalding, J.J.: "Ein Brief an Sülzern über eine an sich selbst gemachte Erfahrung": *Mag. Erfahrungsseelenkunde* I, 1 (1783): 38-43.

377. Spencer, H.:
   a) *Principles of Psychology*: 1855.
   b) *First Principles*: 1862.
   c) *Principles of Biology*: 1864.
   d) *Principles of Sociology*: 1877-1896.
   e) *Principles of Ethics*: 1877-1896.

378. Sperry, R.W.: "In search of psyche": in: *The Neurosciences: Paths of Discovery*: Cambridge, Mass./London: MIT Press.

379. Sperry, R.W., Gazzaniga, M.S., & J.E. Bongen: "Interhemispheric relationships: the neocortical commissures; syndromes of hemisphere disconnections": in: *Handbook of Clinical Neurology IV: Disorders of Speech, Perception and Symbolic Behavior*: Amsterdam: North Holland: pp. 273-290.

380. Spurzheim, G.: see [143].

381. Starobinski, J.: *Les mots sous les mots: les anagrammes de Ferdinand de Saussure*: Paris: Gallimard: 1971.

382. Steinthal, H.:
    a) *Outline of Linguistics*: 1850-1854.
    b) *Origin of Language*: 1851.

383. Steneck, N.: "Albert the Great on the classification and localization of the internal senses": *ISIS* 65, 227 (1974): 193-211.

384. Steno, N.: *Discours sur l'anatomie du cerveau à Messieurs de l'assemblée qui se fait chez M. Thévenot* [April 6, 1665]: Gotfredsen, E. (ed.): Copenhagen: Nyt Nordisk Forlag: 1950.

385. Stern, W. & C.: *Die Kindersprache*: 1907.

386. Stratton, G.: "Brain localization by Albertus Magnus and some earlier writers": *Am. J. Psy.* 43 (1931): 128-131.

387. Silvius (F. de la Boé): *Opera Medica*: Amsterdam: 1679; Geneva: 1681.

388. Tarin, P.:
    a) *Brevis Epistola ad Quattanum de Lithotomia*: Paris: 1748.
    b) "Anatomie"[article in the *Encyclopédie*].
    c) *Anthropotomie, ou l'art de la dissection*: 1750.

389. Ténon, J.R.: *Observations sur les obstacles qui s'opposent aux progrès de l'anatomie*: 1785.

390. Theodorides, J.: see [362].

391. Theophrastus: *Theophrasti Eresii Opera Quae Supersunt Omnia*: Wimmer, F. (ed.): Paris: 1866.

392. Thompson, R.: "The search for the engram" in: *Am. Psych.* (March 1976): pp. 209-226.

393. Tiedemann, F.: *Icones Cerebri Simiarum*: Heidelberg: 1821.

394. Tissot, S.A.: *Traité des nerfs et de leurs maladies*: Paris: F. Didot le Jeune: 1778.

395. Trousseau, A.: "De l'aphasie, maladie décrite récemment sous le nom impropre d'aphémie": *Gaz. des Hôp.* 37 (1864); Clinique médicale: 1865.

396. Trubetzkoy, N.S.: *Grundzüge der Phonologie* (Principles of Phonology): 1938.

397. Valentin, G.G.: "Über den Verlauf und die Letzten Ende der Nerven": in: *Nova Acta Phys.-Med. Acad. Caes. Leopold Carol. Nat. Curiosorum Breslau* 18, i (1836): 51-240.

398. Valin, R.: *Petite introduction à la psychomécanique du langage*: Québec: Presses de l'Univ. Laval: 1954.

399. Vallès, F.: *Sacred Philosophy*: Salamanca: 1588.

400. Valsalva, A.M.: *Treatise on the Human Ear*: Venice: c. 1720.

401. Van Goens, R.M.: "Einige Beispiele von Geistes-oder Gedaechtnissabwesenheit": *Mag. Erfahrungsseelenkunde* 7, 3 (1789): 77-80.

402. Van Helmont, F.M.: *Alphabeti Vere Naturalis Hebraici Brevissima Delineatio*: Sulzbach 1657.

403. Van Swieten, G.: *Commentaria in H. Boerhaavii Aphorismis de Cognoscendis et Curandis Morbis*: Leiden: 1741.

404. Van Woerkom, W.:
    a) "La signification de certains éléments de l'intelligence dans la genèse des troubles aphasiques": *Journ. de Psychol. norm. et pathol.* 18 (1921).
    b) "Sur l'état psychique des aphasiques": *Encéphale* 18 (1923).

405. Varolio, C.: *Anatomiae Sive de Resolutione Corporis Humani Libri iii: de Nervis Opticis*: Frankfurt: 1591.

406. Verduc, J.P.: *Suite de l'ostéologie contenant un traité de myologie raisonnée*: Paris: L. d'Houry: 1698.

407. Vervorn, M.: *Irritability*: New Haven: Yale Univ. Press: 1913.

408. Vetter, H.: see [342].

409. Vesalius, A.: *De Humani Corporis Fabrica*: 1543.

410. Vesling, J.: *Syntagma Anatomica*: Padua: Frambotti: 1647.

411. Vico, G.B.: *Principi di una Scienza Nuova d'Intorno alla Commune Natura*: 1725.

412. Vicq d'Azyr, F.:
    a) *Deux mémoires sur l'organe de la voix*: 1779.
    b) *Quatre mémoires sur la structure du cerveau et de la moelle épinière et sur l'origine des nerfs*: 1781.
    c) *Traité d'anatomie et de physiologie*: 1786.
    d) *Discours sur l'esprit*.

413. Vieussens, R.: *Nevrographia Universalis*: Lyon: Certe: 1684.

414. Vinarskaya, E.N.: *Clinical Problems of Aphasia: Neuropsychological Analysis*: Moscow: Meditsina: 1971.

415. Vygotsky, L.S.: *Thought and Language*: Eng. trans. by E. Hanfmann and G. Vakar: Cambridge, Mass.: MIT Press: 1962.

416. Wada, J.: see [335].

417. Warburton, G.: *The Divine Legation of Moses*: 1737-1741.

418. Weisenburg, T.: see [288].

419. Wernicke, K.:
    a) *Der aphasische Symptomenkomplex*: Breslau: 1881-1883.
    b) *Lehrbuch der Gehirnkrankheiten*: Cassel: 1885-1886.
    c) *Einige neuere Arbeiten über Aphasie*: 1885-1886.

420. Whitaker, H. A.: "A model of neurolinguistics": *Occasional Paper no. 10*: Language Centre: University of Essex: Colchester: 1970.

420'. Whitaker, H.A. & H. (eds.): *Studies in Neurolinguistics*: New York: Academic Press.
    I   (1976)
    II   (1976)
    III (1977)
    IV   (1979).

421. Whytt, R.: *An Essay on the Vital and Other Involuntary Motions of Animals*: Edinburgh: Hamilton, Balfour & Neill: 1751.

422. Wilkins, J.: *An Essay Towards a Real Character and a Philosophical Language*: 1668.

423. Willis, T.:
    a) *Cerebri Anatome*: London: 1664.
    b) *The Anatomy of the Brain and Nerves*: Feindel, W. (ed.): Montreal: McGill Univ. Press.

424. Winslow, J.B.: *Exposition anatomique du corps humain*: Paris: 1732.

425. Wolfson, H.A.: "The internal senses in Latin, Arabic and Hebrew philosophical texts": *Harvard Theological Rev.* 28, 2 (1935): pp. 69-133.

426. Wollock, J.: see [341].

427. Wolpert, L.: "Positional information and the spatial pattern in cellular differentiation": *Journ. of Theoretical Biology* 25 (1969): 1-47.

DICTIONARIES AND ENCYCLOPEDIAS

A- *Grand Vocabulaire Français*: Paris: C. Panckoucke: 1770-.
B- *Encyclopedia Britannica*: London: 1768.
C- *Encyclopédie ou Dictionnaire raisonné des sciences, des arts et des métiers*: Neuchâtel: S. Faulche: 1765-.
D- *Dictionnaire de l'Académie française*: 5th ed.: Paris: Bossange et Masson: 1815.
E- *La Grande Encyclopédie, inventaire raisonné des sciences, des lettres et des arts*: Paris [19th century].
F- Moutier, F.: *Lexique des termes employés dans la nomenclature des troubles du langage*: 1908.
G- *Dictionnaire de Linguistique*: Paris: Larousse: 1972.
H- *Trésor de la Langue Française*: Paris: Gallimard. (currently being published)

Recent publication:
Changeux, J.P.: *L'homme neuronal*:: Paris: Fayard: 1983.

INDEX

Achromatic microscope.
See Microscope; Optics
Agrammatism, 188
Agraphia, Bastian and, 166
Alajouanine, Théophile, 218
Alalia, pathology concepts, 128
Alberti, S., 118
Albertus Magnus, 38, 39
Alcmeon, 4, 19
Aldini, Giovanni, 106
Amman, Johann Konrad, 118-119
Amnesia
aphasia and, 163-164
Bastian and, 166
definitions, 142
Anarthria, aphasia and, 186
Anaxagoras, 5-6, 23
Andral, Gabriel, 140
Anokhin, P. K., 219
Anselm, Saint, 40
Anthropology, 179
Antonio, Nicholas, 119
Aphasia
aphrasia and, 166
Bastian and, 166
Broca and, 134
categories of, 164, 169
classification of, 193-194
Déjérine and, 170
dissolution theory, 172
epilepsy and, 205
hemiplegia and, 210
historical diagnosis, 122
Jackson and, 172-173
Kussmaul and, 167
language theory and, 179, 187, 189
Marie and, 185-186
nosology, 125
operations affected by, 192
phonology and, 191
term of, 162-163
Aphemia
Bastian and, 166
brain lesion, 160-161

Aphemia *(cont'd)*
Broca and, 161-162
head trauma, 160
Aphonia
defined, 120
pathology concepts, 128
Aphrasia, aphasia and, 166
Aquinas, Saint Thomas, 39, 136
Arceo, Francisco, 122
Archambault, Théophile, 165
Archibald, E., 127
Aristotle, 6, 11, 12-13, 21, 26-28, 36, 37, 49, 101, 115, 116, 117, 133, 134
Articulation
Broca and, 157
study of, 119
Asclepiades of Bithynia, 15
Associationism, 165-168, 184-186
Astronomy, antiquity, 15
Asymbolia, 167
Asynergy, definitions, 142
Athenaeus, 15
Atomic theory, antiquity, 4
Auburtin, Simon-Alexandre Ernest, 141, 155-156
Augustine, Saint, 24, 38, 63, 70
Aulus Gellius, 121
Averroes, 39
Avicenna, 28, 35, 37, 46, 121
Axon, observation of, 146

Bacon, Sir Francis, 45, 116
Baillarger, Jules Gabriel François, 145, 163, 164, 171
Bain, Alexander, 166
Bartholin, Gaspard, 98
Basal regulation center, 204
Bastian, Henry Charlton, 165, 166, 171
Baudoin de Courteny, 66, 180, 190, 197
Bauhin, Caspar, 46-47
Baveriis, Baverius de, 121
Bayle, Antoine, Laurent, Jessé, 143
Beauzée, Nicolas, 74, 85, 231

269